PRECIOUS PEARLS

From the Proverbs

GREG HINNANT

CREATION HOUSE
A STRANG COMPANY

PRECIOUS PEARLS FROM THE PROVERBS by Greg Hinnant
Published by Creation House
A Strang Company
600 Rinehart Road
Lake Mary, Florida 32746
www.creationhouse.com

Unless otherwise noted, all Scripture quotations are from *The New Scofield Reference Bible* (New York: Oxford University Press, 1967). *The New Scofield Reference Bible* contains introductions, annotations, subject chain references, and some word changes in the King James Version text that will help the reader.

Scripture quotations marked AMP are from the Amplified Bible: Old Testament © 1965, 1987 by the Zondervan Corporation; New Testament © 1954, 1958, 1987 by the Lockman Foundation. Used by permission.

Scripture quotations marked KJV are from the King James Version of the Bible.

Scripture quotation marked MLB are from the *New Berkeley Version in Modern English*, revised edition, copyright © 1945, 1959, 1969, by Zondervan Publishing House. Used by permission.

Scripture quotations marked MOFFATT are from *A New Translation of the Bible* by James Moffatt, copyright © 1988 by HarperCollins. Used by permission.

Scripture quotations marked NAS are from the New American Standard Bible. Copyright © 1960, 1962, 1963, 1968, 1971, 1972, 1973, 1975, 1977 by the Lockman Foundation. Used by permission. (www.Lockman.org)

Scripture quotations marked NIV are from the Holy Bible, New International Version. Copyright © 1973, 1978, 1984, International Bible Society. Used by permission.

Scripture quotations marked NKJV are from the New King James Version of the Bible. Copyright © 1979, 1980, 1982 by Thomas Nelson, Inc., publishers. Used by permission.

Scripture quotations marked PHILLIPS are from *The New Testament in Modern English*, revised edition. Copyright © 1958, 1960, 1972 by J. B. Phillips. MacMillan Publishing Co. Used by permission.

Scripture quotations marked TLB are from *The Living Bible*. Copyright © 1971. Used by permission of Tyndale House Publishers, Inc., Wheaton, IL 60189. All rights reserved.

Cover design by Terry Clifton

Library of Congress Control Number: 2005930410
International Standard Book Number: 1-59185-900-X

First Edition

05 06 0708 09 — 987654321
Printed in the United States of America

To the four best blessings
I will ever receive, my "olive plants"—
Samuel, Sarah, John,
and Joseph

ACKNOWLEDGMENTS

*W*hat could I possibly do to benefit the body of Christ without the multifaceted daily assistance—praying, giving, proofreading, advising, making tapes, answering letters, preparing mailings, shipping books, running errands—of my faithful friends and fellow laborers at Greg Hinnant Ministries? Surely, less; probably, much less; maybe, nothing! This I know beyond the possibility of doubt.

So it is with a very real awareness of my human limitations and need of other members of Christ's body that I wish to praise God for giving the gift of "helps" (1 Cor. 12:28) to the following believers, giving their gifted service to me temporarily for the ministry's sake, and thus enabling me to give this book to the church permanently for Christ's sake.

To God be the glory and to us the labor—and the joyous privilege of knowing and serving such a wondrous God and His wonderful people! My hearty "Thank you!" goes out, not only to the Lord, but also to:

Alice W. Bosworth
Jean Brock
Suzanne Hinnant
John J. "Jack" McHugh Jr.
Virginia G. McHugh
Kathleen E. McHugh

Phyllis H. McNeill
Mary Ann Mowery
Chris D. Smith
Melissa N. Smith
Evelyn A. Ward

CONTENTS

PREFACE

*I*n one of His brief but memorable parables, Jesus spoke of a jewel merchant "in search of fine and precious pearls" (Matt. 13:45, AMP), who willingly sold everything he had to obtain a single "pearl of great price" (v. 46). That pearl, we know, represents the "kingdom of heaven" (v. 45). This interpretation is confirmed in the Book of Revelation, which describes each of the twelve gates of New Jerusalem as being made "of a single pearl" (Rev. 21:21, NIV). Indeed, heaven is *the* most valuable human attainment, accessible not by our works but only by Christ's work and God's grace.

Just as God's eternal kingdom is uniquely and incomparably valuable, so also is His eternal truth—the Word of God—that is found only in the Bible. Within that vast, sixty-six book repository of inspiring and inerrant divine thought there is one literary jewelry box specially filled with God's peerless and priceless wisdom: the Book of Proverbs. Unashamedly, this little book boasts of the large value of its wisdom:

> Happy is the man that findeth wisdom...for the merchandise of it is better than the merchandise of silver, and the gain thereof than fine gold. She is more precious than

rubies; and *all the things thou canst desire are not to be compared unto her.*
—Proverbs 3:13–15, emphasis added

"Silver," "fine gold," "rubies," and, as if to make the comparison unmistakably clear, the mighty logos declares, "all the things thou canst desire" are "not to be compared" with the wisdom of God recorded in the Book of Proverbs. Thus God has given us His personal evaluation of the spiritual gems in the Bible's jewelry box: they are incomparably valuable!

If we are wise men and women searching for "fine and precious pearls" of divine truth, we shall find them aplenty in the Book of Proverbs. And beginning with chapter two, each chapter of the humble book you now hold in your hand examines one of God's lustrous pearls of truth with close, careful attention to detail. Just as rare natural pearls come in a whole range of colors—black (gray), pink, orange, gold, cream, white, and purple—so these chapters touch on a broad range of important topics: attitudes, marriage, parenting, speech, motives, habits, judgment, mercy, faithfulness, slothfulness, envy, exhortation, and insight, to name a few. Just as pearls are of universal origin and appeal, so these proverbial expositions are of universal application, addressing all phases of the human experience, both profound and practical.

So please ponder these precious pearls from the Book of Proverbs. And then practice them and proclaim them—for your blessing, for others' blessing, for His glory!
—Greg Hinnant

Chapter One

MAY I RECOMMEND
THE PROVERBS?

*L*arge, beautifully crafted, exquisitely gilded, and filled to overflowing with all kinds of priceless gems of eternal truth, the Book of Proverbs is the undisputed jewelry box of biblical wisdom: "The proverbs of Solomon, the son of David…to know wisdom" (Prov. 1:1–2). Chiefly a collection of short, evenly constructed sayings encapsulating vital spiritual and life truths, this invaluable sacred scroll is must reading for every developing disciple, aspiring overcomer, and minister. Why?

We need the Book of Proverbs because we must possess and practice what it proffers—wisdom, knowledge, understanding, and discretion—if we hope to "reign in life by one, Christ Jesus" (Rom. 5:17). King Solomon of Israel, the chief author of the Proverbs, implies that in his work he is passing on some, perhaps many, of the proverbs his godly father, King David, taught him as a young man:

> Hear, ye children, the instruction of a father…for I give you good doctrine…for I was my father's son…[and] he taught me also, and said unto me, Let thine heart retain my words…Get wisdom…
>
> —PROVERBS 4:1–5

3

Why did David instruct and urge his son to learn godly wisdom? He did so to prepare him to reign effectively as king of Israel. And why did Solomon pass on his, and David's, inspired proverbs to us? Because God, his Inspirer, wants to use his writings to prepare us to reign effectively: over sin, folly, adversity, adversaries, Satan, and demons in this present Church Age; over the nations in the thousand-year Day of the Lord; and, at last, over the new earth in the eternal Day of God. If indeed God has given us the Book of Proverbs to fill us with the wisdom He requires and we need to lead, how can we share Christ's authority, in this or the next life, if we ignore this vital book? Truly, for lack of this very wisdom many believers have ruined their lives and ministries, whereas if they had fed on and lived by these inspired truisms, they would have stood every test and emerged more than conquerors and able rulers over the perils of life. Do we understand the kind of wisdom featured in Solomon's proverbs?

THE WISDOM FEATURED IN THE PROVERBS

The "wisdom" presented in the Book of Proverbs is primarily moral in nature. Given from the viewpoint of eternity, it is centered not in one's worldly esteem or success but rather in one's personal relationship to God, the beginning and sustaining of which is the fear of the Lord. This is seen in its initial grand assertion that "the fear of [deep awe of, respect for, and faith in] the LORD is the beginning of [the true] knowledge [of God]" (Prov. 1:7), a central theme which it later restates, "The fear of the LORD is the beginning of [eternal] wisdom" (9:10), and with which it closes its final chapter, "a woman who feareth the LORD, she shall be praised" (31:30). This also accounts for its repeated references to sin versus righteousness and God's blessing as opposed to His judgment. So biblical wisdom, as featured in the Book of Proverbs, is not merely higher intelligence but also higher morality. It emphasizes not merely the quest for information but also the demand for integrity, virtue, and ethics. It is not merely shrewdness but also sanctity;

not only sharpness of wit but also purity of heart. By the work of the Holy Spirit, God's wisdom leads to and produces in us not only exceptionally fast cerebral responses but also extraordinary characters. This *good judgment* distinguishes wise Christians who walk closely with God from foolish ones who follow Him afar off and from infidels who, whatever their intelligence quotient, as complete fools deny the most obvious and ubiquitous facts on the planet—God's very existence and creatorship: "The fool hath said in his heart, There is no God" (Ps. 53:1).

Proverbial or heavenly wisdom is described by the recurring use of four key terms:

1. **Knowledge**, which is *correct information* about God's character, will, values, ways, and judgments, and about the abiding realities, good and evil, of this present world

2. **Wisdom**, which is *good judgment* or *excellent decision making*; the ability to know when, where, and how to apply knowledge to the spontaneous and fluid situations of life

3. **Understanding**, or *insight*, which is the ability to interpret (or sense accurately), see clearly, and grasp firmly the meaning of concepts, words, and events; also *merciful consideration*, which recognizes exceptions and distinctions that call for allowances

4. **Discretion**, which means *to be careful* rather than careless, thoughtful rather than thoughtless as to what one says, does, or believes; to consider consequences before speaking or acting

Not confined to spiritual things, the Book of Proverbs also offers a wide range of subjects pertaining to worldly wisdom. Its numerous themes touch on all the practical trials, temptations, and troubles of life, such as the need for morality and financial prudence; the importance of honesty, especially commercial ethics;

the dangers of immorality, alcoholism, laziness, and sinful companions; the virtues of humility, hard work, and patience; the superiority of eternal wisdom to mere worldly wealth; the importance of right speech; the folly of haste, quick temper, and unchecked anger; the sad prevalence of injustice and respect of persons; the benefits of mercy, justice, and the fear of God; God's hatred of and sure judgment upon pride, covetousness, and lying; the value of virtuous womanhood; the perilous pit of prostitution; and so forth. Such themes help us not only in our relationship with God but also in relating to the people and problems we face every day in this present sinful society and satanic world system. These spiritually rich themes are touched upon not once but many times, and some proverbs are intentionally duplicated verbatim for emphasis.

REASONS TO STUDY THE PROVERBS

There are several other good reasons why we should study the Book of Proverbs.

The Proverbs are an excellent springboard for broad-ranging Bible study. If you study Solomon's pearls of wisdom, you will find the Spirit of God leading you (by chain references or quiet remembrance) all over the Old and New Testaments for confirming, clarifying examples. Repeatedly you will find a proverb's essential truth illustrated perfectly in one of the historical portions or characters of Scripture. Thus, as a kind of thematic "skeleton" of the Bible, the Book of Proverbs reaches out to and holds together the entire, more corpulent body of God's revelation. Studying Proverbs will therefore help you have a more comprehensive Bible knowledge, a better command of key truths, and a greater conviction that the principles of God's Word are truly timeless, as sure and predictable in one century as they are in another.

Also, the brevity of most proverbs makes them easy to commit to memory. This in turn helps us recall them and meditate on them more easily. Rather than advocating any memorization

technique, I recommend simply reading them often and medita-
tively. The Holy Spirit will then quietly bring them to mind just
when we need them for guidance in life, reference in study, or
illustration in counsel or other ministry, just as Jesus promised:
"He [the Holy Spirit] shall...bring all things to your remembrance, whatever I have said unto you" (John 14:26).

Furthermore, Jesus seems to have had a special love for various kinds of proverbs, or concise sayings summarizing important
spiritual and natural truths. In His extensive speaking ministry
He spoke proverbs almost as often as parables. They appear frequently in the Sermon on the Mount, "Blessed are the meek; for
they shall inherit the earth" (Matt. 5:5), and elsewhere in the
Gospels, "Whosoever shall exalt himself shall be abased; and he
that shall humble himself shall be exalted" (Matt. 23:12). Jesus
sometimes summarized the essential meaning of a parable in a
proverb spoken just before or after He told His inspired story. For
instance, He declared, "A man's life consisteth not in the abundance of the things which he possesseth" (Luke 12:15), then told
of a rich man who focused on the abundance of his possessions
and forgot about his soul (vv. 16–21). He also declared, "Men
ought always to pray, and not to faint" (Luke 18:1), then told of
a persistent widow who did precisely that (vv. 2–8). In the Book
of Acts, Luke recorded what was apparently one of Jesus' most
frequently used proverbs, though it was omitted from the Gospel
records: "It is more blessed to give than to receive" (Acts 20:35).
If Jesus loved and often used proverbs, and, as we know, had
access to and was superbly versed in the Old Testament scriptures (John 7:15), He must have also been a committed learner
and lover of the Book of Proverbs, the chief biblical storehouse
of inspired proverbs. It is incredible to think or claim otherwise.
Therefore, if Jesus delighted in and digested the Book of Proverbs, shouldn't we? That is, if we really want to be like Him. With
this high purpose before us, let's look into and learn to love this
book Jesus loved.

Organization of the Book of Proverbs

Organizationally, the Book of Proverbs is arranged in a clear, simple order. In the first nine chapters, Solomon, the chief but not lone author, opens by stating his reasons for publishing his proverbs, emphasizing the grave dangers of ignorance, immorality, and foolishness, and praising the unparalleled importance and benefits of godly wisdom, the knowledge of God, and moral integrity. The bulk of his contribution, including material later discovered and added by Hezekiah's scribes, then follows in chapters 10 through 29. The work closes with a diverse, spiritually fertile two-chapter addendum, which includes the famous description of the "virtuous woman" and other sayings and maxims penned by two unknown but undeniably inspired writers, Agur and Lemuel.

In the chapters that follow in this book, we will concentrate on expounding proverbs taken from the heart, or core chapters (10–29), of Solomon's book of wisdom, in which the Holy Spirit instructs us by using many sharp contrasts between righteousness and sinfulness or wisdom and folly, one or two statements typically being the exact antithesis of those which follow.

Before we consider some of these larger proverbial pearls we have prayerfully selected for fuller examination, let's peruse some smaller, sample pearls of truth.

Sample Proverbial Pearls

Proverbs 13:13

Whoso despiseth the word shall be destroyed, but he that feareth the commandment shall be rewarded.

Paraphrased, this states:

Whoever rejects, belittles, or ignores the Scriptures will ultimately pay for his disrespect in destructive judgments, but the person who honors, studies, and obeys Bible truths will be blessed by God for doing so.

The theme here is our *attitude toward the Bible.* Note the contrasting terms, "despiseth" and "feareth," and "destroyed" and "rewarded." Though characteristically devoted to God's Word, David ignored the written commandment of Moses when he first attempted to bring the ark of the covenant to Jerusalem, and he paid a heavy price—the death of a friend—for doing so. On the second attempt, therefore, he very carefully transported the ark "according to the word of the LORD" (1 Chron. 15:15)—and immediately received God's blessing and a joyous sense of His approval. Are we, like David, becoming people of the Book?

Our attitude toward God's written Word is of utmost importance, because upon it rests every other phase of our walk with God: obedience, prayer, worship, intercession, discernment, knowledge, gifting, and service. Does God's Word mean what it should to us? Do we tremble at its inspired authority or trivialize it? Cling to it or cast it away? Devotedly study it or disrespectfully doubt and shun it?

Proverbs 13:20

> He that walketh with wise men shall be wise, but a companion of fools shall be destroyed.

Paraphrased, this reads:

> If we respect, walk closely with, and obey the counsel of God-fearing, virtuous friends and leaders, we will gradually become like them, but if we befriend and keep company with those who neither know nor respect the Lord, we will soon take on their ways—and eventually their judgment!

The theme here is *the consequences of choosing wise or foolish friends and leaders.* Note the contrasting phrases, "walketh with wise men" and "companion of fools," and "be wise" and "be destroyed." The New Testament calls us to not be "unequally yoked together with unbelievers" (2 Cor. 6:14) and cites the contagiousness of sin as its reason: "Be not deceived: Evil company corrupts good morals" (1 Cor. 15:33). It also calls us to respect, learn from, and spend time with godly elders, ministers, and mentors, just as the apostles first sat at Jesus' feet and, later, the early church's new converts sought the apostles' company and instruction. Because he accompanied, assisted, and humbly learned from Elijah, Elisha one day became like him, and "the sons of the prophets... said, The spirit of Elijah doth rest on Elisha" (2 Kings 2:15). Whose spirit is increasingly resting on us?

Whatever those with whom we associate are like—soberminded or silly, thoughtful or thoughtless, true or treacherous, committed or corrupted—we are being gradually changed into their image. The company and leadership we choose invariably leave their personal stamp on us. Thus says the Book of Proverbs.

Proverbs 13:21

> Evil pursueth sinners; but, to the righteous, good shall be repaid.

Paraphrased, this reveals:

> Everyone is being chased by the fruit of their consistent actions; sinners by troubles, saints by blessings.

The theme here is *the sure consequences of our consistent actions*. Note the contrasting words, "evil" and "good," and "sinners" and "righteous." Didn't God solemnly promise that the consequences of the Israelites' consistent obedience or disobedience would one day "overtake" them? (See Deuteronomy 28:1–2, 15.) And isn't that exactly what biblical history testifies they received time and again? Seasons of rebellion brought needless troubles, enemies, catastrophes, and exile, while times of repentance, faith, and obedience brought long periods of peace, joy, and the wondrous presence and power of God. The same is true for us. One day our "crop" of consequences will, it must, come in: "Be not deceived, God is not mocked, for whatever a man soweth, that shall he also reap" (Gal. 6:7).

What kind of a crop is growing in the field of our lives today? Or, to change the figure, what kind of consequences are chasing us? Whatever they are, they have been determined by the sum of our consistent "yesterdays," and we can't change them now. But we can change our future. If we want a host of angels bearing blessings to overtake us tomorrow, we have only to do God's will today, consistently, enthusiastically, and in faith, knowing His reward *must* meet us farther on: "Thou meetest him [with fresh blessings] who rejoiceth and worketh righteousness…" (Isa. 64:5).

Proverbs 13:22

> A good man leaveth an inheritance to his children's children; and the wealth of the sinner is laid up for the just.

When paraphrased, this says:

> Righteous men leave legacies [of various kinds] to not only their children but also their grandchildren, and [at times] God arranges circumstances so that the wealth of sinners is given [as a legacy] to His righteous ones [apparently when they have no other].

The theme here is *the sure inheritance of the righteous and their children.* Note the contrasting characters, the "good man" and the "sinner," and the implied connection between the sinner's "wealth" and the good man's "inheritance." Godly Christians invariably leave their posterity good inheritances, if not monetary or material in nature (Prov. 19:14), then other kinds. For instance, they may leave a wealth of wisdom; priceless faith; heaps of exemplary good deeds, graciousness, or generosity; large deposits of timely encouragement; valuable practical advice; or treasures of Bible teaching. And when He wills, God sometimes gives favor or works providentially (*not* by human covetous-ness and craft!) to use the wealth of the unrighteous to meet the worldly needs of less prosperous righteous ones. For instance, He caused Laban's sheep to be transferred into Jacob's flocks to feed his growing family; Haman's estate to be given to Mordecai; and the wealth of the royal family of Egypt—palace, servants, chariot, jewelry, and clothing—to be given to Joseph, who had nothing. Why is this justified? Because originally, presently, and forever, God owns *everything and everyone* in this whole wide world: "*The earth* is the LORD's, and the *fullness thereof*" (Ps. 24:1, emphasis added). That's why.

So get to work on your legacy. If your material wealth is great, leave it to your spouse and children. If it's small, don't despair. Leave them a large righteous example to follow and trust God with all your heart to help them monetarily and materially in His own way and time, remembering and believing David's inspired words, "I have been young, and now am old; yet have I not seen the righteous forsaken, nor his seed begging bread" (Ps. 37:25); and again, "The meek shall [one day] inherit the [entire] earth..." (v. 11). That's a large, and fully legal, legacy!

Proverbs 13:25

> The righteous eateth to the satisfying of his soul, but the belly of the wicked shall want.

Paraphrasing this, we discover:

> God gives those who are right with [and close to] Him ample provisions and lasting contentment with whatever He gives them, but unbelievers constantly "want"—lack necessary provisions or satisfaction with the provisions they have [even when they have plenty].

The theme here is *the sure provision and contentment of the righteous*. Note the contrasting terms, "righteous" and "wicked," and "satisfying" and "want." The apostle Paul taught the Philippians that God would provide all their needs and testified that he had learned to be content in "whatever" condition he was in (Phil. 4:11–12, 19). In another letter he declared that "godliness with contentment is great gain [spiritual wealth]" (1 Tim. 6:6). In the same spirit, the writer to the Hebrews commands us to not covet anything, but to "be content with such things as ye have" (Heb. 13:5). How can we do this? Because whatever else we don't have at the moment, every day we have a wondrous, personal, supernatural, untouchable relationship with the greatest Satisfier on earth, Jesus: "For he [Jesus] hath said, I will never leave thee, nor forsake thee" (v. 5). Implied here is that close fellowship with Jesus imparts an overriding contentment. Or in the words of the psalmist, "In thy presence is fullness of joy" (Ps. 16:11). And with that joy in us we always eat to the satisfying of our soul, whether our fare is pinto beans and cornbread or caviar and prime rib.

Are we satiated or insatiable today? Our answer will depend on how often and deeply we are satisfying our hearts with fellowship with *Him*: "Thy words were found, and I did eat them, and thy word was unto me the joy and rejoicing of mine heart" (Jer. 15:16).

Proverbs 14:3

> In the mouth of the foolish is a rod of pride, but the lips of the wise shall preserve them.

We may paraphrase this as follows:

> The boastful, arrogant, defiant, or rude words of foolish [and proud] ones contain a "rod of pride" [a cause of punishment for pride], but the humble speech of God-fearing souls ensures that they will not be punished [for pride].

The theme here is *proud versus humble speech,* which invariably arises from proud versus humble *thoughts.* Jesus taught us,

"Those things which proceed out of the mouth come forth from the heart [or mind]" (Matt. 15:18). Nabal, Pharaoh, and Nebuchadnezzar lived relatively calm lives until they spoke proudly against God and His people. Then God's rod of discipline visited and remained, until their thoughts and words were humble again. But no such rod fell upon Abigail and Daniel, whose thoughts and words were consistently humble. (See 1 Samuel 25:23–24, 41; Daniel 2:30.) This really shouldn't surprise us if we are familiar with the Book of Proverbs. Why? Because Proverbs reveals that, of all sins, God hates pride the *worst*: "These six things doth the Lord hate; yea, seven are an abomination unto him: *a proud look…*" (Prov. 6:16–17, emphasis added). And religious pride is the worst kind! Why? Because of all forms of pride, religious self-exaltation reminds God most poignantly of His age-old enemy, the devil, just as humility reminds Him of Jesus, who was the meekest man to ever live.

So from now on "think soberly" (Rom. 12:3) and speak, not with lofty but with levelheaded and loving words. You don't want to remind God of the devil, do you?

Proverbs 14:8

> The wisdom of the prudent is to understand his way, but the folly of fools is deceit.

Paraphrased, this verse states:

> The God-fearing, obedient attitude of wise ones enables them to understand [generally] what God is doing in their circumstances [and souls], but the rebelliousness of fools causes them to be self-deceived [and left without a clue as to God's workings, or worse, believing the exact opposite of the truth].

The theme here is *wisdom gives spiritual discernment; rebellion, spiritual blindness.* Note the contrasting phrases, "wisdom of the prudent" and "folly of fools," and "understand" and "deceit" (deception). When sinful Hophni and Phinehas visited Israel's camp with the ark of the covenant in tow, the Israelites shouted for joy, confident that victory over the Philistines would follow. But their sin had deceived them, as the next day proved all too rudely and tragically (1 Sam. 4:1–11). Yet when wise King Solomon heard Adonijah's seemingly innocent request to marry Abishag, he instantly discerned that trouble had visited his "way" (circumstances) in the form of yet another attempted coup by his unrepentant older brother. (See 1 Kings 2:13–25.) What about us?

Is our spiritual vision clear or clouded? Are we understanding or misunderstanding what God is doing in our souls and circumstances? The key to this vital discernment is a broken spirit and a humble attitude, which always manifest in a consistently obedient life. For such "prudent" ones, God will send whatever it takes—prophets, pastors, visions, angels, even little boys (Acts 23:16)—to cause them to understand their situations. So let's be wise and prudent, not willful and presumptuous. We don't want to live in a fog, do we?

Proverbs 14:15

> The simple believeth every word, but the prudent man looketh well to his going.

Paraphrased, this maxim teaches:

> Foolishly simple-minded souls [unintelligent, incurious, and gullible] believe everyone and everything they hear at face value, but wise men take a deeper look [examining, considering, and verifying] before acting upon what they hear.

The theme here is *credulity versus cautiousness*. Note the contrasts, "simple[ton]" and "wise," and "believeth [at once]" and "looketh well [waits and examines]." The Old and New Testaments confirm repeatedly that there are many false prophets and deceived teachers running loose among us. The apostle Paul discerned and opposed the false teaching of the Judaizers at Antioch (Acts 15:1–2). John exposed the dangerously proud false leader Diotrephes in his writings (3 John 9–11). The Bible commends the Berean Jews for searching the Scriptures to confirm or deny Paul's teaching (Acts 17:10–12). What about us? Have we heeded the Holy Spirit's call to "test the spirits" (1 John 4:1)?

Do we act or think first? Wait and seek confirmation or impulsively run with every prophecy? Chew and digest counsel by thinking or blindly swallow it whole? Believe every preacher's claim to a divine call or evaluate men by their fruit of the Spirit? Do we believe "every word" of every sermon, or do we differentiate between human opinions and heavenly ordinances? Do we blindly trust long-held denominational views, or do we search the Scriptures to see if they are truly and fully correct? Our answer will reveal if we are cured of spiritual naiveté. If we aren't, there's still hope. We may begin testing spirits and sermons and speakers today—and cross over from the company of simpletons to the ranks of the wise.

Friend, do you want to be like Jesus? Then learn to love the book He loved. Do you want to reign with Him? Then reach out and grasp the wisdom, knowledge, understanding, and discretion He offers us in the Book of Proverbs. With the above sampling fresh in your mind, may I recommend that you eagerly and prayerfully study the Book of Proverbs? My prayer is that the remainder of this book will stir your desire to do just that, and, as you do so, that the Spirit of wisdom will make you as wise as King Solomon.

So peruse these priceless pearls of proverbial wisdom. Ponder them. Practice them. Praise God for them. Preach them. And promote them, just as the Paraclete does every day:

Doth not wisdom cry, and understanding put forth her voice?...She crieth at the gates...Unto you, O men, I call...Hear; for I will speak of excellent things...

—Proverbs 8:1–6

This will benefit not only your soul but also your body.

Chapter Two

FOR YOUR HEALTH'S SAKE

here are many good reasons Christians should trust and obey God: to know God; to please Him; to glorify Him; to have His approval for service; to be a blessing to others; to have God's blessing upon our work, family, and possessions; to avoid judgment; to qualify for rewards in this life and the next; and so forth. But if all these reasons fail to stir you to righteousness, here's another sure motivator: do it for your health's sake!

That's the rationale of wise King Solomon—and more importantly, His infallible Inspirer, the Holy Spirit—in the Book of Proverbs:

> A sound heart is the life of the flesh; but envy, the rottenness of the bones.
>
> —PROVERBS 14:30

Paraphrased, this proverb reads:

> Spiritual, mental, and emotional stability help establish and maintain physical health, but when we let the agitation of envy [or other harmful emotions such as anger, fear, resentment, strife, etc.] rest in our souls, our bodily health eventually breaks down.

18

Does this surprise us?

It shouldn't. This just makes good sense. We are, after all, tripartite beings, every human being having a spirit, a soul, and a body. And all three divisions of our being are inseparably linked. So whatever affects one part of our being will, if not checked, affect all its parts. The presence of a demon in your spirit, for instance, will affect your mind and body. The presence of sinful thoughts or emotions in your soul will affect your spirit and body. And the presence of a disease in your body will often weaken your mind and spirit. This proverb points out that the state of your mind affects the state of your body, if not immediately, then eventually.

Medical science widely acknowledges these illnesses and categorizes them as *psychosomatic diseases*. They are bodily illnesses that spring not from physical causes (injuries, infectious, or noninfectious diseases), but from unhealthy mental or emotional conditions. These intangible but real stimuli cause our brains to send signals (nerve impulses) throughout our nervous systems to various parts of our bodies that cause our glands, muscles, organs, and bodily systems to malfunction, producing chemical imbalances in our blood and distressing physical pain and sickness.

Now here's the point: regenerated, Spirit-baptized, biblically taught Christians need not suffer these kinds of sicknesses! They are entirely avoidable if we will but consistently surrender to God, trust Him, and obey His Word.

This is the theme masterfully expounded by Dr. S. I. McMillen in his classic best-selling, must-read Christian book *None of These Diseases*. A lifelong physician, devoted Christian, and captivating writer, McMillen pinpoints "emotional turmoil" as the real cause of illness so often overlooked in search of purely physical causes. His prescribed antidote is gloriously simple: obedience to the Bible, most specifically the commands of the New Testament epistles that in so many words tell us to, with the Spirit's help, put off the old man and all his carnal attitudes and actions and put on the new man, Christ, and His higher ways of thinking, speaking, and living. (See Colossians 3:1–4:1; Philippians 4:4–9; Ephesians 4:17–6:9.) Why is this helpful? Because prompt and consistent obedience to God's Word minimizes the time during which these harmful thoughts and emotions—imaginations, anxiety, anger, resentment, vengeance, and guilt—rest in our mind, or "heart," thus not permitting them sufficient time to cause "rottenness of the bones" (Prov. 14:30).

Here is the way this plays out in daily living. We get angry at unfairness, offense, or evildoing, but, remembering God's Word, we quickly choose to "fret not thyself because of evildoers" and to "cease from anger, and forsake wrath" (Ps. 37:1, 8). Or we become intimidated, but, remembering that "God hath not given us the spirit of fear" (2 Tim. 1:7) and that "fear hath torment" (1 John 4:18, KJV), we quickly reject fear and choose instead to trust God to help us. Or someone speaks or acts offensively towards us, but we remember Christ's command, "Forgive, if ye have anything against any" (Mark 11:25), and decisively drop the offense, refusing to harbor an unforgiving spirit. Or we get irritated and impatient with a fellow Christian, but, remembering Jesus' principal command that we "love one another; as I have loved you" (John 13:34), we yield to patience and kindness. Or thoughts of likely future financial needs bring us anxiety, but, remembering Jesus' orders to "be, therefore, not anxious about tomorrow" (Matt. 6:34), we firmly reject our anxious thoughts and choose instead to "trust in the LORD with all thine heart" (Prov. 3:5), believing that He will "supply all your need according to his riches in glory" (Phil. 4:19). Or a friend shares how he has been blessed, prospered, or honored, and afterwards, unaccountably, we're in a bad mood; then the Spirit of truth quietly convicts us of envy (discontentment or anger at others' advantages, real or imagined), and we quickly confess our sin to God and resolve to reject envy, remembering the scripture, "Let not thine heart envy sinners [or saints!]" (Prov. 23:17). Or we think, speak, or act sinfully, but, remembering God's promise that "if we confess our sins, he is faithful and just to forgive us our sins and to cleanse us from all unrighteousness" (1 John 1:9), we quickly confess our sins to Him and receive His forgiveness.

Every time we thus obey the Scriptures, we swallow invisible but potent spiritual "pills"—biblical miracle drugs—that bring us immediate supernatural relief. The result? We protect ourselves from the excessive pressures that agitate our emotions, stress our arteries, overload our nerves, disrupt our glands, contaminate our blood, stiffen our joints, ulcerate our stomachs, damage our vital organs, and ruin our physical health.

The Book of Proverbs concurs. It directly links God's Word to our physical health, declaring that the Word is both physically rejuvenating and medicinal in its effects:

> My son, attend to *my words*; incline thine ear unto *my sayings*. Let them not depart from thine eyes; keep them in the midst of thine heart [mind]. For they *are life* unto those that find them, *and health to all their flesh.*
> —PROVERBS 4:20–22, EMPHASIS ADDED

While these verses highlight listening to, reading, and meditating on the Scriptures, we must remember that the context here also heavily emphasizes obedience to the Scriptures. (See Proverbs 4:14–15, 23–27.) Mere Bible reading, no matter how receptive we are, can't give us full life. It is neither awareness nor thought but obedience that releases all the supernatural life of God latent in His Word. Heart surrender, never mere mental assent, gives us abundant life; hearty compliance, not merely heady contemplation, is required. Not only the mind but also the will must be moved if the rivers of healing power flowing through the Bible are to be let loose in us. But returning to the issue before us, why can't our bodies stand the stresses produced by sinful actions and reactions?

The answer lies in our construction. Acknowledging the lofty wonder that is the human body, the psalmist exclaimed,

"I have been fearfully and wonderfully made; marvelous is Thy workmanship" (Ps. 139:14, MLB). Indeed, God made the human body amazingly strong, durable, flexible, and adaptable, able to handle a whole range of mental and physical stresses. But He did not design it to bear the unnatural and excessive stresses caused by sinful thoughts, emotions, speech, and actions.

After Adam sinned, a whole host of excessive psychological pressures came to bear upon him and his posterity: Guilt and fear came first, when Adam hid from God (Gen. 3:8–10); then came prideful self-defense, when Adam and Eve each blamed their disobedience on others (vv. 12–13). After that came anger (envy), when Cain became enraged with God and his brother Abel without cause (Gen. 4:5); then stubbornness, when Cain resisted conviction, despite God lovingly warning him to forsake his sinful attitude (vv. 6–7). After stubbornness came violence, when Cain cruelly murdered Abel (v. 8); then lying, as Cain denied his crime (v. 9). Finally came self-pity and resentment, when Cain complained that God's punishment was unbearable (v. 13).

All these stressful carnal thoughts, emotions, words, and actions put more pressure—psychological, emotional, and physical—on man than he was created to bear. The body was not designed to carry such a "sin load." Through Christ's redemption, we can be free from all of these additional and unnatural stresses—provided we trust Him and obey His Words, all of which are carefully designed to protect us from the crushing burdens of sin.

When in the fear of God we walk in love, fairness, truthfulness, and non-retaliation toward people, and when we maintain close fellowship with Jesus, we are not encumbered with heavy mental and emotional stones. Consequently our blood pressure is normal, our muscles are not contracted, our vital bodily systems (circulatory, respiratory, nervous, glandular, digestive, etc.) function properly, and our energy level is normal. In short, our inward stability preserves our outward health.

In these increasingly health-conscious times, we recognize all the other factors that affect our bodily health: maintaining good nutrition, rest, exercise, and hygiene; avoiding exposure to extreme temperatures, bad weather, and contagious diseases; and shunning harmful substances, such as alcohol, tobacco, and illegal drugs. Shouldn't we also recognize and guard against the destructive emotional agitations caused by yielding to our carnal natures rather than surrendering to the Spirit and Word of God?

If we wisely do so, does this mean that we will never get sick? Or, if we do become sick, does this mean that we must have disobeyed God's Word? Not necessarily. God may test us (and Satan attack us) with physical illness at any time, as He did Job (Job 2:1–10). Or we may occasionally become physically exhausted from excessive labor and need extra rest. Jesus once recommended that His extremely busy disciples "come aside into a desert place, and rest a while" (Mark 6:31), and Paul wrote touchingly of Epaphroditus, who fell sick due to his love-driven yet excessive labors to support Paul's ministry (Phil. 2:25–30). Nonetheless this remains sure: if we consistently yield to and obey God's Word day by day, we will consistently avoid stress-induced and stress-aggravated physical illnesses. The result will be delightful divine health.

So if you want divine health, my friend, you can have it—and for a very low price! Just surrender, trust in God, and obey the exact scripture that applies to the situation at hand. Take this Bible medication "as needed" until the peace of God that passes all understanding keeps your mind and body day by day. I'm no physician, but that's my prescription.

And here's another, directly from the Great Physician, Jehovah-Rapha:

> If thou wilt diligently hearken to the voice of the LORD thy God, and wilt do that which is right in his sight, and wilt give ear to his commandments, and keep all his statutes,

23

I will put none of these diseases upon thee, which I have brought upon the Egyptians; for I am the LORD that healeth thee.

—EXODUS 15:26

For your health's sake, take it! And while you do so, stop and consider your motives.

Chapter Three

WHY AM I DOING THIS?

The issue that weighs most on God's mind is not what we're doing, but why we're doing it. So says the inspired proverb. In the sixteenth chapter of Solomon's writings, we read:

> All the ways [actions, paths] of a man are clean [innocent, justifiable, meritorious] in his own eyes, but the LORD weigheth the spirits [thoughts and motives].
>
> —PROVERBS 16:2

We may paraphrase this sagacious saying as follows:

> We usually assume the correctness of our decisions and actions and therefore justify them, but the Lord's examination of us goes deeper: He judges our acts by the thoughts and motives from which they spring.

Here God's Word informs us that our deeds are "clean," or right, pure, and worthy of divine reward only when our accompanying thoughts and motives are right in God's sight. To emphasize this point, the same truth is duplicated in Solomon's book of wisdom with only slightly different wording (Prov. 21:2). We must remember then that, in God's judgment, wrong motives render otherwise righteous acts unrighteous. And God's judgment, not man's, is the one that ultimately counts. Forever. And ever. And ever.

This standard of evaluation shouldn't surprise us. A well-known Old Testament reference declares, "For the LORD seeth not as man seeth; for man looketh on the outward appearance, but the LORD looketh on the heart" (1 Sam. 16:7). Why does God, and why should we, value right motives so highly? Because God knows, and we must learn, that sometimes we may do right things for wrong reasons, and at other times we may do seemingly wrong things for right reasons. The Bible provides a lot of hard evidence to support these claims.

Mostly it tells of those who did noble deeds with ignoble intentions.

- King Saul seemed so gracious and loving when he proposed to give his daughter Michal to David in marriage. But in his heart Saul was hoping the Philistines would kill David while he attempted to acquire the special dowry he had deviously chosen (1 Sam. 18:20–25).

- In Matthew 23, Jesus said seven times that the Pharisees were "hypocrites," or notorious religious actors! (See Matthew 23:13, 14, 15, 23, 25, 27, 29.) He compared them to "whited sepulchers," or whitewashed tombs, to show how they thought only about clean appearances and not at all about corrupt motives (vv. 25–28). Affirming the outward righteousness of their devotional habits, Jesus credited the Pharisees with frequent prayers, donations, and fasts. Then He exposed their corrupt underlying motive: they did so only to be seen and praised by men, not by God (Matt. 6:2, 5, 16).

- Absalom seemed moved by genuine respect when he bowed low to honor his father-monarch, King David

(2 Sam. 14:33). Yet the next day he proved his reverence was only an act by launching a sinister slander campaign to dishonor and dethrone David (2 Sam. 15:1–6).

- The Herodians sounded like converted men when they praised Jesus as a truthful, unbiased, divinely sent teacher: "Master, we know that thou art true, and teachest the way of God in truth" (Matt. 22:16). But all the while their hearts were yearning for Him to say something, anything, they and the Pharisees could use to incriminate Him (v. 15).

- The sons of Sceva appeared to be merciful ministers as they attempted to deliver a young man from demons in Ephesus. But their real motive was not righteous compassion but religious competition—to outshine Paul's shining deliverance ministry in that city (Acts 19:11–13).

- Judas lifted his voice to protest the apparent "waste" of Mary of Bethany's expensive spikenard, suggesting that it should have been sold and given to the poor. Yet John reveals that Judas' real aim was not charitable but covetous—to pocket the money for himself (John 12:4–6).

All of these good deeds were nullified by unquestionably bad motives. Conversely, the Bible also tells of questionable acts that arose from unquestionably good intentions.

- To casual bystanders, Elijah looked like a conscienceless swindler—just another crass prophet for profit—when he brazenly asked the desperately poor widow of Zarephath to give her and her son's last handful of food to *him* (1 Kings 17:10–16)! But the man of God did so for a spiritual, not selfish, reason. He knew she had to give to get, that only if she gave to God would God reciprocate, according to His timeless principle of giving (Luke 6:38), and give her His miraculous provision to sustain her and her son through the famine.

- Jesus sounded terribly callous when He told an aspiring disciple to *not* attend his own dying father's funeral (Luke 9:59–60). But His intention was not to hurt but to heal—to demonstrate the vital "kingdom first" principle (Matt. 6:32–33), which, if obeyed, would have led the young man into a ministry that would have saved many fathers and sons in Israel.

- Jesus looked like a lawbreaker caught in the act when He first permitted His disciples to glean grain, and then He healed the sick, on the Sabbath (Matt. 12:1–8, 9–13). But such actions were exceptional, not typical. Usually Jesus delighted to rest on the Sabbath, but on these rare occasions He worked only to show mercy on those in need—that they might more fully enter into the true and enduring rest of faith in God.

- When He suddenly and forcefully dismantled the religious marketplace the Jews had placed in the temple courts at Jerusalem, Jesus appeared to be an even worse character: a violent, irrational, sacrilegious blasphemer. His purpose, however, was not to dishonor but to honor His heavenly Father and His house of worship—to demonstrate holy outrage at the unholy commercialism being practiced there unlawfully (John 2:13–17).

Despite their dubious appearances, all these acts were perfectly right in God's eyes.

In his essay "The All-importance of Motive," A. W. Tozer gives some powerful perspectives on the vital importance of right motives:

The test by which all conduct must finally be judged is motive...

As water cannot rise higher than its source, so the moral quality in an act can never be higher than the motive that inspires it. For this reason no act that arises from an evil motive can be good, even though some good may appear to come out of it. Every deed done out of anger or spite, for instance, will be found at last to have been done for the enemy and against the Kingdom of God...

Unfortunately the nature of religious activity is such that much of it can be carried on for reasons that are not good, such as anger, jealousy, ambition, vanity and avarice...

Many a solo is sung to show off; many a sermon is preached as an exhibition of talent; many a church is founded as a slap at some other church. Even missionary activity may become competitive, and soul winning may degenerate into a sort of brush-salesman project to satisfy the flesh...

The apostle takes the highest religious service and consigns it to futility unless it is motivated by love. Lacking love, prophets, teachers, orators, philanthropists and martyrs are sent away without reward...

To sum it up, we may say simply that in the sight of God we are judged not so much by what we do as by our reasons for doing it. Not *what* but *why* will be the important question when we Christians appear at the judgment seat to give account of the deeds done in the body.[1]

You may ask, "How will I know when my motives are not right?" You will know because the Holy Spirit will convict you.

Then just cooperate with Him. When He weighs your acts and thoughts in His balances and your motives come up short, don't resist-His revelations, however humiliating and persistent. Any fool can justify his folly and any carnal Christian his bad motives. It takes a wise and humble soul to acknowledge its own wrong thoughts, intentions, or secret desires. So confess your sin to God, be cleansed, and correct either your motive or your act, or both, as needed. You may wonder, "Do I have to wait for the Spirit to speak to me? Can't I take the initiative myself now?"

Yes, you can, and you should. Be proactive by forming a new habit of motive examination: "Examine yourselves" (2 Cor. 13:5). Every time you undertake a new line of action, ask yourself, "Why am I doing this?" (Or, "Why am I *not* doing this?") If unrighteous motives—vanity, ambition, fear of man, love of money, envy (competitiveness), jealousy, strife, spite, the approval of man—are driving you, stop and go no farther. But if your motives are right—to please God, show faith, be loving or merciful, fulfill your duty, bless others, minister the Word of God, or spread the gospel—go forward with confidence. You may wonder, "How can I ensure that my self-judgments will be accurate?"

Here are some suggestions. First, keep very short accounts with God and man. Don't let any separation remain between you and Jesus. Quickly identify causes of offense and obey God's Word concerning them. Hold no hard attitudes toward anyone for any reason: forgive, forsake anger, refuse fear, and watch for spite and envy. Second, stay very full of the Spirit of God. Prayer, thanksgiving, and worship will permeate you with the Holy Spirit—who is the Convicter. So, "Pray without ceasing" (1 Thess. 5:17). That is, have times of prayer and have prayer all the time, remembering closeness brings fullness. Give thanks to God continually. And worship the Lord regularly. Third, stay full of God's Word. Prayerfully read and study your Bible daily and meditate upon—ponder in pleasure—its statements often. A truly supernatural force, the Word of God (which is full of the Holy Spirit) has an amazingly accurate way of exposing wrong intents and motives. Like a sharp sword, it swiftly penetrates our subconscious and brings to the surface any wrong motives that are driving us, however subtly:

> For the Word that God speaks is alive and full of power [making it active ...]; it is sharper than any two-edged sword,

penetrating… […the deepest parts of our nature], *exposing and sifting and analyzing and judging the very thoughts and purposes of the heart.*
—HEBREWS 4:12, AMP, EMPHASIS ADDED

Finally, remember this unchanging biblical precept: "If we would judge ourselves, we should not be judged" (1 Cor. 11:31). That is, if we will face our true motives now, fully, deeply, honestly, and consistently, we need never worry about facing Jesus.

Provided, of course, that we let Him correct our attitudes.

Chapter Four

ATTITUDES, ATTITUDES, ATTITUDES...

*W*hat your attitudes are, you are—that's the inspired conclusion of wise King Solomon. Or, to put it in his words:

> As he thinketh in his heart, so is he.
>
> —PROVERBS 23:7

Paraphrased, this pearl of wisdom states:

> The way a man thinks is the way he really is [that is, more than what he appears to say or do, what he thinks determines and discloses what he is].

Do we in the church, and especially in the ministry, realize this as we should?

In our zeal to sanctify believers' behavior, we sometimes overlook their being. But God always seeks first to correct the inner man, then to rectify outward appearances and actions: "For the LORD seeth not as man seeth; for man looketh on the outward appearance, but *the LORD looketh on the heart"* (1 Sam. 16:7, emphasis added). Just recently this was brought home to me afresh.

A fellow counselor told me of a Christian sister who failed to give financial aid to her son when asked to do so. Admittedly, the son had proven irresponsible in the past, rarely repaying his debts despite his promises to do so. Nevertheless, Christ's command concerning personal requests for charity remains clear: "Give to every man that [in need, personally] asketh of thee" (Luke 6:30). (This does not obligate us to give to non-necessities or to every fund-raising scheme, ministry request, or large charity, but rather to personal appeals for personal needs, especially from family members.) And her son's request was for a reasonable amount and a legitimate need—his utilities payment. So I felt that, to obey God's Word, she should have given. Upon further inquiry, the real reason for her failure surfaced: "I *hate* my son's wife; I just *despise* her," she admitted, revealing the secret lack of mercy that had held her back. The Lord showed me that this attitude was what He was after all along. Knowing her heart, He had prompted her son's request, not only to give her a chance to do God's Word, but also to expose her wrong attitude that she had long held unconfessed, so she could then be rid of it by confession and repentance. This was no isolated occurrence.

In counseling Christians, I have often noticed the Holy Spirit using circumstances to expose and correct bad attitudes, or *fixed patterns of wrong thinking and feelings toward people or situations.* Indeed, His commission from the heavenly Father probably reads something like this:

> Your assignment during the Church Age is to conform My people to the character-image of My Son. (See Romans 8:29.) For that, You will have to change them substantively, not superficially. Your work must not be religious or ritualistic but revolutionary. You must change not only

my people's behavior but also their very being—and not just positionally, but practically. To reform their consistent actions, You must reform their consistent attitudes. So focus Your work there. Always concentrate on their attitudes...their attitudes...their attitudes...

Why is this likely? Because from the eternal perspective of the Father of spirits, we are bundles of attitudes temporarily inhabiting mortal bodies. When we expire physically, we leave our bodies behind, but we carry our attitudes with us into eternity. Hence, God's evaluation of us for fellowship with and service to Him is based largely upon our attitudes: "The Lord looketh on the heart [attitude, way of thinking, feelings, mood, mental posture]."

Sure that attitudes command actions, A. W. Tozer wrote:

Except for that conduct which springs from our basic natural instincts, all conscious behavior is preceded by and arises out of our thoughts...Thinking stirs feeling and feeling triggers action. That is the way we are made and we may as well accept it.[1]

Perhaps this is why, in His process of sanctification, the Lord seeks to make us thoroughly right from core to cover, beginning with our inward thoughts, motives, and feelings, and then extending to our outward actions. It also explains why David declared, "Thou desirest truth in the inward parts, and in the hidden part" (Ps. 51:6). Clearly, then, we can't be sanctified—or holy, meaning pure in heart and set apart for our holy God and His exclusive use—if our attitudes remain uncorrected in our "inward parts," or hearts and minds. This lack of sanctification causes at least three other major problems in our lives.

First, it causes us not to be fit for divine service. While He saves even the vilest people if they repent, God uses only sanctified souls in His service. "Sanctified, and fit for the master's use" (2 Tim. 2:21) is always heaven's standing, inviolable prerequisite for God-approved ministry. Indeed God won't call us if our attitudes remain uncorrected. And if after entering His service we let sinful attitudes return, we immediately begin losing divine approval and spiritual power for further service. To confirm this, we need only to study the lives of Samson, Eli's sons, and King Saul, whose souls and service were spoiled by anger, greed, and envy respectively.

Second, bad attitudes spoil our worship. Jesus expressly said that the heavenly Father seeks, and requires, that all our worship be rendered "in spirit and in truth" (John 4:23–24). Unspiritual (carnal), untruthful, and ungodly attitudes, then, render our offerings of praise and worship as unacceptable as swine's flesh on the altar of the tabernacle—a distress, not a delight, to God! So we can't be God's "true worshipers" if we let ungodly attitudes rest in our hearts.

Third, bad attitudes create "strongholds" of sin in our lives. "For the weapons of our [spiritual] warfare are…mighty through God to the pulling down of *strongholds*" (2 Cor. 10:4, emphasis added). Besides referring to demonic possession and oppression, the term "strongholds" also speaks of long-standing bad attitudes through which Satan firmly holds and manipulates us at will to speak or act against others and ourselves. I'm sure the apostle Paul had this in mind when he described to Timothy "those that oppose themselves…that they may recover themselves out of the snare of the devil, who are taken captive by him at his will" (2 Tim. 2:25–26, KJV). This state of mind, in which the devil has a spiritual "advantage" (2 Cor. 2:11), or controlling position, over us, results from our having yielded consistently to sinful attitudes or actions. Paul encapsulated this principle that *yielding determines servantship* in his writing to the Romans: "Know ye not that to *whom ye yield* yourselves servants to obey, *his servants ye are* whom ye obey, whether of sin unto death, or of obedience unto righteousness?" (Rom. 6:16, emphasis added). This bondage to carnal attitudes is fully the opposite of the spiritual liberty Jesus came to give us. So we can't be "free indeed" (John 8:36), or thoroughly liberated from sin and its cruel master, if we harbor bad attitudes. You may wonder, "Do other scriptures confirm the vital nature of our attitudes?"

Indeed they do, as the following quotations demonstrate. Each of these Bible references indicates that wrong thoughts or feelings are equally as damaging as wrong words or acts. Jesus taught us, "For out of the heart proceed *evil thoughts* [including attitudes] ... these are the things which defile a man [render him unfit for fellowship with and use by God]" (Matt. 15:19–20, emphasis added). He also said harboring unjustified anger is a cause for divine chastisement: "Whosoever is angry with his brother without a cause shall be in danger of judgment" (Matt. 5:22). Resounding this theme, the apostle John declared that despising a brother or sister in Christ, even if nothing hostile is ever said or done, puts one in the spiritual darkness of sin and deception: "He that saith he is in the light, and hateth his brother, is in darkness even until now ... and walketh in darkness ... because darkness hath blinded his [inner] eyes [of understanding]" (1 John 2:9–11).

COMMON BAD ATTITUDES

What are some of our most common bad attitudes? Consider these.

- **Pride** certainly ranks first among our besetting bad attitudes. To think too highly of ourselves and not highly enough of others or of God renders us an "abomination" to God (Prov. 6:16–17).

- **Prejudice**—harboring preconceived unflattering notions about people because of their race, nationality, occupation, or religion (even Christian denomination!)—also offends Him who is "no respecter of persons" (Acts 10:34–35).

- **Envy** of others' blessings, advantages, achievements, gifts, popularity, promotions, or honors transforms sweet, cooperative friendships into bitter, competitive rivalries.

- **Hardness of heart** (indifference or callousness) toward spouses, children, unpleasant relatives, neighbors, or fellow church members separates us from the God who "is love" (1 John 4:8) and who would have us always will the highest good for every soul.

- **Insubordination** to legitimate human authorities, such as employers, managers, pastors, law enforcement officers, judges, or elected officials, is another unacceptable frame of mind, because all legal human authority is "ordained of God," who has commanded Christians to "be subject unto the higher powers" (Rom. 13:1).

- **Loathing one's occupation** is both an iniquitous and ignorant negative outlook. It is sinful because God commands us, "Whatever ye do, do it heartily, as to the Lord, and not unto men, knowing that of the Lord ye shall receive the reward" (Col. 3:23–24). It is unwise because it causes us to despise, and thus lose the enjoyment of, the very activity at which we spend most of our waking hours.

- **Stubbornness**, or reluctance to enact divinely prompted or humanly required changes, even when we sense they will bring God's blessing, is another nefarious mind-set.

- **Rejecting, denying, or ignoring the arrival of divinely authorized adverse circumstances** is another. While never preferred, periodic visitations of trouble are universally unavoidable in this fallen world, for "man is born unto trouble, as [surely as] the sparks fly upward [from a campfire]" (Job 5:7). And Jesus promised us

they would come: "In the world ye shall have tribulation" (John 16:33).

- **Unforgiveness and resentment** toward personal adversaries are dispositions harbored everywhere...and helpful nowhere.

- **Self-pity**, that subtle but highly destructive self-
sympathy and self-petting that weakens us and halts
all spiritual progress, is another.

Attitudes such as these are the large, strong, and ugly roots
of sin the Holy Spirit seeks to "axe" to the glory of God!

"There was a man sent from God, whose name was John [the
Baptist]" (John 1:6). God sent John to teach us not to deal with
sin at the fruit level but at the root level: "Now also the axe
is laid unto the *root* of the trees [of sin]" (Luke 3:9, emphasis added). Dealing with our bad attitudes—habitually wrong
thoughts and feelings toward people or circumstances—does
just this. If we will humbly and steadily obey the Holy Spirit as
He shows us our wrong viewpoints, the roots of sin in our souls
will be plucked up and new roots of godliness planted—and
our lives will be established in a new, beautiful divine order or
pattern of consistent growth.

Clean, our new roots of righteousness will keep us free from
spiritual contaminants and toxins. Open, they will draw large
amounts of the life of God into our thirsty souls daily. Free, they
will not be entangled any longer by the thorns, thistles, or parasites
of this world. Strong, they will hold us in place when the turbulent
winds of trial blow hard against our faith. Noble, they will make us
like Jesus, the Root of David and most glorious Tree of Righteousness. And as we interact with people daily, they will taste our new
"fruit," that is, our consistently Christlike attitudes, words, and
actions. And, blessed, they will praise and glorify God.

So let the Holy Spirit have His way with you, my friend. Today, yield to His conviction and correct your *attitudes, attitudes, attitudes…*

This will please the Lord—and save you and everyone around you a lot of needless trouble.

Chapter Five

TROUBLE—AND THOSE WHO MAKE IT

*I*n all interpersonal relationships—in our homes, neighborhoods, churches, schools, and places of business—trouble doesn't just accidentally happen. Wherever there is trouble, there is a troublemaker. And wherever there is a troublemaker, there is a troubled soul—someone with an unresolved heart issue that makes his or her spirit restless rather than restful. I remember when the Lord first taught me this.

The year was 1977, the place was Greensboro, North Carolina, the learner was myself, and the subject was one "Bill Marden," a near-retirement-age underwriter who worked for the Shelby Mutual Insurance Company. (I have changed Bill's name to preserve his anonymity.) I first met Bill when visiting Shelby Mutual's regional office in Greensboro with my father, an independent insurance agent. Since I had recently begun working for dad as a bookkeeper and agent in training, he had taken me along to see firsthand the day-to-day activities of an insurance company office. In the previous months, I had conversed and corresponded with several of Shelby Mutual's employees and found them both competent and courteous. But Bill Marden was different. He was in a bad mood almost every time I spoke with him. His manner was curt, his voice was loud and raspy, and his words were abrasive. Even his handwritten memos seemed irritated, so hastily and messily written they were virtually illegible. Nevertheless, a new employee in a new setting and new season of life, I was eager to visit the company and largely unconcerned with Bill's characteristic grumpiness. But the Lord sent me that day to learn not merely about business but about life.

As we circuited the large, unpartitioned, main room filled with wall-to-wall desks and people, the resident manager pointed out who was who, where they sat, and what they did. Noting there were so many people working in such close proximity, I asked if everyone was able to concentrate on their work with noise and motion on every side. Surprisingly, he said they were...most of the time. Then, with a sigh, he disclosed the unpleasant exception. "We get on well in the mornings. Everyone goes about his or her business quietly. Then it starts. Old Bill Marden gets into an argument with an agent or broker over the telephone, and, after listening to his loud, rude comments, the others get so agitated that they start arguing too, with each other or with callers. The whole day seems to go downhill from there." So I listened and learned of the contagion of contention.

After reflection I realized the company's trouble was not vague and unidentifiable, but specific and personal. It was caused by one person, not twenty. It didn't enter the room through a window, but through a body. It wasn't abstract, but real and tangible. It had a name, face, and personality. And it, rather he, made trouble for one reason only: he was a troubled soul. When he didn't make trouble, there was no trouble. Peace, order, and productivity prevailed among the other employees. Years later I discovered that the Bible describes this very principle, the contagion of contention, in both its precepts and historical record.

In our examination of the Book of Proverbs, for instance, we find this prized black pearl of truth:

> Where no wood is, there the fire goeth out; so where there is no talebearer, the strife ceaseth. As coals are to burning coals, and wood to fire, so is a contentious man to kindle strife.
>
> —Proverbs 26:20–21

Paraphrased and inverted, this two-sentence maxim states:

> A gossipy [literally, a whispering] or contentious [pugnacious, belligerent, or rude] person causes and fuels hot arguments and divisions. Remove the contentious or gossipy person, and the contention and controversy will end, just like a fire deprived of its wood and coals.

Only heaven knows what was gnawing at old Bill Marden, but gnawing it was! And angry and contentious he was! And needlessly troubled his colleagues were! Truly, he was our text personified.

Other Old and New Testament references also speak of trouble and those who make it: "A wrathful man *stirreth up strife*" (Prov. 15:18, emphasis added). "There are those who *raise up strife and contention*" (Hab. 1:3, emphasis added). "But unto them that are *contentious…*" (Rom. 2:8, emphasis added).

While any of us may fall headlong into a senseless argument at any time if we don't watch ourselves, there are many people (including Bible-professing, church-going Christians) who are chronically argumentative: "a contentious man" (Prov. 26:21) or "a contentious…woman" (Prov. 21:19). By their repeated life choices, these bellicose battlers have formed a deeply ingrained inclination to controvert. While most people are loath to argue, these determined debaters are exceptionally prone, even driven, to argue over the most trivial matters, even when presently there is absolutely no chance for agreement or a change of mind. Far from eschewing it, they *enjoy* arguing and freely accuse, condemn, berate, and mock the targets of their verbal abuse without a twinge of guilt. The only thing that disturbs them, it seems, is *not* finding someone with whom they can argue. What a pity!

THE HIDDEN TOXINS OF TROUBLEMAKERS

What is it that transforms a pleasant, congenial human being pro-created in the image of God into such a belligerent, problematic son of Belial? The real generators of contentiousness, some of which we introduced in the previous chapter, are always unresolved sin-issues of the heart. Scripture identifies a number of these hidden toxins that transmute potentially sweet peacemakers into incorrigibly bitter strife-mongers. Here are some of them.

- **Unquenched anger** is one sure spiritual poison: "An angry man stirreth up strife" (Prov. 29:22).

- **Unforgiveness, vengeance, and hatred** are three others closely related: "Hatred stirreth up strifes" (Prov. 10:12).

- **Unrequited love or unreturned favors** are two more. When Samson's beloved bride failed to respond to him with affection and loyalty, he was so embittered that he troubled Philistia for twenty years! Though used of God for His larger, loving purposes toward His covenant people, Samson's bad reaction nevertheless left him a troubled soul, pitifully small and persistently driven by bitterness.

- **A proud attitude** is another. One proverb declares, "He that is of a proud heart stirreth up strife" (Prov. 28:25), and another reveals, "Only by pride cometh contention" (Prov. 13:10).

- **Ambition**, whether worldly or religious, is another. As the apostles mused "which of them should be accounted the greatest," trouble suddenly erupted among the holy apostles of peace: "There was ... a strife among them" (Luke 22:24).

- **Thoughts of misjudgment and condemnation** are two more troublous toxins. When Nabal harbored gross mischaracterizations of David as a worthless servant who had rebelled against his loving master (1 Sam. 25:10–11), he cruelly reproached him and lit a potentially deadly firestorm of controversy in David's heart (vv. 12–35).

- **Thoughts of scorn** are another. Haughty, belittling thoughts prompt arrogantly inconsiderate acts and derisive words, two sure social incendiaries: "Cast out the scoffer [mocker], and contention shall go out; yea, strife and reproach shall cease" (Prov. 22:10).

- **Gossip and talebearing**—releasing defaming, shameful, and often partially or completely false information that should be repressed—are two others, as this chapter's sample proverb relates: "Where there is no talebearer [whisperer], the strife ceaseth" (Prov. 26:20).

- **Envy**, a topic discussed more fully later in this book, is a very active source of bitterness and belligerence. The apostle Paul discerned it as a cause of division in the Corinthian church: "There is among you envying, and strife, and divisions" (1 Cor. 3:3).

- **Preoccupation with pet doctrines** is another spiritual poison. Paul warned Titus to "avoid" controversial conversations with those who were obsessed with "contentions, and strivings about the law" (Tit. 3:9). (See also Romans 14:1–6.)

When these or other spiritual contaminates are left unchecked in our hearts, spiritual agitation begins. And instead of being calm and placid, the waters of our soul begin to churn, seethe, and boil—and they are sure to boil over into a controversy.

What can we do to minimize contention, division, and trouble and maximize peace, order, and progress? Here are three proven biblical methods of peacemaking.

First, when contention arises in your home, church, school, neighborhood, or place of employment, seek a real, not a superficial, cure. Aim at rooting out the true, underlying, unresolved issue troubling your troublemaker. Go before God in intercessory prayer about the problem. If He shows you the problem and you have a door to speak, render counsel, or pass along your understanding to one who is better gifted and trained to do so. If counsel is rejected, continue praying in faith for your troublemaker's repentance until God by the pressures of conviction or adversity opens him (or her) up to correction.

Second, watch over your own heart very diligently: "Keep thy heart with all diligence, for out of it are the issues of life" (Prov. 4:23). When the Spirit quietly convicts you of having an unsettled sin-issue, don't play the fool by ignoring Him. Settle the issue scripturally, quickly, and thoroughly. Whatever line of action Christ, the living Word, commands about that issue—confession, restitution, submission, committal, or simply attitude reformation—take it: "Whatever he saith unto you, do it" (John 2:5). And don't stop short. Don't consider your heart-issue settled until God's peace, "the peace of God, which passeth all understanding" (Phil. 4:7), fully and deeply refills and permeates your heart. That alone is proof that your spiritual transaction is complete and all is well.

Third, refuse to enter into senseless strife. The moment you discern that there is presently no way you can reach agreement with someone or change his (or her) mind, drop the matter. Though He was bold and blunt-spoken when necessary, and His ministry was highly controversial, Jesus of Nazareth was not a controversialist. He never purposely sought or stirred contention, though it frequently arose against Him as He humbly taught His Father's truth or did His Father's works. And through the Epistles He has, as Head of the church, ordered us not to give ourselves to contention: "Charging them before the Lord that they strive not about words to no profit, but to the subverting of the hearers" (2 Tim. 2:14). And again, "The servant of the Lord must not strive, but be gentle unto all men, apt to teach, patient" (v. 24). So settle it: there is only one striver you should strive to silence . . . yourself! "If it be possible, *as much as lieth in you*, live peaceably with all men" (Rom. 12:18, emphasis added). Make up your mind, then, and confess, "I can't control whether others forsake or hold their contentiousness, but I can, and will, quench all the strife *that 'lieth in me,'* that is, in my own thoughts and words." (See Proverbs 17:14.) Remember, God commands us not to argue with our testy contradictors for a good reason— so He may argue the matter, or "plead our cause," for us! "I will contend with him that contendeth with thee" (Isa. 49:25).

But will we obey Him? If so, three wonderful blessings will follow. First, we won't be troubled. The inner lake of our spirit will be still and quiet, not swirling or churning. Second, we won't trouble others. We will never unnecessarily disturb the waters of our home, church, school, workplace, or neighborhood. And third, when troubled troublemakers trouble those waters, we'll be ready and able to diffuse the trouble, as did our peacemaking forefather in faith, Abraham, who said to his fellow pilgrim, Lot:

> Let there be no strife, I pray thee, between me and thee . . . for we are brethren.
>
> —GENESIS 13:8

To excel at peacemaking, we must learn to say the right thing to the right person at the right time—and in the right way.

Chapter Six

WORDS FITLY SPOKEN

s the chief biblical repository for God's wisdom, the Book of Proverbs speaks to all aspects of wisdom, or good judgment, and all areas of conduct. One area of conduct it addresses repeatedly is our speech: what we say, when we say it, how we say it, and to whom we say it. Undoubtedly a student of the Book of Proverbs, the prophet Isaiah referred to wise, Spirit-led speakers as possessing "the tongue of the learned." "The Lord GOD hath given me *the tongue of the learned*, that I should know how to speak a word in season to him who is weary" (Isa. 50:4, emphasis added). If we aspire to have and walk in godly wisdom—and every one of us should—we must prayerfully seek and develop "the tongue of the learned."

Succinctly, this means that our speech as well as our thoughts should increasingly reflect that we are becoming spiritually "learned," or taught by God's Spirit in the ways of wisdom and grace. One of Solomon's inspired axioms reveals that God considers wise speech both valuable and beautiful:

A word fitly spoken is like apples of gold in pictures of silver.
—PROVERBS 25:11

Paraphrased, this reads:

> A word [verse, statement, or message] spoken in the right time and way is as beautiful and valuable [to God and the wise] as a table setting [or wall hanging] of golden apples in silver baskets.

The word *pictures* is translated from the Hebrew word *maskiyth*, which means a "figure" carved or modeled; that is, a sculpture. Several expert translators also render the word as "settings" (NIV, NAS, NKJV, MLB). Thus they believe Solomon envisioned a royal place setting consisting of a basket, bowl, or tray made of sterling silver in which were arranged decorative apples molded from pure gold. It is also possible that he envisioned a wall hanging, such as a relief, or sculpted "picture," carved from wood and overlaid with gold and silver. Such an elaborate table setting or wall hanging would have two evident characteristics: high value and immense beauty. Apples of gold in settings of silver would be very costly, since they would be made from two of the three most precious metals naturally occurring on earth. They would also be very beautiful, or aesthetically pleasing to look upon. What is more stunningly attractive than gold or silver jewelry, art, or furniture? From this inspired maxim, therefore, we learn the essential truth that when we speak the right substance in the right season we are very *valuable* and *beautiful* to God and the wise.

Let's take this analysis a little further. By "valuable" we mean facilitating, or something or someone that enables or expedites the performance of a plan, in this case, God's. Words fitly spoken cause God's will to be done and His kingdom to be established in human lives. Conversely, they destroy Satan's work in people, thus decreasing his sphere of control, or kingdom. Every day Jesus released fitly spoken words that utterly dismantled Satan's work of sin and deception in human souls: "For this purpose the Son of God was manifested, that he might destroy the works of the devil" (1 John 3:8).

By "beautiful" we mean pleasing or satisfying. When we gaze at a beautiful sight, such as a mountaintop vista, seascape, or sunset, our minds and bodies receive a very real and permeating sense of satisfaction. Our psychological burdens and emotional agitations are temporarily relieved, and our whole being is lightened and infiltrated with deep, satisfying peace. A beautiful sight, then, is a satisfying experience. Hence, we conclude that words fitly spoken are both *facilitating* and *satisfying* to God and His people. By them, His plan is fulfilled and His heart satisfied, and His people's works are accomplished and their hearts relieved.

WORDS FITLY SPOKEN

Let's consider some biblical examples that illustrate this proverb.

A word of timely instruction

At the very moment the Ethiopian eunuch was reading Isaiah's description of the suffering Savior, Philip met him and explained the passage to his satisfaction and salvation (Acts 8:29–35). The right teaching at the right time for the right student, Philip's timely homily led to the conversion of a believer who later founded an enduring church in Ethiopia. Hence Philip's words delighted the hearts of God, Philip, the Ethiopian, and countless African believers. "A word spoken in due season, how good is it!" (Prov. 15:23). (For other words of timely instruction, see Acts 18:24–26; Revelation 2–3.)

A word of exhortation

The very day David grew weak and weary, Jonathan visited him and "strengthened his hand in God" (1 Sam. 23:16–17) by reassuring him that God would keep His promise to make him king of Israel. Thus he dissuaded from fear and urged forward in faith the man God had chosen to lead and bless His then visible kingdom on earth, the nation of Israel. How priceless

Jonathan's words were and how satisfying to God and to David! (For more words of exhortation, see 1 Chronicles 28:20–21; Nehemiah 4:14; Haggai 2:4–5; Luke 3:7–14; Acts 2:40; 18:9; Hebrews 3:13.)

A word of reconciliation

When the apostle Paul returned Onesimus to Philemon, he sent a letter urging Philemon, his personal friend and fellow minister, to fully receive his now converted and faithful former servant, who had previously robbed and abandoned Philemon. (See Philemon 1–21.) His conciliatory words were the bond of love that re-cemented the two who had been so long and bitterly separated. Paul's epistle was beautifully adorned with gracious words, iridescent pearls of gracious wisdom. And it was highly valuable to Onesimus, Philemon, and those who sat under his subsequent ministry, which was surely enriched by his decision to receive his former offender! (For more words of reconciliation, see Genesis 45:1–15; Matthew 5:23–24; 1 Corinthians 7:11; 2 Corinthians 2:6–7; Galatians 6:1–2.)

A word of prophecy

"He will show you things to come," promised Jesus, as He described the various ministries of the soon coming Holy Spirit (John 16:13). And, indeed, through Agabus and other inspired foretellers of future events the Spirit forewarned Paul of his approaching unjust arrest and incarceration in Jerusalem. (See Acts 21:10–11; 20:22–23.) Though ominous and misinterpreted as a *prohibition* by Paul's understandably concerned brethren (Acts 21:12), this repeated prophecy was invaluable to God's purpose, because it fully *preconditioned* Paul, who, thus strengthened, stood like a rock in the midst of the ensuing storm stirred by his rabid Jewish persecutors! (See Acts 21:27–22:23.) (For more words of prophecy, see Acts 27:21–26; Revelation 1:19.)

A word of wise counsel

The ingenious famine preparation plan Joseph presented to Pharaoh (Gen. 41:33–36) was of great worth to Jehovah, because it facilitated His worldwide plan of redemption by rescuing the people through whom the Savior would eventually come. It was also incalculably valuable to Pharaoh, because it saved his throne and nation. (For more words of wise counsel, see Exodus 10:7; 1 Kings 12:7; Revelation 3:18.)

A word of guidance

When the self-willed, ambitious, insubordinate, and insolent Diotrephes usurped control of the church attended by Gaius, Gaius' teacher, the apostle John, wrote him, exposing Diotrephes for what he was. John graciously but clearly called on Gaius and his fellow congregants to turn away from Diotrephes and call Demetrius, a godly elder, as their new minister. (See 3 John 9–12.) This bold pastoral guidance saved a promising disciple from deception, a church from ruinous leadership, God's kingdom from substantial loss of fruit, and His name from dishonor. It was a golden word from a leader of sterling worth and a magnificently satisfying sight to the eyes of God! (For more words of guidance, see Acts 20:28; 1 Timothy 4:12–16; 2 Timothy 2:15–26; 1 Peter 5:1–4.)

A word of correction

The prophet Nathan's incisive parabolic reproof of David is a thing of exquisite beauty in the sight of both every reader and the Inspirer of Scripture. (See 2 Samuel 12:1–12.) Had he not thrust his razor-sharp spiritual sword, "Thou art the man," straight into David's heart, the anointed king's fruitful multifaceted ministry—as psalmist, musician, writer, prophet, head of state, chief justice, and military commander of the chosen people—may well have ended in shameful judgment. Indeed, it was a pearl of great price. (For other words of correction, see 1 Samuel 25:23–35; 2 Samuel 19:1–7; 24:3; Proverbs 25:12; John 8:7–9; 21:15–17; Galatians 2:11–14; 2 Timothy 3:16; 4:1–2.)

A word of warning

A gifted, prolific, and Spirit-led exhorter and warner of erring believers, Paul cautioned the Corinthians that if they did not receive into fellowship their repentant brother, their unforgiveness would give Satan a spiritual "advantage" (2 Cor. 2:9–11), or an opportunity to deceive, infiltrate, and ruin them. His timely alert was highly valuable to God and to the Corinthians, because if they had remained unmerciful, their shining witness and work in Achaia would have been sadly snuffed out. (For more words of warning, see Esther 4:13–16; Matthew 5:25–26; Acts 20:28–31; 27:9–11; 2 Timothy 4:14–15.)

A word of knowledge

Seen first in Jesus' ministry, all the various gifts of the Holy Spirit, including the "word of knowledge" (1 Cor. 12:8), are irreplaceably valuable to God's work. When by the Spirit alone (without natural means of discovery) the Nazarene revealed Zacchaeus' name (Luke 19:5), Nathaniel's character (John 1:47), and the sin of the woman by the well (John 4:18), they were each immediately gripped by the overwhelming conviction that God saw them, knew them intimately, and wanted to save them—and the Spirit drew them straight into the salvation and kingdom of God! (For other words of knowledge, see 1 Corinthians 14:24–25.)

A word of rebuke

When Spirit-given words of instruction, exhortation, reconciliation, counsel, guidance, correction, and warning are persistently rejected, it's time for the ministry of rebuke. When the Cretan Christians persisted in their besetting sins of lying, laziness, and gluttony, Paul's Spirit-inspired message was not soft but stinging: "Rebuke them sharply!" (Tit. 1:13). When delivered by Titus, Paul's rebuke cut and hurt, I'm sure, but in God's sight it was precious and beautiful, a master stroke sure to save His children from the powerful and deadly vortex of unrestrained carnality. (For more words of rebuke, see Matthew 16:23; 1 Corinthians 5:1–2; 11:17–22; 2 Timothy 4:2.)

A word of judgment

When even rebukes are repeatedly disregarded, only one fitly spoken word remains: a word of judgment. When Ahab's quietly efficient, "professional" elimination of Naboth was finished, the king of Israel confidently went down to take possession of his dead Jewish brother's vineyard. But, to his dismay, God had a disturbing message of judgment awaiting him in the mouth of Elijah. (See 1 Kings 21:1–24.) You may ask how such a word of condemnation and punishment could be beautiful or valuable. Because it was *the truth*—full, accurate, richly deserved, and final—and the truth is always beautiful to the God, Spirit, prophets, and people of truth. God's pronouncements of judgment are His final assessments of human lives and characters, and, complimentary or caustic, they are always pricelessly and beautifully true. (For more words of judgment, see Proverbs 29:1; Isaiah 54:17; Daniel 5:18–28, 30; Matthew 23:13–36; Acts 5:3–5, 9–10; 13:9–11.)

To fully satisfy God and perfectly facilitate His will, all these correct words must also be spoken in the correct spirit. "Fitly spoken" intimates a statement made not only at the right time but also with the right intent, manner, and tone of voice.

This means we should speak the truth with love, not lust, in our hearts; that is, focused on seeking our listener's highest good, not obsessed with proving we are right: "speaking the truth *in love…*" (Eph. 4:15, emphasis added). Oswald Chambers taught that we should identify ourselves with God's interests in every person we meet. This selfless identification with God's purposes in others is a mark of a soul that is maturing into full identity with the Son of God: "…may *grow up* [develop and mature] into him in all things, who is the head, even Christ" (Eph. 4:15, emphasis added).

We should also speak with gentleness, patience, and meekness: "The servant of the Lord must not strive, but be *gentle* unto all men...*patient*, in *meekness* instructing those that oppose him..." (2 Tim. 2:24–25, emphasis added). If we say the right thing proudly, our arrogance repels those who would otherwise listen. If we are in a hurry or preoccupied, we betray our lack of interest—and our listener loses interest. If we speak curtly, angrily, or mockingly, we speak God's truth in the devil's spirit—and offend our listener. By such carnal manners and tones, we drive away the very souls God is trying to draw to Him. By speaking gently, patiently, and meekly, however, we intensify the drawing of the Spirit and facilitate His success, and to His and our delight, "God...will give them repentance to the acknowledging of the truth...that they may recover themselves out of the snare of the devil" (vv. 25–26).

Furthermore, a little wit sometimes facilitates God's purpose. Like a drink with food, humor helps people swallow hard, heavy truths. After Paul graciously appealed to Philemon to forgive Onesimus' debt, he wittily reminded him that he himself was indebted to him! "If he has wronged or cheated you, put it down to my account...I, Paul, hereby promise to repay you. (Of course I'm not stressing the fact that you might be said to owe me your very soul!) Now do grant me this favour, my brother" (Philemon 18–20, PHILLIPS). And in the midst of his catalog of criticisms of the Corinthians, Paul interjected a touch of humor by asking them if they wanted him to come to them with fatherly praises or fatherly paddling rods! "Now it's up to you to choose! Shall I come to you ready to chastise you, or in love and gentleness?" (1 Cor. 4:21, PHILLIPS). A merry heart does good like a medicine—and opens the way for the Word! Sometimes poking fun at someone pokes a hole in their religious armor just wide enough for you to shoot an arrow of truth through to set them free. So make them laugh, then aim and let fly your word fitly spoken!

Finally, there are times when we must resort to pleading. If we're too proud to plead, we're too proud to please—that is, to please God! When the issue is urgent, don't orate or lecture. Get down and plead with your hearer to obey God—for his life's, family's, destiny's, and reward's sake; for Christ's honor and kingdom; and, if all else fails, to avoid the fearsome and uncharacteristic wrath of our characteristically kind heavenly Father! Paul wasn't too proud to do this, master theologian though he was. He told the Ephesian elders, "Watch [over your believer-sheep], and remember, that for the space of three years *I ceased not to warn [you and] everyone night and day with tears*" (Acts 20:31, emphasis added). The words "with tears" denote pleading. Paul reminded these ministers of his humble, frank, and heartfelt emotional appeals in order that they might emulate them when necessary in their own preaching and counsel. And the Holy Spirit incorporated them into Scripture that we might do the same.

When we speak the right words for God at the right time, are we speaking them in the right spirit? Are we speaking them with God's love, with the patience, gentleness, and meekness of the Holy Spirit, and, when appropriate, with humor or pleading? If not, it's time for us to pray.

When he realized it was imperative for him to rule in wisdom, young King Solomon prayed, "Give...thy servant an understanding heart" (1 Kings 3:9). Deeply pleased, God abundantly answered his petition: "Lo, I have given thee a wise and an understanding heart, so that there was none like thee before thee, neither after thee shall any arise like unto thee" (v. 12). Shouldn't we follow Solomon's example?

Let's ask God to give us "the tongue of the learned," so we can increasingly speak the right substance in the right season in the right spirit. Then, as other Spirit-led communicators before and after us, our lives and ministries will be like "apples of gold in settings of silver," to God, to the wise, and to everyone touched by our words. Daily we will facilitate, not frustrate, God's plans and His servants' works in the earth. And continually we will satisfy

His and His people's hearts—until the day we hear these satisfy-ing and priceless words ringing in our ears:

> Well done, thou good and faithful servant…Enter thou into the joy of thy lord.
>
> —MATTHEW 25:21

Until that day, let's focus on and seek spiritual understanding.

Chapter Seven

UNDERSTANDING: A WELLSPRING OF LIFE

*I*f you don't have understanding, you better get it—and soon! Your life, as well as the lives of many others, depends upon it.

The wisest writer and book in the Bible assert that understanding is our spiritual life source:

> Understanding is a wellspring of life unto him that hath it.
> —PROVERBS 16:22

Paraphrased, this means:

> Understanding [insight, interpretation, comprehension] is a springing well [source of life] to those who have it [and to those with whom they share it].

As stated previously, understanding is one of the four major divisions of godly wisdom described for us in the Book of Proverbs. Specifically, *understanding* is "insight," and *insight* is "the ability to comprehend and interpret hidden meanings or obscure messages." Specifically, it is defined as "penetrating mental vision or discernment; [the] faculty of seeing into inner character or

57

underlying truth."[1] Thus, insight is *the ability to go beneath or beyond surface appearances and grasp the inner realities of issues, events, people, statements, or subjects.* As stated earlier, we desperately need understanding. The apostle Paul prayed that "the eyes of your understanding be enlightened" (Eph. 1:18). Why did he do so? Because the two alternatives—having no understanding and having misunderstanding—are not only undesirable, but they are also deadly.

Having no understanding means simply that when presented with something new or different, we have no clue as to what it is or means or how we should relate to it. So we're left in the dark, stymied and stumped. This can be lethal. Jesus said, "When any one heareth the word [gospel] of the kingdom, and *understandeth it not*, then cometh the wicked one, and catcheth away that which was sown in his heart" (Matt. 13:19, emphasis added). Failure to grasp the message of salvation leaves one lost, without God, spiritually dead, and headed for the abyss of eternal torment.

Misunderstanding can be equally fatal. It occurs when our insights are inaccurate: We think we understand a matter correctly, but we're mistaken. We see, but our vision is blurred. We consider and conclude, but our conclusion is errant. After probing, examining, and analyzing Jesus, the learned Pharisees concluded, "Thou…hast a demon" (John 8:48), but it was they, not He, who were under demonic influence. This misunderstanding kept them from believing on and receiving Him, the Life.

When David's servants saw King Saul sleeping and unprotected in David's cave, they took it as a sign that God wanted David to kill Saul (1 Sam. 24:4). But their interpretation of events was inverted: God hoped David would *not* harm Saul. Had David taken their advice, it may have meant death, not only for Saul but also for David—the death of his walk with God, his kingship, and perhaps his physical life.

Just as surely as its alternatives are sources of death, understanding, or insight, is a source of life. Solomon describes insight as a "wellspring" of life. The Hebrew word he used for "wellspring" (*maqowr*) means "something dug; a source (of water, even when naturally flowing)."[2] This speaks of an artesian, or springing, well, a biblical "fountain" commonly referred to as a "spring." Wellsprings are sources of pressurized underground water, which, when tapped naturally by rock fissures or artificially by drilling, spring to the ground and release steady flows of water—from which we drink and live and share with others, who also drink and live. From the wellspring of spiritual understanding comes the precious spiritual water that gives life to us and to others.

That life may take a number of forms. Understanding the gospel of God's saving grace gives eternal life, or spiritual rebirth, to those who receive it. Understanding godly exhortation gives encouragement to discouraged souls. Understanding Bible teaching gives the knowledge of God to those who thirst for it. Understanding corrective counsel gives renewed life to erring Christians. Understanding key spiritual truths from God's Word enables tried believers to drink in refreshing inspiration to see them through their trials of faith and patience, however hot and long.

WE NEED INSIGHT INTO...

Here are some areas in which we all need understanding, or insight into what we read, see, or experience.

Scripture

Biblical insight is the greatest spiritual wellspring. Directly or indirectly, all of God's blessings spring from the living waters of the Word of the living God. The Holy Spirit alone gives us the fullest possible understanding of the Bible. Once grasped, Bible verses not only inspire us, but they also give us inspiration to give others. Philip imparted saving insight into Isaiah's writings to the Ethiopian eunuch only because he had first received it himself (Acts 8:30–31). Have you?

Are you seeking and receiving scriptural insight? "Understandest thou what thou readest?" (Acts 8:30).

Current events

In David's day, the men of Issachar possessed "understanding of the times, to know what Israel ought to do" (1 Chron. 12:32). Evidently they could interpret changing current events in light of the unchanging plan of God. They saw through temporal problems to the eternal solutions that lay back of them—the timeless principles of God's character, ways, judgments, and unfailing prophecies. They discerned the hand of God behind the acts of men and nations. Separated from the lukewarm majority, their vision was not clouded by the popular cravings and cries of their times. Hence, they looked beyond visible events to the invisible God who controlled all things for Israel's good. This penetrating vision enabled them to tell the Israelites where they stood, what was coming, and how to prepare for it. Where are our sons of Issachar today?

We have many pollsters, but few prophets; many statisticians, but few seers. Our leaders see, but few see through. Many are intelligent, but few are insightful. Where are those who can discern and solve our perplexing church, national, and international problems? Will you be one?

People

To succeed in life, we must deal successfully with people. For that, we must have insight into their true natures. We must see not only the persona they project but also the person they are. We must differentiate between their reputation and character. We must look beyond their talk and consider their walk. We must cut through the spin and grasp the substance. We must assess people by their actions, not their assets; their purpose, not their popularity; their commitments, not their chatter. Wrestling with this difficulty of discerning people's true characters, and knowing that only God knows men perfectly, Solomon prayed earnestly for a profound, God-given understanding of human beings: "Give…thy servant an understanding heart to judge thy people, that I may discern between good and bad" (1 Kings 3:9). As stated earlier, his prayer was abundantly answered.

Have you asked God to give you an "understanding heart" so you may deal wisely, fairly, and mercifully with the problematic, perplexing people you face daily? Why not ask Him now?

Adversities

Light is most valuable in the darkness. The darker our circumstances, the more we need the light of insight within. When enveloped by dark trials—rejection, betrayal, defamation, divorce, bereavement, financial collapse, failure, etc.—we must first seek the illumination of insight: "Is this testing or chastening, Lord? What do You want me to do? Shall I wait or move forward, change my modus operandi or maintain it? What is Your purpose in allowing these difficulties? Please give me a Bible verse, passage, or principle that parallels and explains my situation." Then, if we continue abiding, God will send the light.

Just to realize that *God* sends troubles, that He uses them to refine and mold us, that they prepare us to do His will, and that they must one day end, etc.—insights such as these are powerful spiritual light beams that guide us through the darkest storms to bright harbors of fulfillment. By showing us the end from the beginning, they keep us calm, strong, and hopeful in all the dark valleys that contradict and test our bright hopes. Hence, Solomon observed, "Understanding [insight] shall keep thee" (Prov. 2:11).

Are you intimidated by uncertainty or inspired by insight in your present valley of Baca?

A. W. Tozer, the exceptionally gifted twentieth-century writer, preacher, and prophet, wisely noted his (and our) generation's need of spiritual insight:

> We need the gift of discernment again in our pulpits…the anointed eye, the power of spiritual penetration and interpretation, the ability to appraise the religious scene as viewed from God's position, and to tell us what is actually going on…[3]

And for himself, Tozer prayed:

Lord, give me sharp eyes...give me understanding to see and courage to report what I see faithfully.[4]

By such persistent, passionate prayers Tozer drilled and accessed an amazingly deep and pure wellspring of spiritual insight, from which he drank and gave drink to many—including this writer—by the printed and spoken word. What about you?

Have you drilled your spiritual wellspring? Is insight flowing in your life? Are you drinking its clear, cool, reviving waters and sharing them with others? If not, start drilling! Ask for insight: "Give thy servant an understanding heart" (1 Kings 3:9). Search for insights: from God's Word, "Through thy precepts I get understanding" (Ps. 119:104), and from insightful teachers, "A man of understanding will acquire wise counsel" (Prov. 1:5, NAS). Record your insights: "It seemed good to me...having had perfect understanding...to write" (Luke 1:3). Most importantly, obey your insights, for "a good understanding have all they that do his commandments" (Ps. 111:10). And freely share them with others, that they too may drink from your wellspring of life— "What I tell you in darkness [private study], that speak in light [public speaking]" (Matt. 10:27)—knowing that, as you give, God will give you more insights to drink and to share.

> Consider what I say, and *the Lord give thee understanding* in all things.
> —2 TIMOTHY 2:7, EMPHASIS ADDED

Spiritual understanding will enable you to become bold as a lion.

Chapter Eight

FOUR KEY ATTITUDES

FAITH

There are four interrelated key attitudes that every Christian needs to fully understand, quickly recognize in himself, and either continue or change as circumstances may require. They are cowardice, courage, presumption, and intimidation.

Why are these attitudes important? Because they all interact with and are vitally related to our faith, or confidence in God, and nothing is more important than our faith. It is the very basis upon which we live. Four times the Bible declares the primary theme, "The just shall live by his faith" (Hab. 2:4). (See Romans 1:17; Galatians 3:11; Hebrews 10:38.) To help us better understand these four key attitudes, King Solomon directly addressed two of them in one of his most well-known proverbial pearls:

> The wicked flee when no man pursueth, but the righteous are bold as a lion.
>
> —PROVERBS 28:1

Paraphrased, this saying conveys the following message:

> Those who regularly practice sin panic and run away even when no one is chasing them, but those who receive and

63

walk in God's righteousness are bold as lions [who are wisely, not recklessly, bold].

This proverb contrasts cowardice with confidence in God in conflicts. In the same difficult or dangerous circumstances one person stands as still and confident as a lion, the intrepid and intimidating king of beasts, while the other beats a hasty path to safety. Do we know the source and sustenance of our confidence?

The believer's lone source of real confidence is God himself: "God is our refuge and strength, a very present help in trouble. Therefore will not we fear..." (Ps. 46:1–2). He who is utterly faithful, loving, and all-powerful is our unshakable, unmovable rock—not any servant of God, however anointed; or church, however large; or wealth, however great; or nation, however secure. More specifically, our confidence springs from knowing that *God is with us in the moment and matter at hand.* Numerous scriptures are built upon this foundational fact of faith:

And he said, *Certainly I will be with thee...*
—EXODUS 3:12, EMPHASIS ADDED

Be strong...for *the LORD thy God is with thee* wherever thou goest.
—JOSHUA 1:9, EMPHASIS ADDED

Be strong and of good courage...for *the LORD God...will be with thee*; he will not fail thee, nor forsake thee, until thou hast finished all the work...
—1 CHRONICLES 28:20, EMPHASIS ADDED

Fear thou not, for *I am with thee...*
—ISAIAH 41:10, EMPHASIS ADDED

Go ye, therefore, and teach all nations...and, lo, *I am with you always,* even unto the end of the age.
—MATTHEW 28:19–20, EMPHASIS ADDED

If God be for [and with] us, who can be against us?
—ROMANS 8:31, EMPHASIS ADDED

For he hath said, *I will never leave thee, nor forsake thee.*
—HEBREWS 13:5, EMPHASIS ADDED

The more rock-solid this foundation of faith that *God is with us,* the more confident we are. And with confidence come courage and boldness.

Christian boldness springs from complete, confirmed, continuing confidence in God. Bold Christians are distinctively intrepid amid intimidating adversities and associates. This mastery over debilitating fear is one of the less-recognized aspects of the "power" of God we receive when we are filled with the Holy Spirit: "But ye shall receive *power,* after the Holy Spirit is come upon you" (Acts 1:8, emphasis added). When Timothy was tempted to fear, the apostle Paul reminded him, "God hath not given us the spirit of fear, but [the Holy Spirit] of *power,* and of love, and of a sound mind" (2 Tim. 1:7, emphasis added).

Once gained, holy boldness is maintained by sustained closeness to Jesus, who as Son of man was consummately bold. This is how the first Christians, the apostles, received and cultivated their boldness. The first phase of their call was not to go forth and work for Jesus but to come and "be with him" (Mark 3:14) in sustained daily fellowship. After three and one-half years of observing His confident spirit and bold words and acts, His boldness left its imprint on them, and everyone, even their worst enemies, could see it: "When they saw the *boldness* of Peter and John...they marveled; and they took knowledge of them, that *they had been with Jesus* (Acts 4:13, emphasis added). Walking in integrity further establishes our souls in the bravery of the righteous: "Beloved, if our heart condemn us not, then have we confidence toward God...because we keep his commandments, and do those things that are pleasing in his sight" (1 John 3:21–22). And, like the muscles in our bodies, our boldness grows by a proper mixture of steady nourishment and exercise: plenty of time spent in God's presence and Word feeds holy boldness, and plenty of tests, or divinely appointed opportunities to obey God, exercise it to full development. So if we receive the fullness of the Holy Spirit, spend time daily with Jesus and His Word, and obediently endure our tests, we will gradually grow "bold as a lion."

FOUR KEY ATTITUDES

To help us manifest this distinctive Christian valor more consistently, let's consider the four faith-related attitudes mentioned at the beginning of this chapter: cowardice, courage, presumption, and intimidation.

Cowardice

Cowardice is a state of no confidence in God: "How is it that ye have *no faith*?" (Mark 4:40, emphasis added). When cowardly, the believer runs from every challenger, forfeits every contest, and fails his or her calling as an overcomer. Where does this spirit of flight come from? Chiefly, from guilt due to unconfessed, unforsaken sins. As surely as practicing right living edifies our confidence in God, practicing sin—any sin—erodes it. Our text in proverbs brings this out. Commenting on it, Matthew Henry wrote, "Guilt in the conscience makes men a terror to themselves, so that they are ready to flee when none pursues. Sin makes men cowards." God has constructed our souls so that we recognize, subconsciously if not consciously, that when we defy God, we deny ourselves His favor and assistance. So whenever we rebel against Him, we weaken our ability to rely on Him. Consequently, practicing sinners, whether unsaved persons or saved but carnal Christians, are easily put to panic—an unreasonable, hysterical fear that spreads rapidly to others.

The encamped Syrian army arose in the night, left all its provisions and riches, and ran away, though no enemy was anywhere near, only "the noise of a great host" (2 Kings 7:6). Are we following their evasive example, avoiding people and situations that we dread? Or are we trusting God with all our hearts and going on in our normal paths, come friend or foe, delight or difficulty?

Courage

A synonym for boldness, courage is a state of consummate confidence in God. Whatever boldness is, courage is; hence, our previous comments on the one also expound the other. When courageous, we face every adversary, stand fast in our God-ordained places of service, patiently endure till our tests end, and so develop into full-fledged overcomers who are "bold as a lion." King of beasts, the lion is regal in both its appearance and action. And lionlike courage causes Christians to look and live royally, as manifest sons of God the Father and confirmed brethren of His Son, the "King of glory" (Ps. 24:7–10) and the "Lion of the tribe of Judah" (Rev. 5:5).

Lionhearted, Nehemiah roared to himself in soliloquy and to us in Scripture, "Should such a man as I flee?" (Neh. 6:11), and then stood fast, unmoved by the threats and plots of his wily enemies, the Samaritans. Are we imitating his regal example, standing upright and unmoved in devotion and service, boldly roaring our confession of faith before angels, demons, and, when necessary, earthly adversaries?

Presumption

Presumption is a dangerous state of overconfidence in God. Presumptuous Christians foolishly assume God will, or even must, do things He has neither promised nor chosen to do. In this mind-set we forget the vital truth that, although God has promised to be with us always, He has also warned us we must be with Him always. Said the Vine to His branches, "Apart from Me you can do nothing" (John 15:5, NAS). Hence, the Lord is not bound to help us in matters we initiate and pursue in independence or defiance of His revealed will. An anonymous Christian author wisely wrote, "Nothing lies beyond the reach of prayer except that which lies outside the will of God." Presumptuous thinking overemphasizes God's promises and underemphasizes His conditions. As a result, although presumptuous Christians "stand on the promises," as well they should, they stumble over the conditions and so fail to receive the promises. Wise believers learn to focus on God's conditions as much as His promises. Hence, they grow confident, but never cocky; bold, but never belligerent. Why? Because they know their destiny is to be "bold as a lion," and that, confident as they are, lions are not presumptuous.

As the intelligent ruling carnivores of the vast savannas of Africa and India, lions know both their advantages and limitations. To their credit, lions have excellent hearing and exceptional night vision. Their coloration is perfect for concealment in the tan grasses of the field, and they are skilled at hiding in grasses, bushes, trees, and on or behind rocks. Their physical attributes are impressive. Their paws are large, their claws sharp, their jaws strong, and their teeth long; once in their grip, prey animals have virtually no chance of survival. Though they are not exceptionally swift, lions are exceptional leapers (able to leap up to 35 feet). Their family groups, or prides, provide them with valuable assistance on hunts, and their success rate increases significantly when they hunt in groups.

But despite these wonderful advantages, lions have some obvious disadvantages that limit what they will attempt or can achieve in the animal world. They can't outrun any of their preferred prey—antelopes, gazelles, water buffaloes, wildebeest, zebra, giraffe, or even warthogs—over long distances. And in the heat of the day they tire very quickly. Hence, they rest about twenty hours a day and prefer to hunt at night. Though intimidating, lions are not invincible. If weakened by hunger, thirst, or sickness, or if isolated, surrounded, or trapped, single lions may be killed by other very large or strong predators.

For these reasons, lions must not only be bold but also smart. And they are usually just that. Lions are opportunists, following vultures to eat the carcass of downed animals and stealing coveted prey from smaller predators, such as cheetahs and leopards. Lions are strategists, both stalking and "staking out" their victims. They will slowly follow their prey, crawling low to the ground and hiding behind grasses, bushes, or rocks, until they close with them; then, with a sudden, bold leap and brief sprint, they grasp their victims with their large paws and immediately bite down on their necks, holding them still until they suffocate. Or they will lie concealed near places where prey animals are sure to visit, such as food sources or water holes, then leap and take them.

But lions are also prudent, avoiding situations in which they foresee either a futile hunt or their own demise. They will not chase clearly speedier rival predators (for example, cheetahs) for distances over about 100 yards. They will not challenge very large prey, such as adult elephants, rhinos, or hippopotamuses. Normally, they will not brazenly attack large groups of very aggressive carnivores, such as hyenas. Nor will one male lion challenge another's right to rule the pride if the would-be challenger is sick or wounded, or if the currently dominant male has already soundly beaten off his challenger. We see, then, that because lions are not overbold, the proverbial description "bold as a lion" means, "wisely, not recklessly bold." Why are lions not overbold? Because they don't want to die early.

Despite his personal righteousness and the many righteous reforms he instituted in Judah, including his famous restoration of the long-neglected Feast of Passover, King Josiah stepped out of God's will—the only place of safety—when he impetuously challenged Pharaoh Neco to battle in the face of strong warnings. (See 2 Chronicles 35:20–27.) Tragically, the young chief lion of the pride of Judah didn't return from the battle alive. Though characteristically wise in heart, he died like a fool and left his destiny aborted and God's people stunned and saddened. Why? Because he was presumptuous. Apparently, Josiah assumed God would be with him in *whatever* course of action he chose. It was a lethally errant assumption. Though righteous, Josiah was a recklessly bold lion.

69

What kind of Christian lions are we? Are we walking with God, behind Him, or ahead of Him? Are we respecting or breaching the barriers He sets for us? Is our boldness wise or reckless? It's time we thought very seriously about these things.

Intimidation

Intimidation is a state of crumbling confidence in God. When intimidated, our trust in God is under attack, and, though still intact, it is shaking and we are doubting—rethinking our beliefs and beginning to be moved from our Lord, lifestyle, and labor. As believers facing a perilous world, we need to be decisive, sure, and confident in all our decisions, actions, and reactions. Satan constantly tries to rob us of this inner stability by intimidating us, or rendering us timid, hesitant, unsure, weak, indecisive, and worried.

His tools of intimidation are many: fearful imaginations; anxious thoughts; sharp criticisms; false accusations; surprising rejections; failures, real or apparent; and sudden attacks or onsets of adversity. While he uses all these modus operandi, he seems to favor the last one most. All his blitzkriegs, or lightning attacks, are meant to psychologically and emotionally knock us off our feet before we have time to recall God's Word, pray, or remember the reliance on God we've learned and lived in. Don't think this couldn't happen to you: "Let him that thinketh he standeth take heed lest he fall" (1 Cor. 10:12). It can happen to any one of us if we don't watch.

Even Elijah, Esther, and Paul suffered temporary intimidation. When Jezebel suddenly threatened Elijah's life, he immediately became intimidated. Spiraling out of control, his intimidation soon caused a shameful spiritual implosion, and, in a panic, Israel's prophet of great faith fled in great fear. When word of the Jews' stunning death sentence reached Esther, she was clearly rendered hesitant; only Mordecai's sharp rebuke prodded her to regain her courage. When the Jews began plotting yet another attack against Paul in Corinth, he apparently began wondering, and perhaps worrying, if God would yet again let his enemies physically beat him. But the Lord's reassuring word, and Paul's choice to trust it, kept him from being moved by intimidation. Hence, he stood "bold as a lion" and fearlessly labored there for eighteen more months. If even these outstanding overcomers could be intimidated, so can we if we don't remain spiritually alert.

So watch for the insidious stirrings of intimidation in your soul. Be on guard against any timid, weak, pessimistic, or confused thinking. Look out for any altering of your ways merely to appease proud, unreasonable, or oppressive people or your adversaries. When you yield to the fear of man, it only increases its grip on you: "The fear of man bringeth a [new and worse] snare" (Prov. 29:25). To stay free, you must stand firm. So when Satan suddenly shoots his swift spiritual arrows—intimidating thoughts, threatening words, or disturbing occurrences—to jolt you, be still and know that the Lord is God and that He is perfectly unmoved by whatever has occurred. Then refuse to be moved yourself. Firmly confess your determination to reject intimidation: "I have set the LORD always before me; because he is at my right hand, *I shall not be moved*" (Ps. 16:8, emphasis added). By doing this you'll quench your intimidation before it causes a shameful implosion. Remember, the devil is the world's prime bully. If you let him, he'll intimidate you all your days and utterly ruin your rest in God.

"We who have believed do enter into rest" (Heb. 4:3). Are you intimidated or intrepid, nervous or resting?

Please ponder these four key faith-related attitudes until you know them so well that you quickly and easily recognize when they are at work in you. Then either continue or change your mind-set, as necessary.

If you're courageous, stand firm, refusing to be moved by Satan's arrows of intimidation: "Neither be ye of doubtful mind"

(Luke 12:29). And watch for presumption. Remember, "The LORD is with you, while ye are with him" (2 Chron. 15:2), so determine to keep yourself within the safe borders of God's perfect will and guidance for your life. If you find yourself intimidated or acting cowardly, don't deny the Spirit's conviction. Quickly confess the sin of fear—not trusting God—and repent, choosing to immediately face your fear and act as God directs, relying on Him for wisdom, strength, and, if necessary, protection. If you don't know what God wants you to do, follow David's example and ask for God's authorization: "Shall I pursue?" (1 Sam. 30:8). If an answer comes but you're still unsure, ask God for confirmation. Once He gives it, do not hesitate but move with absolute confidence, "bold as a lion," to do as He leads.

This discipline will keep your confidence in God strong, your words and actions sure, and your person "sanctified, and fit for the master's use" (2 Tim. 2:21). Then you'll readily recognize the poor and minister to them for Christ's sake.

Chapter Nine

GIVE TO THE POOR—
AND THE LORD!

*T*he Bible reveals that caring for the poor is God's special interest or cause. Apparently, since no one else is fully willing and able to care for His less-fortunate creatures, the Creator and heavenly Father feels obligated to help them. Hence, His Word repeatedly commands and commends giving to the poor: "Thou shalt open thine hand wide unto thy brother, to thy poor, and to thy needy, in thy land" (Deut. 15:11). One priceless proverb goes a step further.

> He that hath pity upon the poor lendeth unto the LORD, and that which he hath given will he pay him again.
> —PROVERBS 19:17

Paraphrased, this pearl of truth states:

> The person who makes compassionate donations to the poor is really contributing to God [His special charity or "poor fund"], and God will fully reimburse that person.

This reveals that giving to the poor is actually a form of giving to *God*: "He that hath pity upon the poor *lendeth unto the* LORD *[or Lord's cause]* ..." (emphasis added). It then assures us that God will faithfully reciprocate by repaying everything we give to the poor: "...and that which he hath given *will he [God] pay him again*" (emphasis added). But who are these "poor" of whom the Bible speaks?

In the Old Testament, the word *poor* (KJV) is translated from several Hebrew words conveying the thoughts of poverty, lowness, weakness, or oppression. They all describe a *lack* of something necessary to human health and happiness, such as wealth, respect, strength, or justice. Precisely the opposite of the wicked rich, who are arrogantly proud, financially and socially empowered, and seemingly self-sufficient, the poor suffer from some condition of acute need. By every definition, then, they are *needy*. Primarily, they lack some vital need of the body—food, drink, clothing, or shelter. Secondarily, when compared to the normal standard of living, they are monetarily or materially disadvantaged persons. Yet, when we also consider the figurative applications, God seems to define the "poor" much more broadly.

THE POOR ARE...

Consider these poor ones and the people who considered them for the Lord's sake.

Needy in monies or materials

While false prophets typically focused on wooing and winning the rich and powerful, Jesus purposely took His gospel first to Israel's materially disadvantaged masses: "The Spirit of the Lord...hath anointed me to preach the gospel to *the poor*" (Luke 4:18, emphasis added). The leading Pharisees, who were covetous and often rich with ill-gotten gain, turned away. But the common people heard Jesus gladly. After His departure, the apostles diligently cared for the needy ones in their ranks, such as visitors, widows, traveling ministers, and victims of famine.

(See Acts 4:33–35; 11:29–30; 1 Timothy 5:3–16; 3 John 5–8.) And James, the Lord's half-brother and leader of the original Jerusalem Church, pointedly ordered all believers to neither insult nor neglect the poor, nor were they to prefer the rich: "My brethren, have not the faith of our Lord Jesus Christ…with respect of persons…If ye have respect of persons, ye commit sin" (James 2:1–9).

Do we give lower-income believers the same respect we show for wealthier ones? Why not?

Needy in liberty

Liberty—ah, what a great concept! Many countries have warred and combatants died for liberty as down through history tyrants have maliciously stolen it and revolutionaries have militantly taken it back. Wise, lawful living usually preserves our freedom. But sometimes, with or without just cause, liberty is taken from us.

More poignantly than free men, prisoners, especially those incarcerated unjustly or for the gospel's sake, know the value of liberty. Why? Because it is the thing they most lack and want. Behind walls and fences they have very limited rights, few privileges, and no liberty to go and come in society as they please, work in their chosen field or profession, marry, raise children, or travel—until their time is served. Very elderly or crippled people are equally poor in liberty. If you know the value of freedom and love God, you will give to prisoners and shut-ins: phone calls, letters, cards, books, tapes, food, or any other form of kindness. Why? Because it is more blessed to give than to receive. Also, whatever you do to those who are, or later become, Christians, you do to Christ: "I was in prison, and ye came unto me" (Matt. 25:36). (See also Matthew 25:40.)

Will we show kindness to those who, justly or unjustly, are imprisoned? Will we visit and minister to those who are shut in or elderly? Remember, "The goodness of God leadeth thee to repentance" (Rom 2:4).

Needy in health

Whatever our success, riches, or fame, we become poor the day sickness strikes. Naaman was famous, successful, powerful, and wealthy, yet because of his leprosy, he was a very needy man. Hence, by grace and faith, Elisha ministered to his needy health.

Jesus' contributions to people with health needs were prodigious. Repeatedly during His ministry He donated wealthy garments of healing to people wearing the tattered rags of sickness: "And he healed them all" (Matt. 12:15). And later, by submitting to a dreadful scourging and crucifixion, He established an inexhaustible heavenly health fund from which countless others have received the rich benefits of bodily healing: "By whose stripes ye were healed" (1 Pet. 2:24). In James Moffatt's *A New Translation of the Bible*, this verse reads, "The blows that fell to him have brought us healing." The apostles Peter and John made notable disbursements to many who were poor in health: the crippled beggar at the Beautiful Gate, Aeneas, Dorcas, and others. And to this day Scripture authorizes believing elders to continue enriching the infirm with compassionate divine healing: "Is any sick among you? Let him call for the elders of the church; and let them pray over him, anointing him with oil in the name of the Lord. And *the prayer of faith shall save [heal] the sick*" (James 5:14–15, emphasis added).

Are any among us poor in health? Will we, or our elders, give them "the prayer of faith"?

Needy in mind

Wherever there are troubled, broken, or psychotic minds, there are mental and emotional needs of the highest order. People who are tormented by guilt, fear, or delusions need generous grants of intercession, understanding, kindness, truth, and the peace of God that passes all understanding. Some need an even deeper, or spiritual, deliverance.

Troubled, twisted, and tormented in nerves, imaginations,

and body, the "wild man" of Gadara was psychologically and emotionally impoverished—until he met the greatest psychological philanthropist to ever walk this earth. Then, suddenly, after one miraculous donation, he too was rich, or as the Bible puts it, calm, at peace, and "in his right mind" (Mark 5:15).

Do we know anyone who is poor in mind, poor in nerves, poor in emotional stability? Will we give them repeated donations of prayer or mercy for Jesus' sake... until God visits them by the power of His Spirit and does for them what neither they nor any human being, including us, can do for them—that is, set them free?

Needy in spirit

We may be Mr. or Mrs. Successful, but if God has never touched us, our inner spiritual cores are destitute and we are poor, or needy, in spirit. There is but one cure for this spiritual bankruptcy: "Come unto me [Jesus]... and I will give you rest" (Matt. 11:28). When we repent and receive Jesus, the most valuable Spirit in the universe permeates our spirit. And immediately we are enriched in spirit.

Yet, paradoxically, we are not rich. There is still a sense in which we remain poor, or *utterly dependent on God*. Why? Because to become and remain truly spiritually rich—in the faith and knowledge of God, in His ways, and in His truth—and so forever free from our former spiritually impoverished life-style, we must come to the Savior daily and wait upon Him in His Word, in prayer, and in worship so we may draw constantly upon His unlimited spiritual resources: "They that wait upon the LORD shall renew their strength... run, and not be weary, and... walk, and not faint" (Isa. 40:31). It is imperative that we realize just how poor we are without this daily spiritual replenishment: "Apart from Me you can do nothing" (John 15:5, NAS). Are we convinced we need the riches of His grace, strength, and wisdom for every thought, every breath, every word, and every step? If so, we're becoming rich—yet we're still "poor in spirit" and one of God's dependents and blessed: "Blessed are the poor [needy] in spirit" (Matt. 5:3).

Do we recognize the utter spiritual neediness of the lost and the ongoing spiritual needs of every Christian brother and sister we meet? Will we minister to them as occasion serves?

Needy in knowledge

Everyone needs more knowledge of God: non-Christians, Christians, and even our most knowledgeable teachers. Let's allow the Bible to explain this for us.

The lost need to know they "must" be born again and how to receive this experience. So Jesus gave this knowledge to the leading Jewish theologian of His day, Nicodemus (John 3:1–13). The saved need to know they must also be filled with the Holy Spirit. So Peter and John donated this knowledge to the Samaritan converts (Acts 8:14–17), as did Paul to John the Baptist's disciples in Ephesus (Acts 19:1–7). We also need godly, gifted, well-informed, insightful teachers. So Paul contributed loads of inspired information to his brethren through his epistles, which were widely distributed throughout the first-century churches. And sometimes even the wisest teachers need a fuller understanding of certain key doctrines. So Priscilla and Aquila took aside Apollos, a first-rate Bible scholar and zealous minister, and shared with him their knowledge and experience of Jesus and His two works of grace (Acts 18:24–26). Thus all these needy ones gained the knowledge they lacked—because someone gave to the poor.

But we cannot give what we do not have. "Such as I have, give I thee," said Peter in Acts 3:6, unwittingly speaking for all donors everywhere. Are we out digging in our biblical oyster beds, searching diligently for more pearls of truth? If so, we should stay and keep exploring every day. Then, every time God opens a door for us to speak, we should share our growing wealth of knowledge with the poor.

Needy in heart

Every sinful heart is a hard heart—and one desperately in need of the Spirit's softening touch of conviction and repentance. No matter how cold, callous, and calculating people are, God stands amazingly ready to try to mollify their tough, scarred hearts and penetrate their stony fronts. Indeed, "He is kind [even] unto the unthankful and to the evil" (Luke 6:35).

So when wicked King Herod asked John the Baptist to speak, John freely shared "many things" with him (Mark 6:20). And Jesus described heaven's treasure—the gift of the Holy Spirit—to the promiscuous woman at Jacob's well (John 4:5–26). And, when so led by His Father, Jesus lunched with the corrupt, treacherous liar and notorious thief Zacchaeus, whose steely spirit was known throughout Jericho...yet was soon melted by the Master's surprisingly quiet, non-accusatory attitude (Luke 19:1–10). For love of *God*, John the Baptist and Jesus of Nazareth gave to even the hardest hearts.

Will we follow their example and pray, "Lord, help me see through the hardness to the shocking poverty within"?

Needy in friends

Any man without friends is a poor man, for he lacks that human fellowship he so profoundly needs.

Many disciples, ministers, and prophets have found themselves poor—misjudged and rejected of men—because of their uncompromising messages and unpopular stands taken in faithfulness to God and His Word. Gradually their lukewarm peers withdrew one by one to a safe distance. Of his *Christian* friends' disappointing abandonment, the embattled apostle Paul wrote, "All they who are in Asia turned away from me" (2 Tim. 1:15). But always God faithfully prompts someone to give to His faithful ones. Hence, He moved Onesiphorus to lovingly befriend His unloved and friendless servant: "Onesiphorus...often refreshed me, and was not ashamed of my chain, but, when he was in Rome, he sought me out very diligently, and found me" (vv. 16–17). In

His faithfulness the Lord also moved Ebed-melech, the Ethiopian, to assist and befriend the friendless, thirsting, hungering, and fainting prophet Jeremiah just in time to prevent his death (Jer. 38:7–13).

Will we respond to our heavenly Father when He urges us to befriend His friendless but faithful witnesses? Who knows, our humble friendship may be the loving touch that helps save a "Paul" or "Jeremiah"—a powerful but persecuted minister through whom God subsequently releases a mighty river of blessing that flows to the ends of the earth.

Needy in hope

Every despairing person is needy—lacking a hopeful outlook. And great adversities and long trials at some point invariably produce despair.

As Luke sadly penned the words, "All hope that we should be saved was then taken away" (Acts 27:20), Paul stood up to give to the poor—his depressed, storm-weary shipmates. His hardy words of faith, "Be of good cheer; for there shall be no loss of any man's life" (v. 22), cheered their cheerless hearts and saved many from suicidal panic. Joseph's gratis interpretation gave heavenly light to Egypt's butler when in prison he found himself shrouded in the darkness of despondency. It gave a reason to live to a man that had none.

When faced with despondent, depressed souls—oh, so poor in outlook!—do we give them groundless, empty, humanistic optimism, or do we give them powerful words of heavenly hope, credible assurance from the unfailing Word and Spirit of Almighty God? "I will *never* leave thee, nor forsake thee" (Heb. 13:5, emphasis added). "Be not faithless, but believing" (John 20:27). "*God is [utterly] faithful*, who will…make the way to escape" (1 Cor. 10:13).

Needy at our "gate"

Where are these needy ones? The Bible reveals that they are closer than you may think!

The rich man found the needy beggar Lazarus at his "gate" every day (Luke 16:19–20). The Good Samaritan found the wounded Jew by the very road on which he was traveling.

Do we have eyes to see, hearts to pray for, and the will to give to the poor ones God places at our "gates" regularly or by the roads, rails, or airways we travel? To behold the needy, we only have to look around us: our neighbors, co-workers, and fellow commuters and travelers!

Needy at our feet

Ministers, especially pastors, must not overlook those who presently sit under their ministries. So often we're distracted with thoughts of the next open door, event, or conference, while the sheep on the other side of our pulpits are evidently faint, sick, or starving. Any way you rationalize it, that's poor shepherding. It's not like Jesus.

The great Chief Shepherd was always compassionately careful to first feed the sheep at His feet. Whether those gathered before Him were a "minitude," Mary and a few friends listening to His words before dinner, or a multitude, Jesus' response was always the same: "Jesus…was moved with compassion toward them, because they were as sheep not having a shepherd; and *he began to teach them many things*" (Mark 6:34, emphasis added). Here is some rich food for serious pastoral thought.

Pastors, let's honestly inspect our own sheep. Are they nourished or needy, healthy or haggardly? May God help us be compassionate, not careless, shepherds, and selfless, not selfish, keepers of Christ's sheep: "Elders…feed the flock of God which is among you" (1 Pet. 5:1–2).

Needy…every person, every day, in every place

Broadly speaking, therefore, the "poor" are really *everyone*, for everyone has some form of natural or spiritual need. Every person we meet, every day, in every place is one of God's dependents. Whether aware of it or not, their name is written on heaven's support list. And the neediest of all are those who are convinced they have no needs: "Thou sayest, I am rich, and increased with goods, and have need of nothing, and knowest not that thou art wretched, and miserable, and *poor*" (Rev. 3:17, emphasis added).

Let us bear in mind that God has explicitly promised to give special consideration to those who consider the poor.

Specifically, He has vowed the following. He will repay them in the same substance they have given: "That which he hath given will he *pay him again*" (Prov. 19:17, emphasis added) (See also Luke 6:38.) They will never lack any true necessity of life: "He that giveth unto the poor *shall not lack*" (Prov. 28:27, emphasis added). They will be preserved in and delivered from all kinds of trouble: "Blessed is he that considereth the poor; the LORD will *deliver him* in time of trouble. The LORD will *preserve him*, and *keep him* alive" (Ps. 41:1–2, emphasis added). God will never permanently abandon them to their enemies' malicious plans: "Thou wilt *not deliver him* unto the will of his enemies" (v. 2, emphasis added). And He will "bless" them—that is, favor, increase, and prosper them—in this present lifetime: "He shall be *blessed upon the earth*" (v. 2, emphasis added). Those are His precious promises and our powerful prompts!

So let's get moving. As we have opportunities, let's give to the poor—and to the Lord! This will keep our consciences clear and free.

Chapter Ten

THE MINISTRY OF CONSCIENCE

*B*oth the Bible and common sense agree that God uses our consciences to speak to us. But do we understand what conscience is, how it works, and how to keep ours clear?

Conscience can be defined as "the inner sense of what is right or wrong in one's conduct or motives, impelling one toward right action."[1] In *The Philosophy of Sin*, Oswald Chambers taught, "Conscience is that innate faculty in a man's spirit that attaches itself to the highest the man knows, whether he be an atheist or a Christian. The highest the Christian knows is God; the highest the atheist knows is his principles."

As to God's use of our consciences, King Solomon penned the most memorable biblical statement on this topic:

> The spirit of man is the lamp of the Lord, searching all the inward parts.
>
> —PROVERBS 20:27

Paraphrased, this priceless pearl states:

> The human spirit [specifically its faculty of conscience] is the Lord's lamp, with which He searches all our inner thoughts.

Expounding further, this reveals that God uses the human spirit, or "spirit of man," specifically its faculty of conscience, as a man uses a lamp in a dark room. When "lit" by the Spirit or word of truth, a man's conscience exposes, or makes him aware of, all that was previously hidden from him and others, but not from God—his true thoughts, motives, attitudes, emotions, and condition.

This divine revelation tells us that God is the great Searcher of hearts. The God of truth ever loves truth and hates falsehood. Hence, through His redemption He relentlessly seeks to expose and remove unworthy thoughts, attitudes, emotions, and intents from our spirits and replace them with His truth. Or, as David put it, "Thou desirest truth in the inward parts, and in the hidden part [my innermost being, soul, and conscience] thou shalt make me know wisdom [good judgment; or true, accurate, and correct assessment]" (Ps. 51:6). The faculty of conscience in the human spirit is indeed God's lamp. But without a flame, an oil lamp produces no light. So God uses His Holy Spirit—the "Spirit of truth" (John 14:17)—as the "flame," or light, that activates our faculty of conscience. Consequently, the Holy Spirit is the Illuminator.

The Illuminator's work brings about the following results. First, He convicts of sin: "He will reprove [convict]...of sin" (John 16:8). That is, He convinces us of our guilt when we are, or have done, wrong. When Jesus reproved the judgmental scribes and Pharisees, "they who heard it, being convicted by their own conscience, went out one by one" (John 8:9). Second, He convinces people that Jesus is their Savior. When the apostle Paul preached the Christian message to the Philippian jailer's relatives, their consciences testified that his words were true, and they all believed in and received Jesus (Acts 16:30–34). Third, this saving faith results in salvation—by God's grace sinners' transgressions are forgiven, their spirits are regenerated, and their eternal residency in heaven is secured. After Zacchaeus confessed his sins and called Jesus his "Lord," Jesus said, "This day is salvation come to this house" (Luke 19:9). Fourth, conscience delivers, or restrains us, from sin and folly. Moved by Abigail's apology, warning, prophecy, and exhortation, David changed his mind and aborted his hasty assault on Nabal's household (1 Sam. 25:23–35). Fifth, the ministry of conscience brings restoration and reconciliation. When the Illuminator finished His wondrous work in the prodigal son's conscience, the young man "came to himself" (Luke 15:17) and was promptly reconciled with his loving father and restored to his former home, family, friends, and comforts. Do we understand how the Illuminator works?

The Holy Spirit has numerous ways of lighting our consciences. He may work alone, not using any human agent. When the four lepers of Samaria said, "We do not well. This day is a day of good tidings, and we hold our peace" (2 Kings 7:9), not a soul had spoken to them. But God had lit the lamp of their conscience and, by the searching, inner voice of His Spirit, exposed their selfishness. Often, however, the light comes through human channels.

An evangelist's spoken appeal or written gospel tract faces our consciences with the Light of the world and the dark realities of eternity without God. After Peter preached the gospel to the Jews on the Day of Pentecost, "they were pricked in their heart" (Acts 2:37) by his message.

Exhorters are also prime agents of the Illuminator. Believers are explicitly commanded to "exhort one another daily...lest any of you be hardened through the deceitfulness of sin" (Heb. 3:13).

True prophets are key vessels, too. When they speak openly the inner thoughts of unbelievers present in Christian gatherings, those unbelievers are convinced of the reality, omniscience, and love of God and are converted to the faith. (See 1 Corinthians 14:24–25.)

Religious reformers are effective agents of the Illuminator. John the Baptist, Ezra, and Nehemiah were each used to light the heart-lamps of their respective generations with the knowledge that they had strayed far from God and needed to change their ways.

Intercessors also initiate the Illuminator's mystical yet effective works of conscience. "If any man see his brother sin a sin which is not unto death," writes the apostle John, "he shall ask [intercede], and he shall give him life for them that sin not unto death" (1 John 5:16). Commenting on this power of intercession, Oswald Chambers said, "What happens when a saint prays is that the Paraclete's almighty power is brought to bear on the one for whom he is praying."

The Illuminator sometimes uses people's spontaneous, seemingly ordinary, questions. When Jesus asked the man with the withered hand, "*Wilt thou* be made well?" (John 5:6, emphasis added), it exposed his real underlying problem: he really didn't "will," or strongly desire, to be healed! A British Christian related that, when backsliding, he had visited a public house, or "pub." One of the patrons, recognizing him and his Christian profession, said simply, "What are *you* doing *here*?" That was all it took. Instantly, the Illuminator shot His arrow—"You don't belong here!"—and hit His mark.

There are yet more means the Illuminator uses to reach His ends.

Adversity is one of His more powerful tools. Without speaking audibly, the Illuminator conveyed to Joseph's brothers' hearts the exact reason they were caught in a trap in Egypt: they had entrapped their brother and sent him off to Egypt! And one said what all were thinking: "We are verily guilty concerning our brother, in that we saw the anguish of his soul, when he besought us, and we would not hear; *therefore is this distress come upon us*" (Gen. 42:21, emphasis added).

The mere reading or hearing of the words of the Bible also illuminates our consciences. "The entrance of thy words giveth light...[and] understanding" (Ps. 119:130), declared the psalmist. Indeed, God's Word is a living force that acts quickly and powerfully as a "discerner of the [true] thoughts and intents of the heart" (Heb. 4:12).

God's manifest presence also activates our consciences. Jesus said nothing to elicit Zacchaeus' surprising repentance. Oswald Chambers believed that it was merely the presence of Christ that caused the corrupt chief publican to melt and come clean.

Dreams are yet another means by which the Illuminator renders our consciences lucid and responsive. Elihu lectured Job, "For God speaketh...in a dream, in a vision of the night...he openeth the ears of men, and sealeth their instruction, that he may withdraw man from his purpose" (Job 33:14–17). (See also Genesis 20:3–7.) Such are the means by which God seeks to impart enlightenment. And they usually succeed.

But not always. If we are either extraordinarily stubborn or utterly disconsolate, the Spirit of God has been known to speak *audibly* to awaken men's consciences. He called out to Adam, "Where art thou?" (Gen. 3:9), to make him realize that, spiritually, he was not where he once was—in close, trusting, obedient, loving fellowship with God—but had fallen away. He called to Elijah audibly with similarly memorable words, "What doest thou here, Elijah?" (1 Kings 19:9, 13), and achieved similar results. And when Balaam didn't yield to his donkey's stunning sermonette, the angel of the Lord (the preincarnate Christ) Himself spoke audibly to the erring prophet, "Behold, I went out to withstand thee, because thy way was perverse before me" (Num. 22:32). Surprisingly, even these powerful and piercing verbal blows fail to crack the most adamant hearts.

But when all else fails, visitation prevails! That is, when it's necessary, God Himself makes a personal visit. Saul of Tarsus' formerly untouchable conscience was radically readjusted the instant Jesus appeared before him in a blinding, brilliant flash and informed him that, contrary to Saul's raging protests and relentless persecutions, He (Jesus) and Jehovah were one—and both with and among the followers of The Way (Acts 9:1–7). Thereafter Saul's conscience impelled him to bless, not blaspheme, the name of Jesus and to help, not harass, His followers.

What does all this have to do with us?

Paul's Good Warning, Good Resolution, and Good Testimony

The above text helps us understand the ministry of conscience, what it is and how it works. To learn how to keep our consciences clear, let's ponder the apostle Paul's good warning, good resolution, and good testimony.

A good warning

Though innate, the faculty of conscience is not indestructible. It may be developed, damaged, or destroyed at our discretion. Let me explain.

We develop our consciences, or render them softer and more responsive to the Holy Spirit, by such actions as obedience to God's Word (as taught us), kindness to other people, fairness and honesty in our dealings, faithfulness in our duties, and the prompt and frank confession of all our sins to God. (See 1 John 1:9.) As we do these things, we walk in the light as God is in the light, "and the blood of Jesus Christ, his Son, cleanseth us [and our consciences] from all sin" (1 John 1:7). This is how we protect our consciences from harm and restore them when they are damaged. Oswald Chambers wrote:

> The sensitiveness of conscience is maintained by the habit of always being open towards God. At the peril of your soul you allow one thing to obscure your inner communion with God. Drop it whatever it is and see that you keep your inner vision clear...
>
> The saintly conscience means that I maintain an open scrutiny before God, and that I carry out the sensitiveness gained there all through my life...[2]

Whenever we choose the opposite actions—disobedience, unkindness, dishonesty, unfairness, infidelity, etc., and then proudly and persistently deny our sins—we damage our consciences, or render them less susceptible to God. If we persist in this destructive habit, eventually we utterly destroy, or "sear," our consciences. Hence Paul warns of those who "speaking lies in hypocrisy, having their *conscience seared with a hot iron*" (1 Tim. 4:2, emphasis added). Regarding the "seared" conscience, Chambers wrote:

> Conscience is the eye of the soul recording what it looks at, but...the recording of conscience may be distorted. If I continually twist the organ of my soul's recording, it will become perverted. If I do a wrong thing often enough, I cease to realize the wrong in it. A bad man can be perfectly happy in his badness. That is what a seared conscience means.[3]

It is awful yet accurate to say that a persistently sinful human being—yes, even an apostate Christian—can grow as cold and hard and conscienceless as the devil himself! Remember, sin transforms its practitioners into the character image of its prince. Do we believe this warning?

A good resolution

Paul's good resolution is one he personally professed and persistently practiced: "And in this do *I exercise myself, to have always a conscience void of offense* toward God, and toward men" (Acts 24:16, emphasis added). This meant that Paul refused to let any unsurrendered or unconfessed sin stand between him and God. While people *took* offense at him and his message constantly without cause, he was careful not to *give* offense by his words, manners, or actions and, if he did, to quickly put it right with the people he offended, just as Jesus instructed us all: "If...thy brother hath anything against thee...first be reconciled to thy brother" (Matt. 5:23–24).

Will we commit to this "exercise," as Paul did?

A good testimony

If we believe Paul's warning and practice his resolution, quickly resolving all the issues that trouble our consciences, whether regarding our relationships with God or people, we will gain Paul's good testimony: "I have lived in all good conscience before God until this day" (Acts 23:1).

Are we making His testimony ours?

My friend, please ponder the ministry of conscience and Paul's warning. Then begin practicing his resolution. And periodically ask yourself this question: "Is there *anything* more important to me than having a clear conscience before God?"

This little change will make a large difference in your spiritual health.

Chapter Eleven

LITTLE CHANGES, LARGE DIFFERENCES

*L*ittle changes over time make large differences. So taught the wisest man that ever lived.

King Solomon's inspired record relates a pearl of a lesson he learned while passing by the farm of a Jewish man given to laziness: "I went by the field of the slothful, and by the vineyard of the man void of understanding" (Prov. 24:30). It was quite a sad sight. The fields and vineyards of this anonymous son of negligence were in serious disrepair. They were completely covered, not with rich wheat, barley, olives, grapes, and flocks, but with all kinds of worthless thorns, thistles, weeds, and bushes: "Lo, it was all grown over with thorns, and nettles [bushes] had covered the face thereof" (v. 31). The stone wall, which was designed to protect the crops from animal and human thieves and the farm from trespassers and false land claimants (Prov. 23:10–11), was dismantled in numerous places: "And the stone wall thereof was broken down" (Prov. 24:31). Apparently so many trespassers, thieves, and animals had climbed over it uncontested that many of its stones had fallen off—and lain for years just where they fell. Thus the redeemed but unwatchful farmer's wall was incapable of providing any protection for his crops, vines, or herds—or his income. Meditative by nature, Solomon slowly surveyed and thoroughly pondered the whole disappointing scenario: "When I saw, I reflected upon it" (v. 32, NAS).

Then it hit him. In one brief but brilliant burst of revelation he discerned the reason for the man's failure: "And [I] learned a lesson from what I saw" (v. 32, NIV). Laziness? Yes, of course, that was the obvious conclusion. But Solomon's God-given insight enabled him to go deeper, beneath the obvious, to discover the subtler, more specific root cause. *The man in question had failed to realize that little changes over time make large differences.* Hence Solomon quietly recites to himself His conclusion:

> Yet a little sleep, a little slumber, a little folding of the hands to sleep; so shall thy poverty come like one that traveleth, and thy want like an armed man.
> —Proverbs 24:33–34

Paraphrased, this states:

> [Just] a little sleep, [just] a little slumber, [just] a little folding of the hands to sleep, and before long [large or great] failure and poverty storm one's life like a wandering, desperate criminal [unexpected and cruel].

Extrapolating, I believe Solomon also envisioned the negligent farmer saying to himself, years earlier, "My farm is doing well, my fields are full, my vineyards loaded, my herds are growing, and my wall is solidly in place. There's really no need to work so hard. I think I owe it to myself to make some changes in my work schedule: nothing big, just a few small changes. I'll just sleep a little longer and work a little less; have a little more fun and watch the fields a little less. That won't hurt anything. My farm will still be productive. Jehovah, gracious as He is, will surely bless it anyway."

But over time things didn't work out as this heedless Hebrew imagined. Gradually but surely he became fast asleep— indifferent and inattentive to his farm's actual condition. And while he slept, his agricultural enemies worked hard and fast: the weeds, thorns, and bushes grew; the foxes feasted; and the thieves stole whatever and whenever they would. Then one day reality suddenly hit him: his farm, income, security, and future were all gone, thanks to a few little harmless changes!

That this is an important, not impertinent, topic in the Book of Proverbs is seen in two facts. First, God inspired a duplicate passage to be included in Proverbs 6:6–11. Second, the key word *little* is used not once but three times in both passages to capture our sometimes elusive attention: "Yet a *little* sleep, a *little* slumber, a *little* folding of the hands to sleep" (Prov. 24:33, emphasis added).

This lesson on the importance of little changes hits at the very heart of our human tendency to only pay attention to big things. Universally Adam's children love and laud big men, big organizations, big ministries, big offices, big victories, big numbers, big successes, big changes, etc., and they totally overlook small things regardless of their quality or importance. But as we see above, tiny things can sometimes have a tremendous impact. Didn't Jesus try to show us this in His parable of the little mustard seed that grew to be the largest garden plant...by praising the poor widow's little offering that loomed large in God's sight...by teaching us that faithfulness in little duties will bring us large rewards? "Well done, thou good servant; because thou hast been faithful in a *very little*, have thou authority over *ten cities*" (Luke 19:17, emphasis added). Despite His repeated attempts to teach us, few Christians have yet to deeply receive His words about the immense value of certain infinitesimally small things.

If you need further convincing, just look around you and, like Solomon, observe long and consider well what you see. Do your own study and see for yourself how incremental changes make incredible differences in due time.

For instance, a few bitter words spoken repeatedly will eventually destroy a good friendship or marriage, whereas a few kind words will heal it. A little less unnecessary spending and a little more saving of extra funds will balance the family budget and keep those dreaded modern twin thieves, foreclosure and bank-ruptcy, far away. A little less television and a little more reading will eventually produce a much more knowledgeable, interesting, and confident person. A little less snacking and a little more phys-ical recreation will within months produce a more fit, less lethar-gic body. A little housekeeping pursued daily or weekly makes a huge difference in the appearance and hospitableness of the home—and in the confidence of the host when guests suddenly appear at the door. A little more use of the dictionary, researching word meanings daily or whenever they are heard or read but not understood, will make a tremendous difference in one's vocabu-lary in just a few years. A little tooth-brushing and flossing daily will preserve our "grinders" and prevent a large amount of pain and expense in the dentist's chair. In all these matters we see the potentially prodigious consequences of petite changes.

But did the Spirit of God inspire Solomon to make this point in Holy Scripture only to help our budgets, vocabularies, waistlines, and smiles? No, I think He had something far more important foremost in mind, namely, our vital personal relation-ship to God. There, too, little alterations over time make large transformations.

Focusing on this, let's identify the symbols found in this pas-sage. The indolent Hebrew farmer represents a lazy Christian. That the farmer is "void of understanding" speaks of a believer who is spiritually ignorant and specifically lacks insight, which ability we discussed in an earlier chapter. Therefore he has only a superficial, not a profound, understanding of the Bible and life. His "sleep" represents a Christian's inexcusable indifference—to his own soul's true condition, his besetting sins, his human responsibilities, his divine calling, his need of more knowledge, and, in our time especially, to the nearness of Jesus' appearing and the imperative of preparing for it. (See Matthew 25:1–5.) Spiri-tual indifference, ignorance, and laziness are perhaps the biggest causes of spiritual immaturity and lack of spiritual growth among believers. Let's consider more symbols.

The "field" and "vineyard" each represent our spiritual lives, which at all times are either guarded or unprotected, fruitful or barren. The "thorns" and "nettles" represent spiritual spoilers, the distractions, hindrances, carnality, and sins that despiritualize us and ruin our spiritual lives, rendering them empty, displeasing, unusable, and hence unproductive to God. Jesus revealed they are "the cares of this age, and the deceitfulness of riches, and the lusts of other things entering in," which "choke the word," and render us "unfruitful" (Mark 4:19). The "stone wall" represents our personal vigilance with which we protect our souls from disruptive and destructive intrusions by the thief, Satan. The "fruit," which is so evidently missing from the negligent Hebrew's farm, represents believers' "fruit of the Spirit" (Gal. 5:22–23), or the evidences of Christlikeness in our lives; also, the ministry works we accomplish with the Lord's help for the benefit of His people and kingdom.

These symbols translate into the following message: While our salvation, thank God, is beyond the reach of the thief, our souls, our relationships to God, and our fruitfulness in God are not. Like the proverbial farmer's field and vineyard, these things require care to prosper—and become barren if they are neglected. So every effort must be made to take care of our "fields" and "vineyards." Even a little "sleep," or indifference, is dangerous.

We must build and maintain an unbroken "stone wall" of determined, habitual self-examination if we want our spiritual lives to honor God and win His full approval for ever-increasing service. That will mean keeping our hearts clean and ready for the seed of God's Word and watching constantly lest "thorns" and "nettles"—daily problems, worldly interests, bad attitudes, good but despiritualizing activities, or any other spiritual spoilers—begin covering up our potential for God. We must realize that God has established our "farm," or personal relationship with Him, for one primary purpose: fruit that will glorify Him and His kingdom. And, realizing this, we must jealously guard our fellowship with Jesus, taking time daily to talk with Him in prayer, letting Him speak to us through His Word, worshiping Him in song, and working with Him in quiet, faithful service as He directs.

As long as we persistently trust and fully obey Him, no adversity or enemy can spoil our "farm." Unlike the indolent farmer's estate, our soul will produce a rich harvest of Christlikeness and Spirit-led ministry that will glorify God and win us the highest possible human satisfaction, which comes only from knowing God is pleased with us: "Well done, thou good and faithful servant...Enter thou into the joy of thy lord" (Matt. 25:21). All this awaits us, if we learn and practice the lesson Solomon recorded for us.

So watch for small changes, those beginnings of minor modifications in your daily habits, attitudes, or work that, ever so subtly lead you *away* from close fellowship with God and dedication to your present duties or ministries—a little excessive eating, sleeping, or television watching; a little complaining; a little unforgiveness; a little offense at God; a little covetousness, envy, or fear of man; a little impatience, anger, or lust; a little stinginess, misjudgment, or condemnation; a little pride in your accomplishments; or a little doubt of God's Word.

And, conversely, see that you obey the minute changes the Spirit suggests to help you draw *closer* to God and work with Him with greater efficiency—a little more time for Bible study, prayer, or private worshiping of God; a little more patience with and intercession for difficult people; a little more cooperation with your superiors and steadfastness in your work; a little quicker response to the Holy Spirit's checks and prompts; or a little more giving of thanks to God in all situations. Why? Because little changes in your spiritual life over time make a large difference in your fellowship with and fruitfulness for God.

Thus taught wise King Solomon. Will you learn and practice his lesson today? If so, God will be pleased with you—and personally deal with everyone who hinders or persecutes you.

Chapter Twelve

GOT AN ENEMY? PLEASE THE LORD!

*I*f we please the Lord, He will subdue our adversaries, clearing the way for our growth and successful fulfillment of God's plan for our lives.

If anyone should know this, Solomon should. When his father, David, and he pleased the Lord during their successive reigns, the Lord subdued their personal, and Israel's national, enemies. Consequently, Israel grew, matured, prospered, and glorified God during the early period of her monarchy more than at any other time in her history. (See 1 Kings 1–10.)

Hence Solomon spoke and recorded this lustrous pearl of wisdom:

> When a man's ways please the Lord, he maketh even his enemies to be at peace with him.
>
> —PROVERBS 16:7

Paraphrased, this proverb states:

> When our ways [of living, serving, and relating to people and situations] consistently please God, He forces our

97

adversaries to act peaceably toward us [terminating their combative attitudes, unjustified criticisms, and stubborn opposition].

Note carefully what this verse promises. To "be at peace" with us is to stop trying to oppose, attack, defame, or ruin us and to simply leave us alone. This guarantees only that God will render our enemies nonaggressive, not that they will necessarily like, unite with, or assist us (though God sometimes does even this for those who please Him; see Daniel 3:30). This is a very sweet promise to Christians long opposed and oppressed by the bitter contradictions, challenges, schemes, and denunciations of their enemies. But do we know who our "enemies" are?

Our enemies are people who oppose our beliefs, our obedience to God's Word, or our service in His calling. They mock our childlike trust that salvation comes solely through one's personal relationship to Jesus (John 14:6) and our seemingly simplistic faith that He will see us through every problem in life if we but trust and obey Him. They usually reject the authority of the Bible—that it is in fact God's inspired, inerrant, and definitive message to mankind. Hence, they have no respect for our decisions to live by biblical commands and principles or to hope in biblical prophecies. They reject God's demands for holiness and repentance, flatly refusing to relinquish their sins to receive their Savior. Some are apostates, or backslidden Christians, who after their conversions became offended during tests of their faith and stopped walking with the Lord. All of these nemeses disregard our claims that God has called us to specific tasks or ministries in life, and they do everything they can to hinder or halt our Christian walk and work. They hate us without cause and cause others to hate us without knowing us. They trouble us every day. When we succeed, they envy us; when we fail, they mock us; but always, they resist us. These are our "enemies." And we need God's help to deal with them. For that, says Solomon, we must please God in our ways. But what are our "ways"?

Simply put, our ways are *all the normal habitual acts that make up our personal lifestyles*—seeking and worshiping the Lord; discharging our occupational obligations; preparing for or pursuing our ministry duties; relating kindly and faithfully to our spouses, relatives, friends, and associates; and reacting to the trials and triumphs of life. And there's one more very important "way," namely, *how we relate to our enemies*—how we think toward them, speak with them, and act and react toward them. In all these "ways," God's Word lays down specific commands for our thoughts, speech, and actions. If we ignore them, we grieve God. But if we carefully and consistently obey them, we please Him, and, as the proverb teaches, He subdues our enemies.

BIBLICAL EXAMPLES

There are many biblical examples of God making His people's enemies to live at peace with them.

Subduing enemies

Because King Jehoshaphat of Judah walked in God's ways, God caused the fear of God to fall on all the hostile nations surrounding Judah, and "they made no war against Jehoshaphat" (2 Chron. 17:10). God did the same for King Asa, Jehoshaphat's father and predecessor on Judah's throne, because he did what was right in God's sight: "He [Asa] had no war in those years, because the LORD had given him rest" (2 Chron. 14:6). When Isaac consistently refused to contend with his contentious Philistine persecutors and meekly accepted their unreasonable rejection, God eventually forced the Philistines to seek peace with Isaac (Gen. 26:26–31). Because Job humbled himself and confessed his sin, God made his bitterest critics come to him seeking prayer and reconciliation (Job 42:7–9). Because of Moses' uncompromising adherence to God's will, God sent plagues to force Pharaoh to relent and release the Israelites from slavery (Exod. 12:30–32). Because of Nehemiah's courageous and determined effort to rebuild Jerusalem's walls, God made his enemies, the Samaritans, abandon their resistance to his mission (Neh. 6:16). Because of Jesus' gracious and irrefutably wise speech, God made His enemies stop trying to provoke Him to make incriminating statements (Matt. 22:46).

In all of these examples, God graciously *created* peace for His servants where there was no peace: "He *maketh* peace in thy borders" (Ps. 147:14, emphasis added).

Converting enemies

Sometimes God went further, converting adversaries into associates and haters into helpers. These not only stopped resisting, but they also started *assisting* the righteous.

Because David pleased Him, God prompted David's most formidable adversary, Abner, to switch his allegiance from Saul's house to David's fledgling kingship (2 Sam. 3:12); no longer hostile, Abner then pledged to fight for David. Because the Lord was pleased with the early church's faith, loyalty, and sacrificial obedience, He suddenly broke their chief persecutor, Saul of Tarsus (Acts 9:1–6); after this, Saul became their chief promoter (Gal. 1:23). Jesus was so pleased with the Philadelphia Christians' patient endurance that He promised to convert their Jewish enemies and bring them into their assembly (Rev. 3:9); thereafter they would support the very church they had viciously slandered. God was so pleased with Jeremiah's loyalty while suffering bitter persecution in the siege of Jerusalem, He caused the Babylonians to favor Jeremiah after the city fell (Jer. 39:11–14); thus former hostiles treated him hospitably. God was so pleased with the Jewish remnant's steadfast determination to rebuild His temple that He inspired a Persian king to order their opponents, the Samaritans, not only to stop interfering with their effort but also to start funding it with local tax revenues (Ezra 6:6–13); no longer supplanting, the Samaritans then sponsored their work.

In all these cases, God converted His people's foes into "footstools" (Ps. 110:1), or sources of support, comfort, and rest.

Inciting enemies

The opposite side of this proverbial coin is equally true. Solomon could have added: "And when a man's ways displease the Lord, He makes his enemies declare war on him!" Solomon experienced this, too. When in his later years the son of David turned from God to worship idols (1 Kings 11:4–10), the Lord "stirred up" enemies against him; first Hadad (v. 14), then Rezon (v. 23), and finally Jeroboam (v. 26). Other wayward children of God had similar experiences.

When King Saul forsook the Lord and mistreated David, God stirred up the Philistines to attack Saul when he was weak and vulnerable (1 Sam. 28:4–5, 15). When the Lord's anger was "hot against Israel" in the times of the judges, He prompted the Mesopotamians to attack and conquer Israel (Judg. 3:8). And when the Jews returned to their sin time and again, God prompted the Midianites to invade and oppress them (Judg. 6:1). The most obvious and dramatic examples of this were Judah's devastating defeat at the hands of the Babylonians (2 Chron. 36:14–17) and restored Israel's utter dismantling at the hands of the Romans in A.D. 70.

In all these examples, the Lord intervened, not to intimidate but to *incite* Israel's enemies! Why? Because He was using those enemies as a rod to chasten His disobedient children. (This complements, not contradicts, the more commonly seen biblical truth that our enemies usually trouble us because we *are* pleasing God and displeasing the prince of this world!)

So we see before us the whole range of possibilities. God subdues, converts, or incites our enemies, depending on one key factor—our ways, or walk, before Him. It's time for self-examination.

Do you have an enemy, a determined spiritual opponent, in your life? Has the Lord been subduing or stirring that enemy lately? If the former is true, praise God. If the latter is true, practice Proverbs 16:7. For the moment, forget about your enemy's attitude, animosity, and actions, and focus on one thing only: pleasing the Lord. And how can you do that?

Here are four "ways" to focus on pleasing the Lord: obedience, non-retaliation, goodness, and prayer.

First, obey the Lord in every area of your daily life. Seek Him early, comply with all His words, obey His Spirit's guidance, speak rightly, avoid sin, and faithfully pursue your work or ministry. Obedience, especially to God's written Word, is the chief way we show God that we love him: "If a man love me, he will *keep my words*…" (John 14:23, emphasis added). And obeying the Word of God always compels God's attention, affection, fellowship, and response: "…and my Father will love him, and *we will come unto him, and make our abode with him*" (v. 23, emphasis added).

Second, never again retaliate against your enemy. God loves, and has called us to be, gentle lambs, not aggressive wolves. So don't repay evil for evil, rebut word for word, or relish or seek your adversary's downfall. Leave all retaliation to God, and determine to obey Jesus' command, "But I say unto you that ye resist not evil" (Matt. 5:39).

Third, pursue goodness. Every act of goodness you sow, you will reap one day. God assures us that, "*Whatever* a man soweth, *that* shall he also reap" (Gal. 6:7, emphasis added). So as you have opportunity, do your enemy good, rendering assistance whenever asked. This is an act of direct obedience to the Lord's Word, which states, "If thine enemy hunger, feed him; if he thirst, give him drink…" (Rom. 12:20), and it will bring a direct response from God every time. As you thus "overcome evil with good" (v. 21), the Holy Spirit will pour the heat of His conviction on your enemy's conscience day and night to bring him (or her) to repentance: "…in so doing thou shalt heap coals of fire on his head" (v. 21). When these overcoming opportunities arise, your old nature will not want to respond and do good to your enemy. So make it respond. No matter how you feel, follow through and render the assistance requested, knowing that if you hold back from helping your enemy, God must hold back from helping you. And you don't want that, do you? Also, "in so doing," God will change you. And soon you will find yourself without any desire to see your spiritual antagonist reap what they deserve; you will be filled instead with a growing sorrow over their stubborn sinfulness and a Spirit-born desire to see them repent so you may reconcile with them on God's terms.

Fourth, pray persistently for God's help. Prayer moves God's hand. In faith ask Him to strengthen you, subdue your enemy, and give him "repentance to the acknowledging of the truth" (2 Tim. 2:25). As you thus "pray for them who despitefully use you, and persecute you" (Matt. 5:44), God's love is fully released and developed in you. That makes you more like Him, who is love. It also fulfills Jesus' high priestly prayer, which ends with His consummate request, that divine love be both implanted and manifested in every believer's life: "That the love with which thou hast loved me may be in them" (John 17:26). And that deeply pleases your heavenly Father.

Then, pleased with your ways, He will bear down on your enemy with the full power of His hand and, much to your relief, make him or her "be at peace" with you. Or, who knows? He may even make them assist you. In either case, you will be deeply pleased with His intervention.

Then spread the blessing—go sharpen someone else's spirit!

Chapter Thirteen

SHARPENING DULL SPIRITS

*I*n every continent, culture, and climate, iron tools grow dull by use. Whether an axe, saw, or knife, the constant attrition caused by chopping, sawing, or cutting gradually spoils the sharp cutting edge of the implement. This leaves its owner with two options: (1) throw away the instrument; or (2) sharpen and reuse it. Contrary to the increasing use-and-discard tendencies of this decidedly disposable generation, wise tool-masters rarely consider the first option. Typically, they just quietly sharpen their instruments, however dull, and put them back in service.

Similarly, Christians all over the world, each of whom is "an instrument for his work" (Isa. 54:16), grow dull by use. The constant resistance of the labors, cares, and troubles of life steadily wears down our spirits. Eventually we sense that we are losing our cutting edge. Our biblical insight becomes dim, our faith weak, our hope dead, our obedience slow, our love tepid, and our worship dry. With our zeal blunted, we feel, sound, and look dull, or, to use Jesus' adjective of choice, "*lukewarm*...neither cold nor hot" (Rev. 3:16, emphasis added). Christ, the heavenly Tool-master, then has two options: (1) discard us as unfit "castaway(s)" (1 Cor. 9:27); or (2) sharpen and reuse us. If we stubbornly persist in willful independence of Him, disobedience to His Word, or rebellion against our calling, eventually He will reluctantly take the first option and set us aside: "If a man abide not in me, he is *cast forth...*" (John 15:6, emphasis added). But always His preferred option is the second. Why? Because He saved us not only because He loved us but also to use us for His purpose and glory in this world. So, by whatever means available, the Master seeks to restore His instruments' sharpness.

He has many ways to do this. Every time we pray, our spirits are sharpened. Whenever we study our Bibles, prayerfully, patiently, and thoroughly researching the sacred verse, our minds and spirits are sharpened. Whoever worships God "in spirit and in truth," whether privately or publicly, is sharpened in spirit. Whenever we receive the Lord's Supper, our spirits are not only nourished but also sharpened by direct, extraordinary contact with Christ's presence. Whenever we read anointed books and messages penned by Christ's corps of ready writers, our minds and spirits are sharpened. And whenever we listen to His army of ordained preachers, teachers, prophets, and exhorters, we are also restored to our full sharpness and readiness to serve our King and His kingdom.

To these proven sharpening methods, King Solomon adds one more effective, readily available way by which we may restore our spiritual focus. In his Book of Proverbs we read:

> Iron sharpeneth iron; so a man sharpeneth the countenance of his friend.
>
> —Proverbs 27:17

Paraphrased, this pearly revelation says:

> Just as an iron file is used to sharpen the edge of an iron sword, axe, or knife [the rubbing of a similar substance improving its edge], so one man [of God, or believer] sharpens the [mind, faith, hope, resolve, zeal, and] smile of another [the "rubbing"—meaningful conversation or correspondence—of similar spirits improving each other's edge].

To help you understand this paraphrase, please consider that "rubbing" suggests not the adversarial but the *friendly contact, or communion, of meaningful conversation or correspondence.* By "meaningful" conversation or correspondence, we mean *communication that is timely, informative, substantive, supportive, encouraging, edifying, or challenging.* Not all talk is meaningful. Much is idle, foolish, or trivial; some is purely worldly in spirit; and some actively incites us to sin. By "sharpeneth," the son of David, and the Spirit that inspired him, means *stimulates to righteous thought or action.* When our spirits are dull and our cerebral computers slow, our brains and spirits need a prick, spur, or impetus, something to get us moving forward again with invigorating thought and soul-replenishing meditation, something to reconnect us with the perpetual flow of the supernaturally reviving river of God (Ezek. 47:1–12).

What does Solomon recommend in his sacred saying? He suggests meaningful conversation or correspondence with a believer of like mind and commitment to Christ. That, he claims, will help restore our spirits' cutting edges just as surely as the other means listed above. Solomon wasn't the only sacred writer to suggest this.

The prophet Malachi commended, and thus indirectly recommended, the spiritually stimulating conversations the righteous remnant of Jews regularly engaged in during the post-captivity period: "They that feared the LORD *spoke often one to another...*" (Mal. 3:16, emphasis added). These edifying talks were essentially on spiritual matters and centered around the will, works, and "name," or benevolent and faithful nature, of God: "they...that thought upon *his name*" (v. 16, emphasis added). So meaningful were these discussions that God Himself drew near to listen to them: "And the LORD hearkened, and heard it" (v. 16). Blessed by the content of these sharpening sessions, the Lord ordered the angels to record them in their books of history to be kept forever in heaven's library: "And a book of remembrance was written before him for them" (v. 16).

Deeply gratified by their decision to devote their thoughts and conversations to Him, the Lord expressed His highest approval of them in three ways. First, He honored them by recording their honorable actions in the Bible and their words in the angels' books of history we will read and enjoy for perpetuity, as described above. Second, He referred to them honorably as His precious, beautiful "jewels." "And they shall be mine...my jewels" (Mal. 3:17). Third, He promised them special protection and honor in the days to come: "And I will spare them, as a man spareth his own son that serveth him" (v. 17).

This passage makes two truths evident:

1. Remnant believers regularly sharpen their spirits by meaningful conversation.

2. God delights in and richly rewards this practice.

The Spirit resounded this biblical keynote through the apostle Paul, who wrote, "Finally, brethren, whatever things are true, whatever things are honest, whatever things are just, whatever things are pure, whatever things are lovely, whatever things are of good report; if there be any virtue, and if there be any praise, *think on these things*" (Phil. 4:8, emphasis added). Extrapolating, we may surely add the addendum, *"and talk about them."* Why do we suggest this? Because Paul was as extraordinary a conversationalist as he was a thinker and teacher. He was as communicatively active as he was cerebrally active, both his thoughts and words constantly percolating with vital spiritual and natural wisdom. Consequently, he was both spiritually strong and stimulative, always keeping himself sharp and sharpening the believers around him by engaging, edifying conversations. (See Acts 20:11.)

Note also that Paul's apostolic command in Philippians 4:8 does not limit fruitful Christian cogitations or conversations to biblical matters, but rather throws the door wide open to a whole universe of worthy, timely, useful, and virtuous thought stuff: "*whatever* things are true, *whatever* things are honest…" Whatever illustrates sound, historically proven life principles, patterns, and morals, says Paul and the Spirit, "think on these things." And, after pondering them, share your insights, analyses, and conclusions with, and receive the same from, other committed disciples of the Nazarene. By this spiritually and intellectually stimulating exchange, both you and those with whom you converse will be refitted for the Master's use.

Jesus practiced this on the Emmaus Road. (See Luke 24:13–32.) There he engaged two very dull disciples in a broad-ranging biblical discussion that made their "hearts burn" with glowing interest while He explained the Scriptures that most directly applied to their current life-problem—His stunningly sudden betrayal, sufferings, and death. And once their faith and hope were again bright and sharp, "he vanished out of their sight" (v. 31). Shouldn't we follow His example by sharpening one another's minds and spirits as we walk along the road to His kingdom?

By His grace, I've often experienced both the receiving and the giving of this blessed ministry of exhortation. My mother was an extraordinarily gifted exhorter. Countless times as a fledgling Christian I went to her confused and discouraged and, after an iron-to-iron conversation, emerged clear and ready to readdress the race set before me. As a minister, I found Dr. Judson Cornwall a willing fatherly advisor and "file." His conversations, faxes, and e-mails restored the edge to my devotion and ministry on a number of occasions. My readers and students have also sharpened me. Numerous times over the years their timely letters and telephone calls have rekindled my zeal when tribulation, persecution, or monotonous tedious labors had temporarily blunted it. My local fellowship is another source of iron. We regularly lunch together after every Lord's day meeting, and, by hearty conversations on biblical, ecclesiastical, historic, national, and international matters, sharpen each other's resolve for the coming week and work. By the wondrously natural work of the supernatural Holy Spirit, personal spiritual needs not addressed by the morning's teaching are often pinpointed and addressed during these luncheon conversations. Fellow ministers occasionally seek to use me as a "file." By patiently and prayerfully listening to their personal, ministerial, or doctrinal problems and then giving them the biblical passages or principles the Holy Spirit brings to mind, I receive just as much edification from the Lord as He gives through me. Often I have entered these sharpening sessions exhausted from my own ministerial labors and left thoroughly refreshed and reinspired in my walk and work. With less frequency yet equal effectiveness, God has occasionally prompted ministers with genuine prophetic gifts to speak to me concerning things to come in my life or work—and whatever dullness was lingering in my spirit instantly vanished.

Why in all these biblical and experiential examples did the Lord visit and bless both His "iron instrument" and "file"? Because God blesses us whenever we obey His Word. And His Word teaches us to sharpen one another: "Iron sharpeneth iron; *so a man sharpeneth . . . his [believing] friend*" (emphasis added).

So let us ask ourselves, Are we communicative or silent? Engaging or reclusive? Drawing near to commune with one another or pulling back? Starting or shunning worthy conversations or correspondences with our brothers and sisters of iron? As if he anticipated this very question, the writer to the Hebrews commanded us:

> Let us *consider one another to provoke unto love and to good works,* not forsaking the assembling of ourselves together, as the manner of some is, *but exhorting one another, and so much the more, as ye see the day approaching.*
> —HEBREWS 10:24–25, EMPHASIS ADDED

Obeying His injunction will help us lose a lot of unnecessary weight.

Chapter Fourteen

PUT OFF THAT WEIGHT!

*T*his twenty-first century finds millions of American Christians preoccupied with the topic of weight. We're buying books, searching Web sites, or listening intently to popular talk show hosts and physicians to learn how to shed unnecessary, unbeautiful pounds. Or we're spending many hours a week in aerobic dancing, jogging, exercising, or weight lifting in hopes of sculpting our own version of the glorified body.

But centuries ago, as King Solomon was reciting his invaluably wise sayings before his court of hushed listeners, the Spirit enveloped him and enabled him to focus intently on another kind of weighty matter—dealing with angry fools! And the son of David said:

> A stone is heavy, and the sand weighty, but a fool's wrath is heavier than them both.
>
> —PROVERBS 27:3

Paraphrased, this lustrous truism states:

> Stone [or gravel] is heavy to lift or carry, and sand is also very weighty, but being exposed to the [constant] wrath [protestations of anger and provocations to anger] of a

fool is an even heavier, more oppressive and exhausting burden.

If you've never realized just how heavy rock and sand are, I suggest the following abbreviated applied curriculum. Try pushing a wheelbarrow full of gravel for about twenty minutes, and then see how you feel. Next, spend twenty minutes shoveling out a pit along the beach or in a sand dune, and, again, see how you feel. Upon completion of these two tasks you will be sufficiently if not fully educated in load bearing…and ready to blissfully agree with the first half of this proverb: "A stone *is* heavy, and the sand weighty" (emphasis added). Discovering the accuracy of the second half—the greater heaviness of dealing with fools, especially angry ones—should take even less time. But first, we must understand what Solomon meant by the term "fool" and also by the phrase "a fool's wrath."

Literally, "fool" (KJV) is translated from the Hebrew *ewil*, which means, "perverse." So a fool is one that is perverse, or spiritually or morally twisted and wrong, in God's sight. *Vine's Complete Expository Dictionary* defines *ewil* as, "a morally undesirable individual who despises wisdom and discipline…and is quarrelsome."[1] Considering the width of these definitions and the varied contexts in which fools are described in the Book of Proverbs, we may extend our description of a proverbial "fool" to take in several phases of folly. Let's consider them.

Broadly speaking, a fool is a (or an):

- **Rebel**, one given to resisting all forms of authority and those who exercise it

- **Angry person,** who, chronically and emotionally chafed over offenses and injustices, deals angrily with whoever is around him at the moment

- **Envious person**, who, seething inwardly with discontent and rivalry over others' blessings, gifts, advantages, or superiority, is always agitated and agitating

- **Contentious unbeliever**, who loves to mock, misrepresent, belittle, contradict, or contend with anyone, especially "born-again Christians"

- **Carnal Christian,** who is presently ignoring and disobeying His Lord's words or call and therefore dislikes and avoids Christians who fervently trust and obey God

- **Apostate Christian**, who has fully rejected his Lord's will and is thereafter diabolically driven to despise, denounce, defame, and destroy Christians who still hold fast their heavenly Father and faith

- **Irresponsible person**, who never listens or carries out assignments correctly or thoroughly

- **Thoughtless person,** or empty-headed fool, to whom you carefully and repeatedly explain things, and, well, they just don't get it, ever

- **Lazy person**, or sluggard, who works very hard not to work very much

- **Prideful braggart**, who bores everyone within earshot with endless boasting, yet never dreams he or she is a bore

- **Drunkard**, who can't bear to be sober and whom we can't bear when he's not

All of these descriptions of a "vexatious fool," as James Moffatt describes, are very accurate to life. We live, work, travel, socialize, and attend church with these folks every day. When they exercise their folly, they exercise us, driving us up the wall, across the ceiling, down the other wall, and out of the room—and out of the Spirit of Christ! Or, as our proverb states, they laden our souls with oppressive, crushing spiritual boulders and heavy spiritual sandbags filled with frustration, grief, and despair.

As to "a fool's wrath," there are two aspects we wish to consider: First, the angry protestations of fools; second, the provocations to anger they cause.

With regard to the first, fools are always angrily protesting something. Why? Because they are full of anger, and anger, if it is not faced and forsaken, must always come out. Ecclesiastes notes, "Anger resteth in the bosom of fools" (Eccles. 7:9). So fools may be further biblically defined as *those who permit anger to remain ("rest") in their hearts and minds, whether with or without just cause.* The wise learn the extreme danger of holding anger and set their minds to quickly drop it, whenever it arises, whatever the cause, however great the injustice. But fools are otherwise normal folks who unwisely choose to hold their anger; then they begin speaking and acting, well, like self-opposing fools!

They insult the very people they should thank, as Nabal did David. Or they attack those they envy, like King Saul, who thrust his javelin at David. They may lash out with uncalled-for revilings, as Shimei, who mercilessly castigated and cursed David. They sulk selfishly before God when they should be praising Him for His mercy, as Jonah did when God spared Nineveh. They may also mock those who worship God with childlike freedom, as Michal did David when he danced before the Lord. They may explode with arrogant contempt at the humble, helpful instructions of God's servants, as proud Naaman did when Elisha advised him to wash in the Jordan River.

Like heavy stones and weighty sand, these repeated, ridiculous protests make every new day a heavy assignment to those whom God ordains to live, work, or congregate with these foolish ones. Why? You never know when or where something—a word, subtle thought, perceived slight, or passing comment—will set them off on yet another bitter tirade! Matthew Henry wrote, "The wrath of a fool lies heavily upon those he is enraged at." Poor Abigail, living with Nabal! Poor David, working for volatile King Saul! Daily, hourly, momentarily, the prospect of yet another outburst of rage or rancor weighed heavy on their minds.

As to the second aspect, angry fools tend to reproduce their own kind. That is, the angry words and mean-spirited actions of fools often provoke similar manifestations in other normally quiet and docile people. "Grievous words stir up anger," declares Proverbs 15:1, and Proverbs 29:22 adds, "An angry man stirreth up strife."

Angry fools stir our anger in several ways by:

- Flatly rebelling against our appropriate authority in the home, workplace, church, or nation

- Responding with stubborn slowness to even our gentlest, humblest requests for cooperation

- Repeatedly misjudging us after we've graciously befriended, helped, defended, or forgiven them

- Habitually rudely contradicting whatever opinion we express

- Relentlessly misrepresenting and slandering us

Besides these types of vindictive agitators, there are kinder sons of provocation, friendly but thoughtless or irresponsible people who try our patience pitilessly. When these associates begin to drop the ball, we begin to drop the Spirit...and pick up our old ways of whining, wrath, retaliation, and being miserable. And the more we meditate on *their* stupidity, inattention, and ineptness, the more *we* manifest a very similar stupidity of anger, inattention to God's Word, and ineptness as an overcomer. Hence, the Fools' Club gains yet another member. In his lower moments, Solomon must have experienced this.

With a command of detail only discernable by personal experience, his writings describe the irritations of dealing with a whole range of fools, such as:

- **Irresponsible messengers**: "He that sendeth a message by the hand of a fool, cutteth off the [his own] feet, and drinketh damage [poison]" (Prov. 26:6).

- **Lazy employees**, who claim: "There is a lion outside; I shall be slain [if I come to work]" (Prov. 22:13).

- **Inattentive, incurious students**: "Wisdom is too high for a fool [to pursue or perceive]" (Prov. 24:7).

- **Nosey neighbors**: "Withdraw thy foot from thy neighbor's house, lest he be weary of thee, and so hate thee" (Prov. 25:17).

- **Practical jokers**: "As a mad man who casteth firebrands, arrows, and death, so is the man that deceiveth [lies to] his neighbor, and saith, Am not I in sport [kidding]?" (Prov. 26:18–19).

- **Insensitive comforters**: "As he that taketh away a garment in cold weather...so is he that singeth songs to an heavy heart" (Prov. 25:20).

- **Disobedient children**: "A foolish son is the heaviness of his mother" (Prov. 10:1).

- **Argumentative husbands or fathers**: "As coals are to burning coals...so is a contentious man to kindle strife" (Prov. 26:21).

- **Belligerent wives or mothers**: "It is better to dwell in the wilderness, than with a contentious and an angry woman" (Prov. 21:19).

- **Stubborn lawbreakers**: "Stripes [whippings, or punishments, are prepared] for the back of fools" (Prov. 19:29).

- **Influential but ignorant leaders**: "...him that ruleth among fools" (Eccles. 9:17).

That is an impressive litany of fools and their follies!

By these and other irritations, vexatious people produce wrath in us and bring upon us hindering burdens of fretting and frustration. Soon we begin feeling increasingly heavy, oppressed, and exhausted. The apostle Peter knew all about this weightiness: "though now...ye are in heaviness" (1 Pet. 1:6). So did the writer to the Hebrews, who spoke of "every weight...which doth so easily beset us" (Heb. 12:1). King David also bore these burdens in his soul: "I am full of heaviness" (Ps. 69:20). And Job testified that the grief his unfriendly friends put upon him was "heavier than the sand of the sea" (Job 6:3). So what in the world should we do with our fools? Or rather, what should we do with the crushing spiritual and psychological loads they regularly place upon us? Well, what do you do if a huge boulder rolls onto you? You roll it off, and quickly!

That's precisely the advice the Bible gives us. Except it adds that we should roll our burdens not only *off* us but *onto* the Lord, who, being with us always, will faithfully help us bear them in His inexhaustible strength. "Cast thy burden on the LORD, and he shall sustain thee" (Ps. 55:22), sang the psalmist. Peter continued his biblical melody, "Casting all your care upon him; for he careth for you" (1 Pet. 5:7). The writer to the Hebrews sang along, harmonizing with the verse, "Let us lay aside every weight, and the sin which doth so easily beset us" (Heb. 12:1). And Jesus finished their heavenly song by inviting us to put on His liberating yoke and let Him bear every burden with and for us: "Come unto me, all ye that labor and are heavy laden, and I will give you rest. Take my yoke upon you and learn of me...and ye shall find rest unto your souls. For my yoke is easy, and my burden is light" (Matt. 11:28–30). But how? How do we enter into Jesus' yoke and lay aside our weights? That's the question we need answered.

We must quickly rule out two popular ways of dealing with fools: unprincipled appeasement and unrestrained retaliation. If we just pliably do or say whatever will for the moment make our fool happy, we're walking in the flesh, not the Spirit. We're not overcoming our tests as we should, nor are we finding relief from our burdens. Why? Because trying ever so carefully to prevent the angry protests of fools is a form of the fear of man, and if we succumb to it, it will leave us trapped in tormenting intimidation, constantly worried, consciously or subconsciously, that another unpleasant episode may erupt. Hence Solomon warned us, "The fear of man bringeth a snare" (Prov. 29:25). Conversely, if we give in and verbally blast fools with the angry reproach they deserve, we're certainly not walking in either the light or love of Jesus. Indeed, "The wrath of man worketh not the righteousness of God" (James 1:20). Such responses only add the additional burden of guilt to our consciences and leave us feeling like foolish failures. Hence we are also warned, "Answer not a fool according to his folly, lest thou also be like unto him" (Prov. 26:4). We will never overcome if we pursue either of these flawed, fleshly methods of handling fools. We need a better idea.

And God has one waiting for us in His Word. His method for shedding spiritual weights is recorded in Psalm 37. Penned by inspiration through David, a man who laid aside more spiritual weights than most of us will ever encounter, this epic Bible poem serves as a virtual deliverance manual for overburdened Christians. With beautiful biblical simplicity, it gives us step-by-step instructions on how to unload our burdens.

Let the Lord speak to you as you ponder these seven biblical steps to freedom given in the opening verses of Psalm 37, bearing in mind that they are written in the imperative mood—if we want to be rid of our burdens, we *must* do these things:

1. **Stop fretting.** Refuse to fret any more at the foolish one that is frustrating you: "*Fret not* thyself because of evil-doers…" (Ps. 37:1, emphasis added). If you realize your anger at him (or her) is partly rooted in the subtle envy of sinners, don't deny your envy, but confess it and repent: "…*neither be thou envious* against the workers of iniquity" (v. 1, emphasis added). (See Proverbs 23:17–19; 24:1.)

2. **Start believing.** To help you stop fretting, believe God's promises to reckon with your (unjust, oppressive, or hostile) fool: "For *they shall soon be cut down* like the grass, *and wither* like the green herb" (Ps. 37:2, emphasis added). And choose to fully trust God's goodness and honesty: "*Trust* in the LORD…" (v. 3, emphasis added).

3. **Do good.** With your trust in God's goodness settled, turn your full attention to your personal responsibility to "do good," meaning your threefold duty of abandon-ing your besetting sins, abiding in Christ, and pursuing the tasks He has given you: "…and *do good*…" (v. 3, emphasis added). This will enable God to fully provide your present needs: "…so shalt thou dwell in the land, and *verily thou shalt be fed*" (v. 3, emphasis added).

4. **Delight in the Lord.** Delight—satisfy, ravish, rejoice—your soul in your sweet personal fellowship with Jesus, believing that He will likewise delight to give you every sweet personal blessing you long for: "*Delight thyself* also in the LORD, and *he shall give thee* the desires of thine heart" (v. 4, emphasis added).

5. **Commit your way.** As new questions or difficulties arise in your "way" (circumstances), "commit" (roll or transfer) them completely into the Lord's all-powerful hands, relying on His faithfulness alone to deliver you in His time and way, and give you full vindication and justice: "*Commit thy way* unto the LORD; trust also in him, and he shall bring it [your release] to pass. And he

shall bring forth thy righteousness [uprightness] as the light, and thy justice [vindication] as the noonday" (vv. 5–6, emphasis added).

6. **Rest in the Lord.** Then "rest" about the whole matter, believing that God has fully granted and begun answering the requests you have committed to Him and that the matter is finished *now* already by faith. (See Mark 11:24.) Refuse to reopen old questions or renew old agitations, and settle down instead in the spirit of patient trust to maturely endure until God acts, meanwhile refusing to fear or fret that your fool looks wise and his (or her) diabolical plans successful, while you appear a foolish failure! "*Rest in the LORD, and wait patiently for him; fret not thyself because of him who prospereth in his way, because of the man who bringeth wicked devices to pass*" (Ps. 37:7, emphasis added).

7. **Continue the above.** Finally, continue doing all these things—quenching all anger and envy, refusing all retaliation, believing all God's promises, expecting His intervention, patiently occupying, and enjoying God's presence and peace—until God changes your situation (vv. 8–11).

Meanwhile, the Lord is busy doing something much more important than relieving you: He's remaking you so that you may be "conformed to the image of his Son" (Rom. 8:29).

That's how to live in Jesus' yoke, deal wisely with fools, and efficiently put off every burden they put on you. Then, with the spirit of heaviness gone, you can put on the garment of praise and run patiently the race set before you!

So be a good twenty-first century Christian. Put off that weight! And put on a new appreciation for your true friends.

Chapter Fifteen

ABOUT TRUE FRIENDS

*N*ext to God, the angels, your salvation, and the Bible, the best blessings you have are your true Christian friends. Do you know who yours are?

The Bible affirms that trouble will reveal them. Like a dependable litmus test, it clearly and definitively distinguishes your true friends from your false ones:

> A friend loveth at all times, and a brother is born for adversity.
>
> —PROVERBS 17:17

Paraphrased, this pearl of great price declares:

> A true friend will love and stand by you at all times, good and bad; God sends [or births] true brothers [and sisters] into our lives [and they assist us most] during times of trouble.

Here the faithful Word of the faithful God praises faithful friends—specifically our loyal comrades in the faith. It frames for our viewing a beautiful word portrait of true friends, who stand by us not only in prosperity but also in adversity. What it does not say is also worthy of consideration.

Implied is that false friends and brothers love and stand by us only when things go well. When we're prosperous or popular, they appear. As long as the good times last, they linger. When troubles enter our lives, they exit. When triumphs return, they reenter. When troubles revisit us again, they exit—again! Why the vacillation? Because their dominating motives are not love and faithfulness, but self-preservation and self-advantage. They will be our friends if it doesn't cost them anything or if they can gain by it, but on no other terms. The word *loyalty* is simply not in their vocabulary. If they foresee any kind of stormy water ahead, they just jump ship and sail on . . . without us. Fair-weather friends such as these have burdened us all.

It lightens our burden, however, to realize that others before us also suffered in the house of their friends. Demas, the apostle Paul's ministerial assistant, walked away from Paul during his period of unjust Roman imprisonment. After David and his men saved the city of Keilah from the Philistines, God warned David that the Keilahites would soon turn him over to his wicked yet still popular persecutor, King Saul. Though David's men had kindly protected Nabal's herds from predators, Nabal misjudged David as a rebel, refused to feed his hungry men, and roundly reproached him. When horrific losses suddenly struck Job, despite his friends' firsthand knowledge of his long-standing righteousness and fruitful ministry, they soon began bitterly accusing and misjudging him. When David reigned over Israel, Ahithophel fellowshiped with and counseled him daily, but when Absalom took control, Ahithophel quietly forsook David and began serving the new and wildly popular monarch. Wounded by Ahithophel's false friendship, David lamented, "Yea, mine own familiar friend, in whom I trusted, who did eat of my bread, hath lifted up his heel against me" (Ps. 41:9). More relief comes to us as we recall the true friends God birthed into the lives of His troubled but faithful servants.

Jonathan, for instance, was indeed a true friend to David,

coming to him when many ran from him and reassuring David of his destiny when thousands doubted the son of Jesse would ever see a throne (1 Sam. 23:16–18). After forty years' separation, Aaron, Moses' younger sibling, reentered Moses' life just when he faced his greatest challenge—his mission to return to Egypt, confront Pharaoh, and end the Israelites' bondage. Notwithstanding his weaknesses, Aaron proved a godsend for Moses, standing lovingly and loyally by him through battles, complaints, rebellions, and long seasons of delay. The elders of Judah and, later, Barzillai, lovingly befriended and loyally supported David throughout his decade of wilderness trials. And while Judas betrayed Jesus and Peter denied him, John stood true to his maligned teacher from the garden to the trial to the cross. These were not merely loyal men. They were human expressions, or agents, of the loving loyalty of God Himself. He sent them to His servants in their lowest hour as incarnations of His unfailing promise, "I will never leave thee, nor forsake thee" (Heb. 13:5). With their examples fresh in our minds, let's consider the facts of friendship.

The Facts of Friendship

Concerning both true and false friends, the Book of Proverbs has much to teach us. Prayerfully meditate on these proverbial facts of friendship.

False friends

- **The attraction of false friends:** "Many will entreat the favor of the prince, and every man is a friend to him that giveth gifts" (Prov. 19:6). The "prince" spoken of has power and the gift-giver wealth. Power, wealth, popularity—these are the baits that attract friends of dubious character. Oh, they may genuinely admire those they cling to, but not nearly as much as they love the authority, money, or fame they possess. When prospering, beware of human leeches!

- **The hypocrisy of false friends:** "The flatterer who loudly praises and glorifies his neighbor, rising early in the morning, it shall be counted as cursing him [for he will be suspected of sinister purposes]" (Prov. 27:14, AMP). When your friends go out of their way to flatter you in front of others, watch out! And watch them! Their walk may be faithless while their talk is friendly: "Whoever flatters his neighbor is spreading a net for his feet" (Prov. 29:5, NIV). Treachery rarely announces its approach. Remember, actions, not words, always reveal the true state of our hearts. (See Psalms 28:3–4; 41:5–6; 55:20–21.) So look past profuse praises of love to see if there are positive proofs of genuine loyalty.

True friends

- **The forge of true friends:** "A man who has friends must himself be friendly" (Prov. 18:24, NKJV). Warm congeniality, not cold self-consciousness, breeds lasting, high-quality friendships. Talkative, outgoing persons invariably gravitate toward each other, while overly quiet, sullen, unfriendly types polarize everyone. If you want friends, be friendly! Don't withdraw; warm up to others of like mind and faith! And you will reap exactly what you sow—true friendship.

- **The attraction of true friends:** "He who loves purity of heart and whose speech is gracious, the king is his friend" (Prov. 22:11, NAS). Honesty, purity, and graciousness appeal to persons of similar integrity. If our motives are right, our meditations pure, and our conversations consistently spiritual, we may expect "kings"—persons of authority and noble Christians fit to rule and reign with Jesus—to invite us into their circle of companions and confidants.

- **The counsel of true friends:** "Open rebuke is better than secret love. Faithful [edifying, helpful] are the [verbal] wounds of a friend; but the [literal and figurative] kisses of an enemy are deceitful [misleading]" (Prov. 27:5–6). The one sure test of a true friend is that he or she will talk to you "straight up" when you need it…no sugar, no honey, just solid salt—unvarnished truth. I'd rather be told off by a friend than talked up by an enemy. I may hurt now, but I'll be healthy later. Said David, "Let the righteous smite me; it shall be a kindness. And let him reprove me; it shall be an excellent oil" (Ps. 141:5). Paul gave just such counsel to his good friend Peter, when he needed it (Gal. 2:11–14). Bluntness is better than blindness.

- **The satisfaction of true friends:** "Oil and perfume make the heart glad, so a man's counsel is sweet to his friend" (Prov. 27:9, NAS). This inspired truism describes the satisfaction of sweet smells and sounds; just as sweet perfumes satisfy us, so do our friends' loving words of counsel. When eulogizing Jonathan, David spoke of this: "Jonathan; very pleasant [pleasing] hast thou [thy companionship] been unto me. Thy love [loving counsel] to me was wonderful, passing the love [physical pleasure] of women" (2 Sam. 1:26).

- **The benefit of true friends:** "As iron sharpens iron, so a man sharpens the countenance of his friend" (Prov. 27:17, NKJV). As we have fully explained previously in this book, when rubbed together, iron-sharpening agents may be used to sharpen iron knives. Similarly, when devoted Christians (of iron-like strength of spirit) converse, their spirits are sharpened and their smiles brightened. Spiritual edification, intellectual stimulation, joy, peace, a comforting sense of camaraderie—all these benefits are ours every time we "interface" and exchange biblical or other worthy data with our believing friends. Are you thankful for wise, faithful believers with whom you may share God's truth? Do you go to your own "company" frequently for meaningful fellowship? "And being let go, they went to their own company, and reported…" (Acts 4:23).

- **The preservation of true friends:** "Never abandon a friend—either yours or your father's. Then you won't need to go to a distant relative for help in your time of need" (Prov. 27:10, TLB). Our friendships are so precious that we should diligently nourish them—and our parents' friendships, too! Then our companionships will extend to bless not one but multiple generations: our children will enjoy fellowship with our friends' children, and so forth. This is why David carefully cared for Mephibosheth, Jonathan's son, and Chimham, the son of Barzillai. (See 2 Samuel 9:1–13; 19:31–40.) Are you perpetuating or terminating your good friendships?

- **The consummate true Friend:** "There is a [supernatural, spiritual] friend who sticketh closer than a [natural or Christian] brother" (Prov. 18:24). In this verse the Spirit of God looks beyond natural, even Christian, friends to the One who said, "I have called you friends" (John 15:15). Loving, trusting obedience to God's Word enables us to enter into Jesus' house of friends: "Ye are my friends, if ye do whatever I command you" (v. 14). And it's the only way to abide there. This is the ultimate true friendship—it can't get any better!

Now do you know who your true friends are? I know mine and will never forget them! You'll know yours when trouble comes. Your true friends will stick with you through thick and thin…and thinner…and thinnest…and nothing! Don't worry if they are few. A few true friends are worth far more than legions of false ones, who, in your day of battle, will sweetly kiss you and march away to a safe distance.

So when adversity reveals your true friends, never forget them—who they are to you and what they have done for you. Thank God for them often. Treasure them. Love them. Honor them. Pray for them. And stand by them in their evil day. Most importantly, ever see behind their faithful presence and ministry your greatest Friend, and theirs, Jesus!

That's one way to buy the truth and never sell it.

Chapter Sixteen

ARE YOU BUYING GOD'S TRUTH?

*I*n numerous ways the Book of Proverbs urges us to find and firmly grasp God's truth and never part with it under any circumstances.

For instance, it exhorts us to <u>search for truth as earnestly as we would for precious metals and hidden treasure</u>: "If thou seekest her as silver, and searchest for her as for hidden treasures" (Prov. 2:4). It advises us to receive wise counsel from godly parents: "My son, hear the instruction of thy father, and forsake not the law of thy mother" (Prov. 1:8). It instructs us to be teachable and receive the instruction of wise teachers: "Bow down thine ear, and <u>hear the words of the wise</u>" (Prov. 22:17).   ✗ It warns us that it is foolish and self-opposing to despise such godly instruction: "Fools despise wisdom and instruction" (Prov. 1:7); or to reject correction, "He that hateth reproof is stupid" (Prov. 12:1). And it informs us that the knowledge, understanding, and wisdom of God are supremely and incomparably valuable—"All the things thou canst desire are not to be compared to her" (Prov. 3:15)—and therefore urges us to seek, grasp, and retain them at any cost: "Get wisdom, get understanding; forget it not, neither decline from the words of my mouth" (Prov. 4:5). Thus its point is well made—and well taken. Yet God's book of wisdom has more to say.

Another proverb commands us to "buy" the truth and never "sell" it:

> Buy the truth, and sell it not; also wisdom, and instruction, and understanding.
>
> —Proverbs 23:23

Paraphrased, this command says:

> Pay whatever price is necessary to obtain God's truth [Word] and make it a part of your daily living, and never, ever compromise, disobey, or abandon it to gain anything desirable [yet of merely temporal value]; do the same regarding God's wisdom [good judgment], instruction [proficient, godly teaching], and understanding [insight].

As interpreted in this paraphrase, "buy" means simply to pay whatever price is necessary to obtain. We know how to buy material things, such as clothes, food, and other consumer goods. But how do we buy such intangibles as divine truth, wisdom, instruction, and understanding?

The Price of God's Truth

Consider these four aspects of the price of truth.

The personal price

Obtaining and retaining God's truth will cost us time, energy, desires, thought, and comfort. In short, this will mean a complete rearrangement of our personal lives. New priorities must be set that favor God's way of living over ours.

We must take time from other things and use it to seek God. We should commune with Him—not the newspaper, television, radio, or Internet—first thing every morning in personal prayer, worship, and Bible meditation: "Seek ye first [every day] the kingdom of God [and its King]" (Matt. 6:33). (See also Proverbs 8:17.) We should also make time to "study to show thyself approved unto God" (2 Tim. 2:15) and "give thyself wholly" (1 Tim. 4:15) to diligently search for biblical treasures of truth. This will demand a sustained determined effort. We will have to sacrifice some personal desires, reduce our involvement in selected outside interests and pastimes, and drop other activities altogether. We will have to become serious spiritual thinkers—curious, prayerful, meditative, studious, and reflective—eager to prayerfully examine the whole Bible, slowly thinking through the biblical phrases and words the Spirit quickens to us, thoroughly researching the lines of study we discover, and reflecting on the biblical truths and patterns we see being fulfilled in our lives and the lives of others. And we will have to throw open our lives to God's testing process. With every truth comes a test, which God uses to establish the reality of that truth in our lives and characters. These tests will bring disruption, as difficulties, challenges, and at times losses and sorrows disturb our former status quo.

But we need never fear. God's grace is always sufficient for us, and His Word grows clearer and His presence stronger with every trial: "Fear thou not; for I am with thee…I will strengthen thee…help thee…uphold thee" (Isa. 41:10). More valuable than any price we pay, His presence is truly priceless: "In thy presence is fullness of joy" (Ps. 16:11).

The social price

With blessed bluntness, the apostle Paul faced us with the big question regarding our social lives: "For do I now seek the favor of men, or of God? Or do I seek to please men?" (Gal. 1:10). Whose approval do we want most, the crowd's or the Christ's? He then added that if we try to keep everybody happy with us, we will not be true servants of Jesus: "If I yet pleased men, I should not be the servant of Christ" (v. 10). So what will it be? Will we please Jesus always, no matter who is displeased? It is a question we must decide. Why?

When we begin seriously learning and living in God's truth, some people will begin taking us less seriously. Others will seriously leave us alone: "Blessed are ye, when men shall...separate you from their company" (Luke 6:22). We may well find our social life sinking as our spiritual life rises. Why? Because the ruling spirit in our former friends will disapprove of our new quest to have and hold the knowledge of God—something they consider an absurd and passing religious obsession. We may expect to be snubbed, laughed at, contradicted, or constantly criticized by lukewarm Christians and unbelieving neighbors and relatives: "And [men] shall reproach you" (v. 22). Others will be preferred over us; they will be invited to activities, programs, and parties instead of us and receive offices and honors we would otherwise receive. Are we prepared for this? Are we willing to lose face and favors to passionately pursue gaining the greatest word of approval human ears will ever hear, "Well done, thou good and faithful servant" (Matt. 25:21)?

Here too we have a consolation. God won't leave us without any human support. When old friends fall away, new ones who share our passion for God's truth will draw near, as described in the last chapter. Sent by God's faithfulness, this new society of believing friends, whether large or small, will provide us with a distinctly higher quality of friendship, and one that will last forever.

The religious price

Religiousness and righteousness are not the same. Some religious persons are righteous; others are not. Some want God's truth with all their heart; others do not.

For this reason, we should realize that our quest for God's wisdom will not go over big with religious people who have no interest in eternal truth or, worse, have rejected it. How many times have newly reborn or spiritually naïve Christians been offended by corrupt clerics, carnal deacons, lukewarm elders, backslidden bishops, or spiritually dead theologians whose flames of faith were extinguished years ago? Have we forgotten that, throughout the Church Age, those who sought, held, and dispensed God's truth were persistently hated and opposed most vehemently by the *religious*, not the irreligious, crowd? "Then the high priest rose up, and all they that were with him...and laid their hands on the apostles" (Acts 5:17–18). If we're fervent for truth, we must watch for offenses in God's house, lest we allow the lukewarmness or coldness of our fellow churchmen or church leaders to quench our faith, love, and fervor. Jesus warned us that Satan would use people—including professing Christians and professional clergymen—to try to steal God's truth and its rewards from us: "Hold that fast which thou hast, that no *man* take thy crown" (Rev. 3:11, emphasis added).

The monetary price

One sure way to discover someone's heart is to read their checkbook register. Where is their money going? That's where their real desires are, despite their protests to the contrary. Said Jesus, "Where your treasure is [or financial resources are], there will your heart [affections, interests, values] be also" (Matt. 6:21).

So if we say our heart is hungry for God's truth, we should be willing to put our checkbook where our mouth is. Translated, this means we should freely spend the nominal fees charged to purchase Bibles and other spiritually edifying materials. We pay lavishly for pizzas, sodas, athletic events, and entertainment; why not for seminar fees, Bible school tuition, Christian books, and tapes? And paying our tithes is required if we want God's truth. God will not release the full knowledge of His Word to those who will not release their full tithes and offerings: "Freely ye have received, freely give" (Matt. 10:8). Are we hungry for more of God's wisdom, knowledge, and insights? Then let's joyfully pay the monetary price! And remember: once you've bought God's truth, never sell it.

THE SELLING OF GOD'S TRUTH

Once we have purchased a thing, it is ours to keep, use, or share. Or if we no longer consider it valuable or useful, we may sell it.

Like material possessions, spiritual possessions—God's wisdom, knowledge, and understanding—may be sold. This usually occurs after we change our minds about its value, and this change in attitude usually arises when we have reacted carnally toward some adversity or offensive person and have failed to examine ourselves. After sin lodges within our hearts, spiritual regression begins. First we doubt, then we disbelieve, and finally we despise and avoid the Bible Words we formerly treasured and the teachers, churches, and ministries through which we received them. Thus we "sell" them by compromising, disobeying, or abandoning them in order to gain things we now consider more desirable. And what are they? Usually they are the very things we previously gave up or set aside to buy the truth.

In practical experience the selling of God's truth works like this. We abandon God's ways of disciplined living and rearrange our days again solely for our own pleasure and comfort, leaving off time for God, His Word, His people, and His work. We stop seeking God's approval and begin craving the approval of people, starting with those who disapproved the loudest when we began buying God's truth. Our satisfaction in God's presence gone, we become gregarious and ingratiatory, always going with the social or religious "herd" and saying and doing whatever gains us favor with people of influence. We abandon all semblance of trying to work out the salvation God's work of grace has deposited in us, and we settle for being saved and comfortably conformed to our generation's religious norm. We see our money once more as "mine," using it selfishly, without any consideration for God's claims, ministry needs, or the pursuit of His truth. So we gradually sell out—lock, stock, and barrel—every precious biblical truth we previously paid to have and live in. Why?

Our sellout has occurred because, consciously or unconsciously, our values have changed. We used to believe "all the things thou canst desire" are not to be compared with the knowledge and wisdom of God. But now we consider other things, the things of this present world, more valuable and vital. And we have been deceived. It is precisely this that Proverbs 23:23 warns against.

Why is it so important to us in these last days that we buy the truth and never sell it? Because learning and living in eternal truth is the only way to be prepared for Jesus' appearing, also known as the rapture of the church. At least two New Testament passages make this clear.

First, in Revelation 3:14–22, Jesus speaks prophetically to our generation of Christians. The historic church at Laodicea was the last of the seven churches of Asia Jesus addressed. (See Revelation 2–3.) From a prophetic perspective His seven messages describe the seven successive periods comprising the Church Age, beginning with the first-century church and ending with the church extant when Jesus appears. Because Jesus' message to the Laodiceans was the last of the seven, it represents His message to the last period in church history—the period in which undoubtedly we now live. The distinguishing theme of the Laodicean letter is the satiation and self-deception of excessive materialism that was spoiling the Laodiceans' spiritual maturity and full fruitfulness in God—exactly the major problem that has for decades now kept so many (especially American) Christians from spiritual maturity. So after chiding the Laodiceans, and, by the Spirit, us, for living for materialism and being spiritually and morally lukewarm, Jesus challenges them, and us, to "buy" what He describes as "gold tried in the fire," so we may become spiritually wealthy, or rich in God. "Gold tried in the fire" represents *the faith and truth of God tested in fiery tests,* and we "buy" it exactly as described in this chapter you are now reading. The larger context of Jesus' message to the Laodiceans (Rev. 2–3) implies that this "gold tried in the fire" will prepare us to be kept "from" the coming time of tribulation, just as it did the Philadelphian Christians, who Scripture implies bought God's truth and refused to sell it: "Thou hast...*kept* my word...*kept* the word of my patience" (Rev. 3:8, 10, emphasis added).

Second, in Matthew 25:1–13, Jesus taught that in these last days a great "midnight cry," a disturbing alarm in the darkest hour of apostasy, will awaken all of God's born-again children—the present-day spiritual "virgins" (2 Cor. 11:2) whose prime hope is to be wed to Jesus, the Bridegroom, after His appearing and intimately live and work with Him forever—from the sleep of spiritual indifference and indolence. The entire body of Christ, wise and foolish Christians alike, will then immediately and fully realize two things:

1. Though long delayed, Jesus' appearing is now truly imminent: "Behold, the *bridegroom cometh*..." (Matt. 25:6, emphasis added).

2. It is very urgent now that we prepare ourselves, or "go out" of our lukewarm comfort zone, to meet Him: "*Go ye out* to meet him" (v. 6, emphasis added).

Stirred by this undeniably heavenly revelation-command, foolish Christians (who have never before taken preparation for Jesus' appearing seriously) will then ask wise ones to give them the "oil"—here used not as a symbol for the fullness of the Spirit but for the purpose of His coming into our lives, that is, *comprehensive spiritual preparation*—that will enable their spiritual lives to burn as brightly as theirs. To their dismay, the foolish will then be informed that this oil of preparation, unlike the Holy Spirit Himself, cannot be *given,* but must be *bought*: "Not so...but go rather...and *buy* for yourselves" (v. 9, emphasis added). This is another direct reference to the truth-buying process described in our text proverb (Prov. 23:23).

From these two timely prophetic passages we conclude that unless we "buy" gold tried in the fire and the precious oil of spiritual preparation, we will not be ready for Jesus' appearing, which means we will be left behind to endure at least the first half of the tribulation period, something God never intended Christians to experience: "For God hath not appointed [planned for] us to [experience the time of] wrath but to [instead] obtain salvation [deliverance] by [the appearing of] our Lord Jesus Christ...[that we may then] live together with him" (1 Thess. 5:9–10). Most of us don't need much prodding to buy literal gold or oil.

If we crave a prized material object—fine gold jewelry, exquisite crystal, celebrated art works, rare pottery, designer clothing, antique automobiles, oil-rich properties, etc.—badly enough, even though we would prefer a bargain, we'll pay whatever we have to pay to obtain it. Because our desire is intense, we abandon our normal sense of reserve and acquire a new and passionate rationale: no price is too high to have this thing.

So let's ask the question of the hour: Are we busy buying God's truth with the same passionate sense of abandon? Or are we selling the precious truths we used to love and live by to appease an unspiritual parent, spouse, or child; to have a larger income; to gain social or religious favor with lukewarm, hypocritical Christians or practicing sinners; or to simply revert to easy, self-indulgent living? If this is the case, we need to repent and "buy the truth, and sell it not; also wisdom, and instruction, and understanding," while there's still time. And if we've already been buying God's truth, let's go buy more! And more! And more!

Then we'll never fear having to endure a period of divine judgment.

Chapter Seventeen

IF GOD JUDGED ISRAEL...

*A*n important fact revealed repeatedly in Scripture is that God deals with nations just as He deals with individual people. Depending upon a nation's character, God responds to it by sending blessings or chastisements. And the chief factor in determining His attitude and actions toward every nation is its reception or rejection of His righteousness.

The Book of Proverbs teaches:

> Righteousness exalteth a [any] nation, but sin is a reproach to any people.
>
> —PROVERBS 14:34

Paraphrased, this states the following:

> [No respecter of persons or nations,] God will honor and elevate any nation in which His righteousness proliferates, prevails, and is promoted; but if sin becomes popular, proliferates, and prevails in that same nation, [despite its previous righteousness and blessings,] God will bring it low with disgrace and contempt.

Here is a beautifully round and flawlessly unspotted pearl of wisdom every nation and its leaders should purchase, ponder, and put on public display.

Its radiant luster tells us that if any nation receives, respects, and raises God's righteousness, God will receive, respect, and raise that nation to prominence in the community of nations. Conversely, if any nation disrespects God's righteousness by practicing sin, He will dishonor and demote it. In this Church Age, God's "righteousness" has a twofold meaning:

1. *Right relationship with God,* by His grace and through faith in His Son, Jesus, and in His work of redemption on the cross

2. *Right living before God and man,* by loving, loyal obedience to the teachings of God's Word, the Bible

Notice the perfect balance in our text proverb: God both honors and dishonors nations, raising and lowering their prestige as He wills. Observe also how fair God is: He dishonors "any people" that dishonor His righteousness, no matter how numerous or few they are, and He will honor "a nation," or better, *any nation*, that embraces His righteousness, whether it is despised or delighted in by other nations. This perfect equality is a distinctive hallmark of God's character. He is always thoroughly fair and just in all His dealings.

Unlike Adam's children, whose viewpoints are perpetually skewed by pride, prejudice, and preference, God is absolutely without favoritism: "Of a truth … God is no respecter of persons; but in every nation he that feareth him, and worketh righteousness, is accepted with him" (Acts 10:34–35). In this New Testament text God specifically promises to accept, and by implication bless, any person of *any* nationality who fears Him and receives and obeys His righteousness: "But in *every* nation…" (v. 35, emphasis added). That He willingly receives believers from "every" nation reveals that He favors no nation, ethnic group, race, or culture above another. All may come unto Him, but all must come on His terms. To emphasize this prime truth, God inspired the biblical writers to declare that He is "no respecter of persons" no less than *seven times* in the Bible! (See Deuteronomy 10:17; 2 Chronicles 19:7; Acts 10:34–35; Romans 2:11; Ephesians 6:9; Colossians 3:25; 1 Peter 1:17.) Since seven is the number of completion and perfection, God wants us to be completely convinced and perfectly sure that He harbors no favoritism.

The principle here is that God favors not nations but *righteousness,* whenever, wherever, and in whomever He finds it. He will never continue favoring any nation that turns away from His righteousness, no matter how much He has favored it in the past. Nor will He accept any other admirable or impressive national attribute—democracy, intelligence, wealth, technological advances, military power, charitable works, advocacy of peace, or religious heritage—as a substitute for current righteousness. And this, His way of dealing with nations, is universal. No nation is exempt from it.

That includes His only chosen nation. While God has shed His grace on many nations throughout the long course of human history, only one has received the distinction of being "chosen" of God. That nation is Israel: "Yet now hear... Israel, whom I have *chosen*" (Isa. 44:1, emphasis added). If God were to show favoritism toward any nation, He would surely do so toward Israel! But the biblical history of Israel proves to the contrary: He showed Israel favor, but never favoritism! Why? Because He will never break the universal rule He has set forth in Proverbs 14:34. When Israel tested Him by turning to sin and idolatry for long periods of time, God, true to His loving nature, was extremely gracious and purposely slow to move against His rebellious children. But ultimately, true to His holy and just character, He fulfilled this maxim to the letter by bringing Israel into utter reproach and contempt for her persisting unrighteousness. And to make the lesson exceedingly clear to sacred and secular historians alike, He did so not once but three times.

THE CHOSEN NATION…CHASTENED FOR ITS SINS

Let's have a brief biblical history lesson on the chastening of the chosen nation.

Philistine captivity

After establishing His covenant people in the Promised Land, God selected Shiloh as Israel's new center of worship and ordered His people to erect the tabernacle there. But though God had given them such a good land, the Israelites failed to give God good faith. Their obedience was lax instead of loyal. Soon they adopted the evil ways, false gods, and corrupt sins of the Canaanites. In the days of Eli, the Israelites' corruption reached intolerable depths of iniquity (1 Sam. 2:12–36). So, just as He had warned through Samuel (1 Sam. 3:3–18), God did the unthinkable: He delivered His precious people, the Jews, into the hands of their spiritually polluted enemies, the Philistines (1 Sam. 4:1–22). This "ear-tingling" military defeat was made even more shocking when the Philistines stole Israel's most prized holy possession, the ark of the covenant (1 Sam. 5:1–2).

O how Israel had fallen from grace! Once celebrated and renowned among the nations for her glorious exodus from Egypt and conquering of the Canaanites, Israel was now covered with a thick, black cloud of reproach and her tabernacle at Shiloh was left utterly desolate. Tragically, every good thing was gone from Israel. The glory of God's presence was gone. The ark of His covenant was gone. The unique peace and security of the land was gone. God's chosen and once godly high priest Eli was gone. And the precious word of the Lord was gone. But, thank God, one evil thing was also gone now: Israel's foolish presumption, at least for the time being.

This humiliating Philistine captivity lasted twenty years (1 Sam. 7:1–13). (See also Psalm 78:55–64.)

Assyrian and Babylonian captivities

After 120 years of united righteousness under kings Saul, David, and Solomon, the chosen people split into two kingdoms, the northern kingdom of Israel and the southern kingdom of Judah, and began reverting to their carnal ways. Despite brief subsequent revivals under kings Asa, Jehoshaphat, Uzziah, Hezekiah, and Josiah, both kingdoms continued backsliding for the next two hundred years, eventually falling headlong into total idolatry and corruption. During this long, sad, spiritual decline, God graciously forbore with His wayward people, withholding deserved judgment in hopes of inducing repentance through the inspired warnings of His faithful prophets, whom He steadily sent one after another. But despite His grace, the Jews didn't repent. So God did exactly what He had said He would do in the Law: He brought foreign invaders to conquer and deport His chosen people. (See Deuteronomy 28:49–57.) First, the Assyrians came and dismantled the northern kingdom of Israel in 722 B.C. Then, over a century later (586 B.C.), the Babylonians defeated the southern kingdom of Judah, utterly destroying its capital and temple at Jerusalem. It was another stunning defeat.

O how the nation had fallen…again! Once so honored and feared that Gentile kings rushed to pay tributes to her kings, now Israel was so lightly esteemed that her once-prosperous population was deemed good for nothing but slavery. And that's just where they went—into bitter Babylonian captivity, this time for seventy years. (See 2 Chron. 36:14–21.)

Roman captivity

When centuries later the reunited nation of Israel violently rejected Jesus of Nazareth—God's righteousness incarnate!—in A.D. 30, Israel turned again from what (and who) had made her great. Even then the Lord graciously and patiently deferred His judgment for forty years, hoping, as He had before, that His children would yet change their minds and believe in, receive, and obey His righteousness, which was being persistently offered them day by day through the ministries of the newly formed church. But, while many individual Jews were converted, the nation as a whole chose once again to remain proud and stubborn. So in A.D. 70, and no doubt with the greatest reluctance, Jehovah permitted the Roman armies to utterly dismantle Jerusalem and King Herod's beautiful, white marble, partly gilded and much-gloried-in temple, one of the resplendent wonders of the ancient world.

"This just can't be true," I'm sure many Jews mumbled to themselves in numb disbelief as they watched Titus' soldiers gleefully loot and burn their capital city and their national house of worship. But it was true—sadly, tragically true. Once more unrighteousness had brought the chosen nation down to the dust. And this time, as if to underscore His wrath, God left the Jews dispersed throughout the Gentile world for nearly 1,900 years. Not until 1948 did they recover the homeland they had so foolishly forfeited through unrighteousness. (See Luke 19:41–44.)

So there you have it. When Israel, God's only chosen nation, persistently spurned His righteousness, God brought her down to the dust—not once but *three* times in her long history. That's the Bible. That's irrefutable truth. That's a powerful lesson. And it's a timely one.

Today all Christians must realize that if God judged even *Israel* according to Proverbs 14:34, how much more, not less, will He judge any other nation that ignores or mocks His righteousness? How can the people of any other nation—America, Canada, England, Australia, New Zealand, South Africa, and so forth—presume to think they will be exempt from His righteous judgments if in their laws, courts, schools, and prevailing social practices they doubt His existence, deny His creatorship, discredit His Word (the Bible), mock His moral standards, and thus utterly reject and defy His righteousness? The stunning events of

September 11, 2001 are all the confirmation any discerning Christian should need in this matter. Sadly, many American Christians failed to realize why God permitted this nation's defenses to be breeched by overtly cruel and evilly possessed religious madmen, preferring to focus only on the surface issues of national immigration and security procedures and ignoring the deeper causes of persisting, wanton national unrighteousness—and that brought on by a shallow, comfortably compromised church that has generally been asleep to the deeper truths and purposes of God for decades now.

But saints, it's time we wake up and understand. Promoting Darwinism, abortion, homosexuality, occultism, fornication, a spirit of national superiority (repeatedly boasting that our nation is the "greatest," "strongest," or "best")—these things cause spiritual and moral blindness, stir God's slow but sure wrath, and ultimately result in tragic consequences. And politics is not the answer! It is, has been, and forever will be merely a means of restraining societal behavior, not of changing our society's deep underlying spiritual being and bent. By its very nature political action is carnal, not spiritual; a human, not divine, method; a temporal solution, not a lasting one. And the broader evangelical church's headlong dive into the turbulent and filthy pool of intense political lobbying is glaringly without biblical or historical precedent. (And we are the people who preach that Christians should have biblical authority for their faith, teaching, and ways of living!) Despite our generation's earnest committal to aggressive political action, our nation's complex and rapidly growing problems cannot be permanently cured merely by having better legislators and better laws. Moral lawmakers and laws are good, but they are not good enough.

Lasting change comes only from God being at work within the hearts of men, and that must begin among Christians. We who name the name of Christ, who call ourselves born-again Christians, must first repent of our own besetting sins and fully restore God's righteousness and order within the house of God—our own private lives, families, and churches. Why? Because God's Word declares, "For the time is come that *judgment* [divinely prompted and enforced restoration of divine order] *must begin at the house of God* [among God's own redeemed people]" (1 Pet. 4:17, emphasis added). Then we will have a weapon to use against the forces of liberalism, atheism, and New Age-ism far more powerful than any new law or court order: the Spirit-empowered gospel of Jesus Christ. And we will have a method of changing the moral face of our nation that is far more effective than political action: godly prayer. (This is the biblical method that the saints have used and God has blessed in centuries past!) And we will find that our prayers will do what no Christian president, congressman, or judge, however wise or bold, could ever do—move the hand of God to sovereignly give repentance to large numbers of otherwise unreachable sinners across our land, just as He did for us one day and just has He has done before in many nations, according to His clear and oft-repeated biblical promise:

> If my people [the redeemed], who are called by my name, shall humble themselves, and pray, and seek my face, and turn from their wicked ways, then will I hear from heaven, and will forgive their sin, and will heal their land.
> —2 CHRONICLES 7:14

American Christians, it's time we fully believe and fully obey this promise. And it's time we fully fear the Lord—that is, stand in awe of His power and judgments and believe not just all His pleasant promises but also all His woeful warnings.

It's also time for Christians in every other nation to fully wake up. Believers who consistently walk in God's righteousness, who obey His call, who study and spread His Word, and who intercede in the Spirit and in faith daily for the conviction and repentance of their respective leaders and nations are needed greatly in this, the final and "midnight" hour of the Church Age.

They are wise. Their presumption is cured. They believe Proverbs 14:34—that righteousness exalts any nation and sin brings any nation into reproach. And by their righteous walk, witness, and persisting prayers, they're doing everything they can to save their respective nations from judgment and reproach.

Be one of them! Conduct yourself always as a child of God.

Chapter Eighteen

DON'T ACT LIKE THE DEVIL'S CHILDREN!

*D*on't seek or spread bad reports about good people! That's the way the devil's children act, not God's. So teaches the Book of Proverbs.

Among King Solomon's many short, powerful sermonettes on human speech and behavior, we find the following consecutive declarations, which, though they seem unrelated, are integrally linked:

> An ungodly man diggeth up evil, and in his lips there is as a burning fire. A perverse man soweth strife, and a whisperer separateth chief friends.
>
> —PROVERBS 16:27–28

We may paraphrase these two pearls of wisdom as follows:

> The sons of Belial [children of the devil] search for buried [past, forgiven, forgotten] evil reports—uncharacteristic sins, misstatements, missteps, failures, reproaches, etc.— about good people and slander them with burning hatred and disdain [creating firestorms of controversy]. Other

worthless ones, twisted, whispering gossips, spread their misrepresentations further, creating contentions that divide even the best of friends.

Here's the explanation for this interpretation. "Diggeth up" can only refer to a search for something buried, or hidden and not apparent. We don't dig for things that are already above ground. They're already visible and plainly known. "Evil" refers to adverse reports or bad news: rumors or reports of statements or actions that present one in an unflattering, defaming, or potentially ruinous light. "Ungodly" is translated from the Hebrew word *Beliyaal,* which means literally "worthless" or "good for nothing." Symbolically, however, this word refers to Satan, or the devil. How do we know this?

This is made clear by its use elsewhere in the Bible. The apostle Paul used its Greek equivalent (*Belial*) when clearly speaking of Satan and his opposition to Christ: "What concord hath Christ with Belial?" (2 Cor. 6:15). Also, the Hebrew *Beliyaal* is frequently used in the Old Testament to describe the lowest, meanest, most despicable and devilish characters in Israel's history, the notorious "sons of Belial." Among this impish rabble were the likes of:

- Nabal (1 Sam. 25:17, 25)

- Eli's sons (1 Sam. 2:12)

- The homosexuals in Gibeah who brutally raped and killed the anonymous Levite's concubine and sparked Israel's bloody civil war (Judg. 19:22)

- The conscienceless false witnesses whose lies led to the wrongful conviction and execution of righteous Naboth (1 Kings 21:9–13)

So an "ungodly man" is one whose character and actions are not only consistently worthless but are also like the devil himself! Hence the "ungodly" or "sons of Belial" represent *the devil's children*. And since these twin proverbs speak of them seeking and spreading evil reports about good people, it is especially fitting that we call them the devil's children, because the devil's chief name and pastime is "the accuser of our brethren" (Rev. 12:10). He began this dark pursuit by personally slandering God, first to the angels in heaven and later to Adam in Eden. And he continues his obsessive and compulsive work to this day by using his children, the sons of Belial, to slander God's children, the redeemed, or any other innocent or decent souls that stand in his way to anyone who will drink in his putrid river of misrepresentations. The Pharisees clearly fitted this description.

They were obsessed with trying to dig up dirt on the cleanest man that ever lived. Wherever Jesus went, they were there, watching, listening, longing to dig up anything—past or present, stated or implied, confirmed or unconfirmed—that they could publicize to His shame. But the Nazarene was so clean that the Pharisees, clearly frustrated, finally resorted to hostile digging, accosting Jesus with mean-spirited interrogations:

> And as he said these things unto them, the scribes and the Pharisees began to oppose him vehemently, and to provoke him to speak of many things, laying wait for him, and seeking to catch something out of his mouth, that they might accuse him.
>
> —Luke 11:53–54

Their zealous quest for defamatory information was reminiscent of the search undertaken by Daniel's envious rivals. When King Darius the Mede was about to promote Daniel to higher office (Dan. 6:1–3), the presidents and princes who would have been under Daniel's authority "sought to find occasion against Daniel concerning [his performance in] the [Babylonian] kingdom" (v. 4). In a classic malicious "dig," they turned Babylon's

147

archives upside down, trying to find even a fragment of a scroll inscribed with hard evidence that Daniel had done something, anything, they could put a negative spin on. But "they could find no occasion nor fault, forasmuch as he was faithful, neither was there any error or fault found in him" (v. 4). So the devil's children were left without any legitimate controversy to discover and disseminate about God's child. Does this story sound familiar?

It should. It reoccurs almost every day in this nation. Just turn on the nearest cable news report or talk show, pick up the latest newspaper, magazine, best-selling nonfiction book, or tabloid, or log on to the politically charged Web site of your choice, and...behold! American politicians, journalists, and public relations experts not only practice the art of defamation, but they have also perfected it. Negative politicking has virtually bottomed out over the last thirty years. Exceedingly low, it can get no lower. Democrats, Republicans, and Independents alike have so often dug so deep that political historians may well satirize our generation as the "Journey to the Center of the Earth!" We may strike flowing magma at any moment! I'm speaking humorously, but God knows, there's really nothing funny about negative politics.

How many times have qualified, dedicated, intelligent, experienced, decent men or women come before congressional committees for confirmation as judicial, executive, or administrative appointees, only to be verbally tarred and feathered and sent packing. And why did they suffer such shameful treatment? Was it because they were evil, self-serving, corrupt, irresponsible, or a threat to the nation? Not at all! Typically, the official reason cited is some unacceptable statement, decision, vote, or other action, which usually has been skillfully and willfully misrepresented, occurred many years, even decades ago, and in no way reflects the nominee's current character, perspective, or value as a public servant. But in actuality they were rejected because their political, religious, or moral views differed from those of the committee's majority; so they just dug up a bad report and, with the help of their biased friends, lit and spread a burning controversy that consumed a good man or woman's opportunity to aid his country. It would be nice if sons of Belial existed only in the pages of sacred literature! But I'm afraid they're loose and running free among us—even in the highest places of power. But that is them, and this is written to us.

So what do these two proverbs say directly to us as God's children? I hear three vital communiqués coming through loud and clear. They are:

1. *Stay clean!* Don't bury your sins; purge them! Don't hide wrongdoing; abandon it! By confession and repentance, leave nothing for the devil's children to dig up. Like Daniel, be righteous in your walk and faithful in your duties. Allow no besetting (constantly recurring) sins to remain in your lifestyle, and examine, reexamine, and correct your work until you eliminate all your errors. Don't assume that the sons of Belial won't find your dirt. They're experienced excavators, real experts at their work. If there's dirt in your life, they'll unearth it and do away with you with relish. So be wise and "abstain from all appearance of evil" (1 Thess. 5:22).

2. *Don't dig up evil reports!* Don't lower yourself to practice the works of sons of Belial. No matter how low and painful your valley of testing, or how deeply and persistently others try to dig up trouble for you, always take the highest way. Jesus did this. So did His apostles. And so have spiritually minded overcomers throughout the Church Age. Make no attempt to slander your personal, religious, or political opponents, even when they are busily and effectively slandering you. Leave them in God's able hands. Let Him dig up their faults for you. He can expose their malicious designs at any moment—and will do so in His time. Moses wrote, "And thine enemies shall be found [exposed as] liars unto thee" (Deut. 33:29). And Jesus added, "Fear them not... for there is nothing covered

that shall not be revealed; and hidden, that shall not be known" (Matt. 10:26). (See also Proverbs 26:26.) Believe them!

And fear God! That is, stand in awe of His fixed ways of judgment. Never dig pits (plans or plots) to entrap and ruin others, because God has decreed that if you try to set them up for a fall, you will—you must!—ultimately fall in connection with your very effort to harm them: "Whoso diggeth a pit shall fall *therein* [in that very pit!]" (Prov. 26:27, emphasis added). (See also Galatians 6:7.) So fear Him, keep your eyes on your Savior, and stay away from your shovel!

3. *Don't spread evil reports!* Never spread slanderous reports others have dug up on anyone, including your personal adversaries: "Neither be partaker of other men's sins; keep thyself pure" (1 Tim. 5:22). When whisperers are working, Satan is working. So quench your human curiosity and walk away, and keep yourself "sanctified, and fit for the master's use" (2 Tim. 2:21).

Jesus pointedly warned us against making firm, final judgments based solely on first impressions, unsubstantiated rumors, or isolated acts: "Judge not according to the appearance, but judge righteous judgment" (John 7:24). Hence, we should learn and practice the ways of just judgment.

When required to make judgments, wise souls judge a person's character by weighing all of their actions, whereas fools assess them only by selected words, decisions, or acts. "Sound-bite" judgments are unsound judgments, so never stamp "Bad" across someone's good name because of isolated statements, failures, weaknesses, or sins buried decades in their past and long since forsaken. You wouldn't want to be judged like that, would you? And frankly, who can bear such a standard? Who hasn't had incidents, however small, in their past that, if isolated and blown out of proportion, would grossly misrepresent their present character? *Current* sinful practices, prejudices, errant beliefs, and irresponsibility are legitimate causes for current concern and disqualification for current service or fellowship, but, generally speaking, someone's past failures are not by themselves cause for present rejection, especially when sincere, sustained repentance has clearly distinguished the person they were from the person they are. Isn't this just, or fair, judgment? Isn't this the way God evaluates us?

May the Judge of all the earth help us evaluate others as He does us. And may we avoid all the ways of the sons of Belial. We're saints, not imps; God's children, not the devil's. May our heavenly Father help us consistently act like it! The benefits will be many and marvelous.

One big plus is that we will be unhindered by needless strife.

Chapter Nineteen

ANYTHING BUT STRIFE!

*L*ord, give me *anything* but strife!" seems to be the heart cry of numerous debate-weary biblical characters and writers.

Abraham, for example, pleaded with his spiritual brother, Lot, for an end to the contention between their herdsmen: "Let there be no strife, I pray thee, between me and thee...for we are brethren" (Gen. 13:8). When continually accosted by argumentative, unreasonable, and physically aggressive Philistines, who stubbornly charged that Isaac's inherited wells were really theirs, Isaac quietly turned away, preferring to waive his rights rather than indulge in a disruptive, potentially violent debate (Gen. 26:17–22). Distressed by lengthy exposure to excessively contentious companions, an anonymous psalmist lamented, "My soul hath long dwelt with him that hateth peace. I am for peace; but when I speak, they are for war [strife]" (Ps. 120:6–7). Why did these believers decry debate?

They recognized what too many Christians today fail to see: God has created us to be people of peace, not strife. Like olive trees planted in the temple courts, we thrive in an atmosphere of calm, not contention; peace and quiet, not constant disruption; order, not chaos. Strife and debate are two of Satan's prime uprooting tools, implements with which he seeks to disturb and steal the Word of God every time it is planted in our hearts through Spirit-blessed reading, teaching, counsel, or fellowship. Once well nourished and deeply rooted, we trees of righteousness can withstand great storms of controversy, tribulation, and persecution. But in order to become established, we must learn to never cause contention needlessly or escalate or perpetuate it when it is thrust upon us. Why? Because the fallout of strife is too costly. It produces only destructive, not constructive, results. Never helpful, it always hinders us. Truly, every time we indulge in strife we come away the worse for it. Heated verbal sparrings leave us self-cursed with mental confusion, injured feelings, chaffed emotions, hostile attitudes, and damaged relationships. Hence, the wise learn to avoid all unnecessary contention. Thank God, we too can always opt for the way of peace. In the Book of Proverbs, divine wisdom bids us choose the wisdom of peacemaking rather than the folly of strife: "Her [wisdom's] ways are ways of pleasantness, and all her paths are peace" (Prov. 3:17).

In fact, wisdom declares emphatically that *anything* is better—spiritually, psychologically, and physically more beneficial—than a contentious atmosphere, even lonely solitude! In one of its twenty pearls of truth revealing the "better" options in life, the Book of Proverbs declares:

> Better is a dry morsel, and quietness [solitude] therewith, than a house full of sacrifices, with strife.
>
> —PROVERBS 17:1

Paraphrased, this tells us:

> It is better to dine on a small amount of stale, tasteless bread in peace and quiet, than to feast on large, delicious portions of [meats offered as] holy sacrifices in a tense, contentious atmosphere.

King Solomon repeated this same truth in substance in Proverbs 15:17, "Better is a dinner of herbs [simple vegetables] where love is, than a stalled ox [choice steaks or roasts] and hatred therewith"; and twice more, in the context of marriage, in two identical proverbs, "It is better to dwell in a corner of the housetop, than with a brawling woman [contesting, quarreling, overruling wife of discord] in a wide house" (Prov. 21:9; 25:24). A man of strong appetite (as we see in Ecclesiastes 2:24–25) accustomed to the finest royal fare and numerous state dinners, Solomon must have felt very strongly about this issue to say he would rather eat a bland, dry crust of bread, if need be, to be free of verbal agitation!

If we too desire strongly to escape the pit of fruitless, frustrating contention, we can. For that, we must learn how to use calm, gentle speech to overcome people given to contentious words and belligerent attitudes. But first, let's examine the causes of contention.

THE CAUSES: SOURCES OF STRIFE AND CONTENTION

While anything may cause a war of words, the Bible reveals that certain attitudes and actions are almost sure to cause one. They are:

- **Pride**: Arrogantly self-confident fools, who never admit the possibility that they may be wrong, are arguments waiting to happen. Truly, "only by pride cometh contention" (Prov. 13:10) and "a [proud] fool's lips enter into contention" (Prov. 18:6). And at any moment any of us may play the fool by contending that we are right when inwardly we know we are wrong.

- **Self-vindication**: It was self-vindication—the lust to prove his righteousness to merciless false accusers—that drove Job to his epic argument with Eliphaz, Bildad, and Zophar. Though he was just a young man, Elihu discerned correctly that Job "justified himself rather than God" (Job 32:2).

154

- **Mocking**: When mocked, we often react by angrily contending with those who have parodied, lampooned, or scoffed at us. Why? Insulted and offended, we're using contention as a convenient weapon with which to exact our spontaneously aroused vengeance. And too often the strife doesn't end until the scoffer exits: "Cast out the scoffer, and contention shall go out; yea, strife...shall cease" (Prov. 22:10).

- **Ambition**: The apostles' religious ambition to be "the greatest" caused "a strife among them" (Luke 22:24). Years later, unbridled hunger for ministerial preeminence moved Diotrephes to contend with and denounce even his elder, the saintly apostle John, and no longer receive him, his fellow apostles, or their friends (3 John 9–11).

- **Envy**: By inspiration James twice lists strife as a sister sin to envy, implying that, wherever one is, the other is also: "But if ye have bitter *envying and strife* in your hearts...where *envy and strife* are" (James 3:14, 16, emphasis added). Invariably, envy provokes otherwise unexplainable eruptions of contention. We eventually misjudge, criticize, and challenge whomever we envy. (See Numbers 12:2.)

- **Drunkenness**: "Who hath contentions?...They that tarry long at the wine" (Prov. 23:29–30). Well knowing this truism long before Solomon inscribed it, Abigail wisely chose not to discuss controversial matters with Nabal when he was inebriated (1 Sam. 25:36). It is unreasonable to reason with a drunk—and sure to spark a quarrel.

- **Selfishness**: We often bite and devour one another verbally because we are competing to possess the same object, be that an occupational, political, or ministerial office; an award; a sale; or a spouse. Hence, Abram's and

Lot's herdsmen fought verbally, and perhaps physically too, over the precious pasturage they each strongly desired to have (Gen. 13:5–7).

- **Love of money**: "The love of money is the root of all [kinds of] evil" (1 Tim. 6:10), and one of its evil fruits is strife. Where there is financial contentment, there is peace and cooperation, but when coveting begins, contention visits: "He that is greedy for gain troubleth his own house" (Prov. 15:27). A wise man learns that he and his family need peace far more than prosperity, a few loving moments rather than many extra dollars.

- **Unbelief**: Every time the Israelites doubted God's character or promises, they fell into contentiousness and argued rudely with their gracious leader, Moses (Num. 20:2–5). And on the few occasions when, disappointed at their carnality, his faith lapsed, he fell headlong into their pit of contention and vigorously argued back (vv. 10–12).

- **Fear**: When by the Red Sea the Israelites suddenly thought they were hopelessly trapped, they immediately began contending with Moses (Exod. 14:10–12). Whenever anxiety or terror grips us and we fail to cast our burden on the Lord, we too are prone to lash out at those around us without cause.

- **Anger**: "A wrathful man stirreth up strife" (Prov. 15:18). Watch yourself and learn. If you let anger rest in your heart, within fifteen minutes you'll be arguing with someone—usually the next person you meet—over nothing.

- **Hatred**: "Hatred stirs up strifes" (Prov. 10:12), concluded Solomon. Harboring hatred for anyone lets spiritual darkness in (1 John 2:11), and soon the devil himself finds "place" (Eph. 4:26–27)—a point of entry, influence, and manipulation—in our souls. Then, with the arch-controversialist urging us on from within, we become unnaturally quick to indulge in hateful, hot-tempered strife.

- **Ill-temper:** Domineering, bossy wives and mean, pugnacious husbands are each sure to ignite many an argument. (See Prov. 19:13; 26:21). Peace-loving spouses beware!

- **Foolish questions**: Questions on very controversial or complicated issues or on unrevealed and hence unknowable matters are like a lighted match nearing flammable liquid. To prevent unprofitable explosions of strife, the wise apostle Paul commanded, "But foolish and unlearned questions avoid, knowing that they breed strifes" (2 Tim. 2:23).

- **Irreconcilable Bible doctrines**: When Christians are intransigently cemented into opposing doctrinal trenches, attempts to find common ground usually end up exposing common hostility. Hence, we are com-manded to "avoid...contentions, and strivings about the law [or any scriptures]" (Titus 3:9). (Polemicists and apologists are exempted from this apostolic order, provided they too "contend for the faith" with grace and not arrogance.)

- **Fanaticism**: A fanatic is one who becomes obsessed with one little phase of Bible truth and cannot think, preach, write, testify, or even converse about anything else. If you feel specially ordained to correct their lop-sided view, please, *save your breath!* It's easier to wrestle with an angry bear than to correct a confirmed fanatic: "Let a bear robbed of her whelps meet a man, rather than a fool in his folly" (Prov. 17:12).

We should watch for these causes of contention in others, and, more importantly, in ourselves! If so, with the Holy Spirit's help, we will recognize more readily the real, underlying reasons people are unreasonable with us—and discern when the same spiritual drivers are urging us forward in the folly of contention!

But understanding contention is not enough. We need to overcome it. For that, let's examine the biblical solution to the problem of strife.

THE SOLUTION: OVERCOMING CONTENTIOUSNESS WITH CALMNESS

The best scriptural antidote for the dreaded spiritual sickness of strife is found in 2 Timothy 2:14, 24–26. There, through the apostle Paul, the Head of the Church commands us, His body, to do the following:

Never argue to prove your point!

"The servant of the Lord *must not strive*" (2 Tim. 2:24, emphasis added). When conversing, speak freely to explain your, or correct your listener's, views. But if stubbornness or rejection arises, stop immediately. For the time being, God has closed your "door of utterance" (Col. 4:3). Leave your hearer in His mighty hands, trust Him to confirm the truth you've spoken, and go your way. But don't give up. Instead, step over onto the spiritual battlefield of intercession and resume your war of liberation through prayer. In Jesus' name, bind that soul's errant view(s), loose them to receive the truths they need (Matt. 18:18), and begin praying for them daily "in the Spirit" (Eph. 6:18). Don't be anxious to speak to them or try to pry open further doors of utterance by cleverness. Fully commit them to God. (Remember, He may want to use someone else to help them!) But if the Lord gives you another opportunity to speak, repeat the entire process described above: talking freely, and, if necessary, stopping your explanations and starting your intercession again. Then several wonderful things are happening.

First, you are sowing God's truth in the field of your hearer's heart as he or she is able to hear it. Both Christ and the apostle Paul followed this method. Jesus always spoke the word, "as they [His hearers] were able to hear it" (Mark 4:33). And Paul informed the Corinthian Christians that he withheld numerous deeper truths from them because they "were not able to bear it" (1 Cor. 3:1–2). Second, you are *not* damaging your listener's soul by willful insistence or rudeness. Many Christians damage the very ones they hope to deliver because of their carnal contentiousness. Third, your tongue is becoming fully "bridled" to the will of God (James 1:26), and you are growing spiritually mature or "perfect." "If any man offend not in word, the same is *a perfect man*, and able also to *bridle* [control] the whole body" (James 3:2, emphasis added). Fourth, as we will examine in greater detail in a later chapter, you are growing in the grace of Spirit-led ministry, learning to let the Holy Spirit show you when, what, how, and to whom to speak. And fifth, you are becoming more pleasing and useful to Jesus, who needs in His service every gracious, Spirit-led speaker He can find. His harvest is large and ripe, and sensitive laborers are few.

Don't allow contentious people to draw you into strife!
"Strive not about words to *no profit*" (2 Tim. 2:14, emphasis added). Strife is highly infectious. Even men of peace are tempted to indulge in strife when skilled strivers contradict and accuse them profusely. So when someone lets loose a flood of contentious and accusatory language upon your head, don't drown. Stay away from the slippery riverbank of excessive clarification. And never dive into the powerful current of passionate self-vindication. It will swiftly take you where you don't want to go—into a wild, confusing whirlpool of "no profit," for you, your listener, God, and His kingdom!

Be gentle!
"But *be gentle* unto all men" (2 Tim. 2:24, emphasis added). Be loving and kind, never curt and callous, in your words and

manner. Gentleness softens even the hardest, most bone-like, resistance: "A soft tongue breaketh the bone" (Prov. 25:15). But rudeness only stirs more revolt against you and everything you say, no matter how biblically correct! The spirit of what we say is just as important as the substance.

Be instructive!

"*Apt to teach... instructing* those that oppose him" (2 Tim. 2:24–25, emphasis added). Instruct, don't confuse, your antagonist. Explain your points with clarity and order. For that, you must understand what you're talking about. If you don't, "study to show yourself approved unto God" (v.15), until your mind is fully informed, organized, and confident. Then you'll be "ready always to give an answer to every man that asketh you" (1 Pet. 3:15).

Be patient!

"Be... *patient*" (2 Tim. 2:24, emphasis added). That is, be willing to wait for your view to be justified at a later time if it is not accepted presently. Give God time to work and your listener time to think. Remember, his stubbornness is just like yours and mine. We didn't accept every truth immediately, did we? Why should you demand that he do so? Learn to be as patient with your listener as God has been with you. Translated, that means, be very, very, very, very patient!

Be meek!

"In *meekness...*" (2 Tim. 2:25, emphasis added). Be humble, not haughty, and willing to appear to be wrong or lose the argument. Oswald Chambers said, "The only result of arguing is to prove to your own mind that you are right and the other fellow wrong." Are you more interested in saving your face or saving the faith of the captive soul before you? Meek souls always yield and obey God's will, no matter how foolish, weak, or defeated they may look. Translated, this means that, if God says stop talking, stop!—and don't worry if it looks like you lost the debate.

Be spiritually minded!

"If God, perhaps, will *give* them repentance to the acknowledging of the truth" (2 Tim. 2:25, emphasis added). When will we learn that God must "give" repentance and admission of the truth to unreasonable or deceived people? Their underlying problem is spiritual, not intellectual. Hence, the solution is not more debate but more prayer, more faith, more patience, and more goodness, for "the goodness of God leadeth thee to repentance" (Rom. 2:4). The more I do good to my unbroken opponent, the more God breaks and melts their stubborn opposition and "gives" them recognition of the truth and repentance. To believe this is to be spiritually, not carnally, minded, and to be spiritually minded is "life and peace" (Rom. 8:6).

If you want to be free and set others free from the destructive atmosphere of strife, watch for its causes and apply these solutions faithfully. Who knows, you may be the means of delivering your most contentious adversary. You may even deliver the most chronic controversialist you know... that person in your mirror every morning! And if in the meantime you must dine alone on dry, stale bread to have peace, well, thank God for your crusty bread and *enjoy!*

To your surprise, you will find yourself not morose, but merry.

Chapter Twenty

IS YOUR HEART MERRY?

*L*et me ask you, is your spirit merry or morose? Bright or broken? Lively or lame? If it is gloomy instead of glad, take heed to this pearl of truth. King Solomon wrote:

> A merry heart doeth good like a medicine, but a broken spirit drieth the bones.
>
> —PROVERBS 17:22

Paraphrased, this text reads:

> A glad, cheerful heart is like effective medicine to the body, but a discouraged, despairing spirit has just the opposite effect: it dries up our health!

The Hebrew word from which "merry" is translated is *same-ach*, which means "gleeful," and is derived from the word *samach*, which means, "to brighten up." A merry heart, then, is a bright, gleeful heart, or a glad, joyful, or cheerful heart. This describes a fully liberated spirit, unfettered with either cares or wrath. It is the opposite of a "broken spirit," which is a heavy heart that is bound and limited by frustration, discouragement, or despair. Neither is it a heart filled with mere worldly merriment.

This present world's merrymaking is a passing, not a permanent, joy. It springs from a whole host of natural causes, good and bad, such as:

- **Good harvests**: "Nevertheless, he [God]…gave us rain from heaven, and *fruitful seasons*, filling our hearts with food *and gladness*" (Acts 14:17, emphasis added).

- **Feasting**: "And bring the fatted calf, and kill it; and let us *eat [feast], and be merry*…And they began to *be merry*" (Luke 15:23–24, emphasis added).

- **Wine**: "When the heart of the king was *merry with wine*" (Esther 1:10, emphasis added); and, "*wine that maketh glad* the heart of man" (Ps. 104:15).

- **Humor, jesting, or comedy**: "I said of laughter, It is mad; and of mirth, What doeth it?" (Eccles. 2:2).

- **Dancing**: "O virgin of Israel; thou shalt again…go forth in *the dances of those who make merry*" (Jer. 31:4, emphasis added).

- **Extramarital sexual indulgence**: "The people sat down to eat and to drink, and rose up *to play* [or for sex-play]" (Exod. 32:6, emphasis added). (See Exodus 32:25.)

- **Good-natured partying**: "…that I might *make merry* with my friends" (Luke 15:29, emphasis added).

- **Leisure**: "Take thine ease. Eat, drink, and *be merry*" (Luke 12:19, emphasis added).

- **Victory at athletic competition**: "…rejoiceth like a strong man to run [and anticipate winning] a race" (Ps. 19:5).

- **Marriage**: "...as the bridegroom rejoiceth over the bride" (Isa. 62:5).

These and other kinds of merely worldly merriment are often without any substance. They consist of nothing more than silliness, comedic trivia, purely worldly attainments, or in some cases, downright debauchery. But the biblical merry heart is filled with an entirely different kind of glee, namely, holy gladness—godly joy springing from an unshakable assurance in God. Why do we need this joy?

WHY DO WE NEED MERRY HEARTS?

Our text for this chapter reveals three benefits derived from a merry heart. It states that a merry heart:

Is like effective medicine

Here the Bible attests to something we discussed in an earlier chapter: the fact of psychosomatic diseases, or bodily illnesses that are caused by sustained mental or emotional stresses.

Like a well-prescribed drug or other helpful treatment, joy and gladness of heart improve our physical health: "A merry heart doeth good [to the body] like a medicine..." (Incidentally, this also affirms the divine recognition and limited benefits of well-prescribed medicines—"doeth good like a medicine"—as well as other beneficial medical and paramedical activities, such as: surgery [Gen. 2:21]; emergency medicine [Luke 10:33–34]; and nursing [Luke 10:34].) On the other hand, a troubled, depressed, self-pitying, or oppressed mind drains and spoils our health: "...but a broken spirit drieth the bones"; or, "a broken spirit saps vitality" (MOFFATT). Note the connection this verse makes between our bodily health and our bones. Why the link? It is because "the life of the flesh [health of the body] is in the blood" (Lev. 17:11). The key to our physical health lies largely in, and can be known by, the condition of our blood, especially our vital red blood cells, which carry oxygen from our lungs throughout our entire bodies and carry carbon dioxide gathered from all over our bodies to our lungs. These red blood cells are formed in the red marrow of our bones. So there is a direct link between the state of our health, the condition of our blood, and the functioning of our bone marrow. When our red bone marrow produces enough red blood cells, our blood, and our bodily health, is normal; when it produces less than it should, we're anemic, or weak.

So this proverb declares that a merry heart "helps and heals" (MOFFATT) our bodily health; that is, it causes our bone marrow to produce red blood cells at a normal rate. But when we indulge in a depressed mind-set, our sick psychological state "saps vitality"; that is, it may cause our bone marrow to produce a deficient number of red blood cells.

We conclude, then, that gladness of heart is an effective medicine. And every Christian should take it regularly, because it's not only healthful, it's also free! And that should make you even merrier!

Makes our faces cheerful

"A merry heart maketh a cheerful countenance," Solomon tells us (Prov. 15:13). Indeed our faces reflect the state of our hearts. When our spirits are broken, our countenances fall (Gen. 4:6); but when our spirits are glad, our faces smile and shine. This is why the psalmist referred to God as his "face-healer" (Ps. 42:11, MLB). He realized that hope in God removed his frown and restored his smile, thus "healing" his face. Why is this important?

It is significant because looks are contagious. When our faces look sad, others around us are inclined to be gloomy; when our countenances are joyful, our companions are lifted. Do we want to spread glee or gloom? Do we want our entrance into a room to bring joy or oppression, life or death?

Leaders especially should consider that *gloomy-faced leaders can't inspire others*. Dwight D. Eisenhower, Supreme European Allied Commander during World War II, learned this lesson. Early in the North Africa campaign, he grew depressed over the

American forces' initially excessively heavy losses at the hands of German Field Marshal Erwin Rommel's famed Africa Corps. Eisenhower's deathly grim face betrayed his personal gloom to his staff, who then became infected with his negative attitude. Noting the undesirable effects on his associates, Ike decided that, to be an effective leader of men, he couldn't afford to look discouraged any more. From then on, no matter how difficult the situation or troubled his heart, he put on a cheerful face. Thus was born the wide, affable, infectiously optimistic, trademark "Eisenhower smile," which thereafter lifted many a hopeless, heavy heart.

Gives us overcoming strength

"He that is of a merry heart hath a continual feast" (Prov. 15:15). This reference reveals that maintaining a merry heart enables us to live every day in a festive mood, as if we were enjoying a free-spirited banquet all day long! Why is this important?

This is vital because steady joy provides steady, overcoming strength. No matter what adversities or adversaries confront us, festive hearts give us the energy to *flow on in joy* and overcome them: "He who has a glad heart has a continual feast [regardless of circumstances]" (v. 15, AMP). A biblically merry heart, or one filled with godly joy springing from unshakable assurance in God, is an undefeatable, irrepressible spirit, a joy so powerful it overrides and overrules any and all trouble.

Joseph obviously had this in Potiphar's prison. If he had been sad, he would never have noticed that the butler and baker of Egypt had broken spirits. He would never have asked them, "Wherefore look ye so sad today?" (Gen. 40:7). Paul too had this overcoming energy in the Philippian jail. Though stripped of his rights, beaten, bloodied, banished to a dark, filthy "inner prison," and bound tightly in painful stocks, he and Silas still *flowed on in joy*, praising and praying to God at midnight! Amazingly, Paul's continual feast of worship never ended! And what he practiced, he preached: "Rejoice in the Lord always; and again I say, Rejoice" (Phil. 4:4).

WHAT MAKES OUR HEARTS MERRY?

The Bible also reveals a number of things that gladden or rejoice our hearts as Christians. Please consider these biblical merry-makers.

More than anything else, feasting on God's Word gladdens our hearts. Jeremiah testified, "Thy words were found, and I did eat them, and thy word was unto me *the joy and rejoicing of mine heart*" (Jer. 15:16, emphasis added). Sustained prayer in the presence of God also imparts sustaining, superior joy. David testified, "In thy presence is *fullness of joy*" (Ps. 16:11, emphasis added). Walking uprightly, in ethical and moral integrity, gladdens our hearts: "Light is sown for the righteous, and *gladness [is sown] for the upright in heart*" (Ps. 97:11, emphasis added). Zeal for God's righteousness in His church (temple) enables Him to imbue us with special joy: "Thou hast loved righteousness, and hated iniquity; therefore, God...hath anointed thee with the *oil of gladness* above thy fellows" (Heb. 1:9, emphasis added). Answers to prayer fill us with joy. So overjoyed was Rhoda when Peter stood at the door, delivered by prayer, that she "opened not the gate *for gladness*, but ran in, and told how Peter stood before the gate" (Acts 12:14, emphasis added). Good news also brightens our spirits: "Heaviness in the heart of man maketh it stoop, but *a good word [encouraging report] maketh it glad*" (Prov. 12:25, emphasis added). Visible fulfillments of divine plans and promises also enrapture our hearts. The psalmist described Israel's euphoric release from captivity: "When the LORD turned again the captivity of Zion, we were like them that dream. Then was our mouth filled with laughter, and our tongue with singing" (Ps. 126:1–2). And there are more causes of godly joy.

Heavenly visions and divine visitations make our hearts merry. When Jesus suddenly appeared among His disciples, "then were the disciples *glad*, when they saw the Lord" (John 20:20, emphasis added). Fresh anointings and refillings of the Holy Spirit, the "new wine" of Christianity, also make our hearts

167

joyful: "And wine that *maketh glad* the heart of man" (Ps. 104:15, emphasis added). (See Acts 2:13, 15–17.) And finally, the salvation of lost souls (Luke 15:3–10) and the restoration of backslidden believers should produce great joy in our hearts: "Let us…be *merry*. For this, my son, was dead; and is alive again; he was lost, and is found. And they began to be *merry*" (Luke 15:23–24, emphasis added). All these things make Christians' hearts *sameach*—or gleeful and bright!

IS YOUR HEART MERRY?

Does your spiritual life, your inner man, need some effective medicine, my friend? Do you need a spiritual face-lift? Time and again, do you lack the joy to rise above the adversities of life? If your answer to any of these questions is "yes," may I recommend that you make your heart merry?

Feed slowly and thoughtfully on God's Word until it becomes in fact the "joy and rejoicing of my [your] heart." Take time from trivial pursuits and give it instead to soaking in God's presence in private prayer and worship until His joy permeates your inner man. Walk uprightly, according to the biblical ethics and morality ("light") you hold, so your conscience may rejoice in freedom from guilt. Pay your vows (duties, pledges), and complete your obedience so God can give you joyous fulfillments of His promises and visions for your life. Choose to be zealous for God's holiness in His "temples," standing for "his righteousness" (Matt. 6:33) in your bodily life, your local church, and the body of Christ at large. Deliberately rejoice over every answer to prayer. Ask for, and expect, good reports from the "far country" of heaven. Ask for and seek fresh anointings and refillings of the "wine" of the Spirit constantly. Be glad whenever the lost are saved or the backslidden restored: "Rejoice with them that do rejoice" (Rom. 12:15). If you persistently do these things, your heart will grow increasingly merrier. And merrier. And merrier. Until it's, well, very merry!

Then your inner cup will run over with joy: "My cup runneth over" (Ps. 23:5). Your bodily health will benefit from the powerful new medicine you're taking daily. Anemia, both physical and spiritual, will become a thing of the past. Your countenance will no longer scowl but shine. And your new psychological "driver"—an undefeatable, irrepressible, supernatural divine joy within—will enable you to move through even the most difficult trials of life with the grace, agility, and speed of a hind traversing a high and treacherous mountain pass to elude a mountain lion. The prophet Habakkuk described this for us:

> Although the fig tree shall not blossom, neither shall fruit be in the vines; the labor of the olive shall fail, and the fields shall yield no food; the flock shall be cut off from the fold, and there shall be no herd in the stalls; *yet shall I rejoice in the L*ORD, *I will joy in the God of my salvation.* The LORD God is my strength, and *he will make my feet like hinds' feet, and he will make me walk [freely and easily] upon mine high places [of difficulty and danger].*
> —HABAKKUK 3:17–19, EMPHASIS ADDED

So, my friend, get merry! And expect God to open doors for you.

Chapter Twenty-one

OUR GIFTS OPEN DOORS FOR US

*T*he gifts God gives us, and sometimes the gifts we give, open doors for us. King Solomon encapsulated this thought for us in this priceless pearl of truth:

> A man's gift maketh room for him, and bringeth him before great men.
>
> —PROVERBS 18:16

Paraphrased, this proverb teaches us:

> A man's gift [given to or by him] creates a place [opportunity, position, office] for him [not previously open] and causes him to be recognized [commended, befriended, commissioned, employed] by people of prominence, prestige, or power.

Admittedly, some expositors believe this "gift" refers to a bribe, while others hold, and I agree, that it refers to a talent or ability, or a gift freely given. *The Spirit-Filled Life Bible* notes, "This gift is not a bribe, but an asset or talent which opens the way." I believe that both language and context confirm that the latter interpretation is correct.

The Hebrew word used here for "gift" is *mattan* and means "present." In numerous Old Testament references, the King James Version refers to "gifts" that are clearly bribes. (See Exodus 23:8; Deuteronomy 16:19; 2 Chronicles 19:7; Proverbs 6:35; Isaiah 1:23; Ezekiel 22:12.) In each of these texts, another Hebrew word, *shachad*, which means "donation," is used. Thus the language used in our text does not specifically or definitively refer to a bribe. There is also nothing about the immediate context that implies the author had the topic of bribery in mind. Proverbs 18:16 is neither preceded nor followed by verses discussing plotting or injustice. Furthermore, the larger context, the entire Bible, repeatedly gives us illustrations that support the interpretation of "gift," not as a bribe, but as a special ability divinely given or a human gift sincerely given.

It was Abigail's sincere gift of food supplies, for instance, that brought her to the attention of David, an up-and-coming great man in Judah! (See 1 Samuel 25:1–42.) While hurrying to bring David bread, wine, mutton, raisins, and figs, Abigail had no ulterior motive whatsoever. Her aims were only to grant David's request for food, turn him from revenge, and live! A very godly and very married woman, Abigail wasn't looking for another man, despite her "Nabal" of a husband! But knowing what would follow, God graciously put her in touch with David just before He removed her evil and oppressive spouse. And it was her gift—present of food and drink innocently given—that opened the door for her to meet her future husband. David had had a similar experience years earlier.

Wanting to bless his soldier-sons and know their condition, Jesse sent young David to find his older brothers and give them and their commanding officer portions of bread, grain, and cheese. It was while dutifully delivering these gifts that David heard Goliath's threats, saw the Israelites' cowardice, and realized that Jehovah was being shamefully reproached. (See 1 Samuel 17:1–26.) Though he was already known to and employed by King Saul as his court musician and armor bearer, David's slaying of Goliath impressed Saul with David's additional gifts of faith and valor and his natural leadership skills, and it prompted him to "set him over the men of war" (1 Sam. 18:5). Suddenly David found himself the General of the Army of Israel and, soon thereafter, the son-in-law to the king—thanks to the door opened by the simple gifts he brought to his brothers in Jesse's name. Hence, David's presents created an opportunity for him and brought him yet again before the great man, Saul. (Perhaps Solomon had this, his father's early meteoric rise to power, in mind when he penned Proverbs 18:16.)

In both Abigail's and David's cases we see Jesus' principle of giving at work: "Give, and it shall be given unto you" (Luke 6:38). When Abigail and David gave people gifts, God gave them gifts. And it must be noted that their gifts were without selfish motives. They gave, not to get but to give; not to advance themselves but to assist others. If they had intended to garner favor for themselves, God wouldn't have opened such wonderful opportunities for them. Besides using the sincere gifts His servants give, God also creates opportunities for His servants through the gifts He gives them.

For example, it was David's musical talent that first brought Him to King Saul's attention and won him the dual posts of the king's musician and his armor bearer. Daniel and his three Hebrew friends won favor with King Nebuchadnezzar and advisory positions in his cabinet because God had given all of them "skill in all learning and wisdom" and had given Daniel "understanding in all visions and dreams" (Dan. 1:17). Joseph's similar interpretive and administrative gifts won him favor with and a commission from the sitting Pharaoh of Egypt. The elders of Israel ordained Moses as their nation's spiritual shepherd after witnessing his amazing dual gifts of supernatural spiritual power and heavenly words (Exod. 4:29–31). Israel's tribal heads made Jephthah their leader because of his twin gifts of courage and military expertise. Isaac's God-given grace and abundant blessings won the attention and respect of Abimelech, the leader of the Philistines. Isaac spoke for all God's gifted ones when he exclaimed, "Rehoboth [lit. *plenty of room*]... For now the LORD hath made room for us, and we shall be fruitful in the land" (Gen. 26:22). Indeed, if we stay faithful, our God-given gifts will bring us before people of authority and make plenty of room for us to live, work, and minister just as God has planned. Thus, as in these examples, we will fulfill the purpose of our creation.

"But I don't have any gifts," you may claim. Oh, yes, you do! We all have gifts—natural or redemptive presents from God— that bless both unbelievers and believers and help directly or indirectly to build God's kingdom. "Every good gift and every perfect gift is from above... from the Father" (James 1:17). The abilities we are born with are natural gifts; those we are reborn with are spiritual gifts.

The spiritual abilities the Holy Spirit gives Christians are listed for us in Romans 12:3–8 and 1 Corinthians 12:4–11, 27–31. The fivefold ministry—apostles, prophets, evangelists, pastors, and teachers—is comprised of gifted ministers who are themselves gifts from the risen Christ to His bride, the church (Eph. 4:11–13). Whether we are in the fivefold ministry or not, whatever ability God gives us helps the overall functioning of the body of Christ, just as the various invisible but vital parts of our bodies help us maintain the balance of health, without which we could not function. How can any church, ministry, or minister function without fellow believers possessing gifts of helps, administrations, giving, exhortation, and wisdom? So, whatever our Christian talents may be, they make room for us before the greatest man, Jesus, and those who are great in *His* sight—born-again believers and their anointed leaders. And they enable us to be a functioning part of the greatest body of people on earth: the body and church of Jesus Christ. Our natural gifts are equally important.

By them, we acquire employments and earn our livings, whether by programming computers, drafting building plans, hanging wallpaper, selling bottled soft drinks, preparing meals, laundering, managing businesses, or working in industrial plants. Without these and other natural employment gifts—medical, technical, mechanical, mathematical, scientific, inventive, artistic, athletic, academic, communicative, organizational, managerial, industrial, political, commercial, or public relations skills—we could not survive in this very pragmatic, material world, much less support the spreading of the gospel, the teaching of the saints, or the sustenance of the poor. These natural gifts, therefore, are just as necessary as their spiritual counterparts. How can our spiritual lives thrive if the needs of our bodies are not met? Truly, our families, local churches, nations, and the church at large all depend upon these natural talents, and they will continue to do so until the trump of God sounds.

But until that much-anticipated, heavenly day arrives, God's plan is that our gifts create opportunities of advantage for us and for His work on earth. And this will surely happen if we do three things:

1. Continue walking with God
2. Practice our special abilities or gifts
3. Await God's time

Why do these three conditions apply, you ask? Please consider these explanations.

First, gifts from God thrive only as we stay in touch with the God who gave them. Hence, in John 15 Jesus repeatedly urges us to "abide in me" (vv. 4, 7). As we, the branches, remain very, very close to Jesus, the Vine, the Spirit of His life flows through us constantly. As a result, both our natural and spiritual talents gradually manifest, blossom, and bear fruit abundantly.

Second, whether ours are natural or spiritual gifts, only frequent use increases, sharpens, and perfects them. Both in the world and in grace, practice makes perfect. Jesus commended the servants who used their talents, not those who hid them. (See Matthew 25:14–30.) Joseph continued practicing his gifts of interpretation and administration even when he was seemingly forgotten in Potiphar's prison. And the major-league apostle Paul urged his friend and understudy, Timothy, to "neglect not the gift that is in thee," but to "give thyself wholly...that thy profiting may appear to all" (1 Tim. 4:14–15), though he was presently in the ministerial minor leagues. All these recognized that gifts neglected die on the vine, but gifts practiced grow and develop to full fruition. Then they open doors, bless those who possess them, bless God's children, and glorify God.

Third, Ecclesiastes teaches, "To every thing there is a season" (Eccles. 3:1), and for every gift there is an appointed time for its optimum use. Paul's apostolic gift didn't blossom until after God's Spirit moved and began saving Gentiles en masse, because his special abilities as apostle to the Gentiles were not needed until that hour. Joseph's interpretive and administrative gifts didn't open a royal door for him until Pharaoh needed an interpreter for his dreams and an administrator for Egypt's famine preparation program. Jephthah's valor and military genius didn't open a door of leadership for him until war challenged the chosen people. (See Judges 11:1–11.) These and many other biblical and historical examples show us that, if our gifts don't make room for us now, they will do so in the hour they're needed. That is, if we stay very close to Jesus, use our gifts often, and wait patiently for our appointed season of service. And that will challenge our love for Jesus, our submission to His will, and our willingness to endure.

So let me—no, let the Spirit of God!—challenge you, my friend! Abide very close to the Giver of your gifts so they may be fully activated and sustained. Recognize your personal natural and spiritual talents, and practice them regularly; concentrate, "give yourself wholly" to them, and refuse to be distracted or discouraged. And then do the greatest thing a believer can do: *believe* that your gifts will open doors for you! In God's time. In God's way. For your blessing. For others' blessing. For God's glory. Let the Spirit of God through Habakkuk exhort and encourage you:

For the vision is yet for an appointed time, but at the end it shall speak, and not lie; though it tarry, wait for it, because it will surely come, it will not tarry.

—HABAKKUK 2:3

And one of the best gifts God may give you—or make you— is a godly wife.

Chapter Twenty-two

GOOD WIFE, GOOD BLESSING

good wife is a great blessing to a man and a sign of favor with God. A bad wife, well, we'll address that sad subject later in this chapter.

But for now let's accentuate the positive. King Solomon did this. A man with no less than seven hundred wives and three hundred concubines, Solomon was uniquely fitted to speak authoritatively on marriage matters. (Although, I'm sure, many wives in this era of prevailing monogamy would just love to wring his polygamous neck!) And he believed firmly that a good wife was a good blessing from God.

Whoso findeth a wife findeth a good thing, and obtaineth favor from the LORD.

—PROVERBS 18:22

Paraphrased, this matrimonial maxim states:

Whoever finds a good [loving, faithful, and godly] wife has found a great benefit; she is a great favor [token of gracious approval] from the Lord.

177

Other proverbs by Solomon and statements by other sacred writers only confirm this high opinion of a good wife:

> A prudent wife is from the LORD...The heart of her husband doth safely trust in her... *she will do him good, and not evil*, all the days of her life.
> —PROVERBS 19:14; 31:11–12, EMPHASIS ADDED

> Thy [loving] wife shall be as a fruitful vine by the sides of thine house... *thus shall the man be blessed* who feareth the LORD.
> —PSALM 128:3–4, EMPHASIS ADDED

> Ye wives, be in subjection to your own husbands...while they behold your chaste conduct coupled with fear [of God]; whose adorning...let it be...even the ornament of a meek and quiet spirit, *which is in the sight of God of great price*.
> —1 PETER 3:1–4, EMPHASIS ADDED

The current divorce rate in North America, including that among Bible-professing Christians, seems to laugh raucously in the face of these blessed biblical facts. But despite our society's rude and contradictory challenge, these proverbs stand true and accurate as originally written. Yes, marriage is under a vicious assault from the kingdom of darkness, but it still remains a beautiful thing of light. If so, let us ask, "In what ways are good wives blessings to their husbands?"

Here are some ways identified for us in the Holy Scriptures.

THE BLESSINGS OF A GOOD WIFE

Joy

"Live *joyfully* with the wife whom thou lovest all the days of [thy] life" (Eccles. 9:9, emphasis added). Here the Bible notes the obvious: the sheer, overflowing delight of a newly married man. For him, life is full of hope. His best days lie ahead. The loneliness of his single life is gone...and good riddance! He is filled with a fresh and invigorating sense of fulfillment: at long last, he has found his soul- and life-mate, his "better half," his divinely recreated "rib." This joy is real and strong. And, as stated above, it is of God: "A prudent wife is *from the* LORD" (Prov. 19:14, emphasis added). But the joy of marriage is not indestructible.

So, wisely, husbands should cultivate it, cheering, pleasing, and caring for their wives for the rest of their earthly journey: "Live joyfully with [thy] wife... *all the days.*"

Fruit

Clearly, one primary purpose of marriage is procreation. Hence, the psalmist prophesies, "Thy wife shall be as a fruitful vine by the sides of thine house," and soon, "thy children [shall be] like [delightful, valuable, useful] olive plants round about thy table" (Ps. 128:3). What a blessing that the Creator should permit us the joy of creating little creatures in our own image! (Remember this the next time their inner "image," or attitude, irritates you!) Thank God for good wives that bear, birth, nurse, raise, and lovingly teach children! Their ministry to tomorrow's laborers and leaders is incalculable. And its rewards are rich and many and sure.

One of them is reciprocity, "for whatever a man soweth, that shall he also reap" (Gal. 6:7). If parents faithfully love and teach their growing children, their children will faithfully love and help their parents, should trouble visit, for the rest of their lives: "Lo, children are an heritage from the LORD... they shall not be ashamed [of their embattled or maligned parents], but they shall speak with the enemies in the gate" (Ps. 127:3–5).

Help

After observing, "It is not good that the man should be alone," God declared, "I will make him an help fit for him" (Gen. 2:18). Thus the Creator's stated purpose for Eve, the first good wife, was that she be a "help fit for" her husband. She was perfectly suited to complement and complete him—physically, psychologically, and spiritually—just as he was her perfect match. And no doubt Eve, aware of this divine word, lived the rest of her life with the holy objective of assisting Adam in his life calling. Many "liberated" women today would feel that by doing so Eve lost her identity and wasted her individual potential. But to the contrary, Eve didn't lose anything. She gained her true personality, fulfilled her divine call, and found her ultimate satisfaction as a woman specially created and predestined for marriage. Other great wives were great helpers.

The anonymous "virtuous woman," or virtuous *wife*, of Proverbs 31 stands alone as the consummately complementary mate. She was:

- **God-fearing:** "A woman who feareth the Lord" (v. 30). She believed in and stood in awe of God's power, authority, and judgments and dared not defy His will. This holy respect was the primary wellspring of her "virtue," or moral power, and godly wisdom. Without it, none of her other admirable natural qualities would be praiseworthy, for God honors no one, however diligent, if they do not fear Him.

- **A devoted seeker of God:** "She riseth also while it is yet night" (v. 15). This verse says she rose early to prepare food for her household. Another reveals she held and spoke of God's wisdom (v. 26). To have God's wisdom, she must have spent time in God's presence and word daily. So she rose early enough to first seek God and His Word amply, and then to see to her day's business, which began with feeding her children: "And giveth food to her household" (v. 15). (See Proverbs 8:17; Matthew 6:33.)

- **Of strong character:** "A virtuous woman" (Prov. 31:10). Fear of and daily fellowship with God instilled in her soul faith, hope, and love—the sure foundations of enduring strong character. Hence, she was a "woman of strength";[1] or a "wife with strength of character" (MLB); or a "wife of noble character" (NIV). Her name was synonymous with integrity.

- **Not necessarily a beauty queen:** "Beauty is vain" (v. 30). By inspiration, this wife of strength's physical beauty is *not* described, implying it may or may not have been exceptional. It is surely not nefarious for the female creature to be "fair to look upon," for this is ascribed to such holy wives as Sarah, Abigail, and Esther. But neither is it a prerequisite of virtue. Hence the reader is reminded that physical beauty is "vain," or only of temporal, not eternal, value. What is God saying here? Simply that exquisite looks are not required for exceptional virtue. Whether of ordinary or extraordinary body, the virtuous woman is a beautiful *person*. (See 1 Peter 3:1–6.) Not every wife can be voluptuous, but every wife can be virtuous.

- **Faithful:** "Her husband doth safely trust in her" (Prov. 31:11). Because she was *faithful*—utterly reliable and thoroughly loyal—her husband didn't worry about her committing sexual, financial, or verbal unfaithfulness; that is, having illicit affairs, misspending family wealth, or lying to or about him. From a financial standpoint, then, he had "no need [want] of spoil"; that is, no lack of surplus financial resources and hence no temptation to seek unjust "spoil."

- **Stable:** "She will do him good . . . *all the days* of her life" (v. 12, emphasis added). Her close walk with God made her spiritually, emotionally, and mentally stable. She was consistently and persistently good-hearted, well-intentioned, and without spite toward her husband and children, not some days but "all" her days.

- **A dutiful cook of delicious food:** "She . . . giveth food to her household" (v. 15). Realizing that good food well prepared is a central feature of every happy family, she dutifully prepared her family's meals. That her husband and children subsequently praised her (vv. 27–28) implies that her meals were full, nutritious, and delicious.

- **A prudent planner and purchaser:** "She considereth a field and buyeth it" (v. 16). She prayerfully considered her family's approaching needs in real estate, merchandise (v. 18), clothing (v. 21), and food (v. 16), and she met them with the help of God's providential and precise guidance. She was a smart shopper, accurately appraising values and comparing prices.

- **A humble, hardworking laborer:** "She…worketh willingly with her hands" (v. 13). Not too proud to work manually, she rose early (v. 15) and "[set] about her work vigorously" (v. 17, NIV), preparing food (v. 15), gardening (v. 16), spinning yarn (v. 19), weaving (vv. 22, 24), and cleaning and keeping the house (v. 27). Conquered by neither bed nor couch, she took rest without indulging in it.

- **A committed intercessor:** "She looketh well to the ways of her household" (v. 27). All spiritually minded women of God know that their family's most basic and indispensable need is God's favor and blessing on their souls, which is accessible only through prayer. So the wife of strength "looked well" to her family's soul-needs first by intercession; then she attended to all the needs of their bodies.

- **A teacher of her children:** "She openeth her mouth with wisdom, and…looketh well to the ways of her household" (vv. 26–27). She "looked well" to her children's spiritual needs also by teaching them God's Word and ways, both systematically and as their situational needs required. (See Proverbs 31:1.)

- **A watchful and attentive domestic minister:** "She looketh well to the ways of her household" (v. 27). More than the proficient keeper of a house, she was the persistent builder of a *home*. As a good shepherdess, she constantly watched for and addressed her domestic flock's situational needs—nixing, not exacerbating, sibling rivalries; settling, not starting, disputes; explaining, not ignoring, confusing problems; lovingly exhorting, not lambasting, her husband when he faltered or failed. Like Jesus and the Holy Spirit, she was there, "not to be ministered unto, but to minister, and to give" (Matt. 20:28).

- **An able part-time businesswoman:** "She maketh fine linen, and selleth it" (Prov. 31:24). Before and after her child-rearing years, and, in the interim whenever her daily family duties were discharged, she made and marketed clothing products to earn extra money for personal and family needs. She discriminatingly bought or traded wool and flax (vv. 13, 18), from which she spun yarn and wove cloth, and crafted high-quality dresses, bedspreads, cloaks (v. 22), and "girdles," or colorful sashes (v. 24), which she then sold in the marketplace as time allowed. (See Acts 16:14.)

- **Knowledgeable:** "She openeth her mouth with wisdom" (Prov. 31:26). Hungry for more vital knowledge, she listened to and questioned wise teachers, pondered their teachings, read (though reading was very limited and usually for men only in her day), and so learned much about many worthy topics, both spiritual and natural. Hence, when she discussed or dispensed divine or human knowledge, she did so competently and confidently.

- **A compassionate donor:** "She *stretcheth out* her hand to the [materially and spiritually] poor; yea, she *reacheth forth*" (v. 20, emphasis added). Freely initiating

183

assistance—"stretching…reaching forth"—to materially and spiritually needy ones as God enabled her, her love was real and her pity practical. Neither cruel, selfish, nor hypocritical, she shared her fortune with the unfortunate and her faith with the faithless. Like God, she so loved that she gave.

- **Prepared for predictable adversity:** "She is not afraid of the snow…all her household are clothed with scarlet [adequate or fine clothing, often crimson in color]" (v. 21). Throughout history, winter has been a predictable, potentially lethal test for human kind. If wood, food, drink, and clothing were not prepared before the advent of snow, the unprepared never saw the spring. Though Palestine was of moderate climate, the wife of strength nevertheless "girded her loins…and strengthened her arms" (v. 17) to prepare in summer sunshine the warm clothing her family would need in winter snowfalls.

- **Kind and wise in speech:** "When she speaks, her words are wise" (v. 26, TLB), and "she…offers kindly counsel" (v. 26, MOFFATT). Mindful of her heavenly Master, the wife of strength watched her earthly mood and manners. She spoke wisely and discreetly, as I have described previously in this book. When she disagreed with her husband, she did so with a courteous, not a belligerent, spirit. And she typically spoke kindly, not curtly; gently, not abrasively. The Modern Language Bible's translation reads, "Gentle teaching is in her tongue." Its annotation adds, "She is not domineering as such an energetic woman often is." As a result, her words always healed and helped, and never hurt.

- **A wise manager of time:** "Her lamp goeth not out by night" (v. 18). An incremental, not impulsive, worker, she used every available time slot to further her necessary work. Note that this verse does not say she worked "all" night, but rather "by" (or at) night, meaning that she didn't quit working at sundown but rather lit her oil lamp to make wise use of her after-dinner hours. Since we know she was both an early riser (v. 15) and wise (v. 26), she must have broken off her evening labor while there was enough time to be with her husband and then take rest, because to either ignore his needs or persist in overwork would have been unwise and self-opposing.

- **An honor to her husband:** "Her husband is respected at the city gate" (v. 23, NIV). Like a beautiful bejeweled and shining "crown" (Prov. 12:4) on her husband's head, she only adorned his reputation and never embarrassed or maligned him by unfaithfulness, slander, rebellion against his authority, neglect of their children (Prov. 29:15), or mistreatment of others. Thus she helped God make her man. That is, by constantly loving, cooperating with, working for, and counseling her husband, and by consistently walking close with and praying to God, she helped her husband become what God wanted him to be—a better man, and, in this case, a leader of men. Thus, her excellent wifehood lifted him to sit "among the elders [leaders]" (Prov. 31:23).

- **Adored and honored by her children and husband:** "Her children...call her blessed; her husband also...praiseth her" (v. 28). Eventually the law of reaping overtook this wife of strength, and all the love and honor she had sowed in her children and husband returned to her. Her children began praying for her blessing, seeking to be with her, and respectfully remembering her wise counsel and reciting and reproducing it in their own families (v. 1). And her husband just couldn't stop boasting about her! For him, the only accurate description of her was, "The best!" "Many daughters have done virtuously, but *thou excellest them all*" (v. 29, emphasis added).

- **Honored by others:** "Let her own works praise her *in the gates*" (v. 31, emphasis added). Because her husband persistently praised her in the city gates and people everywhere noticed her good works, she became lauded throughout her neighborhood, synagogue, and city as a model wife. This was no accident; God's principle of giving was behind this: "Give, and it shall be given unto you" (Luke 6:38). Because she had given her husband a good name, God gave her a good name. And "in the gates" the city leaders said to her, as Boaz said to Ruth, "All the city of my people doth know that *thou art a virtuous woman*" (Ruth 3:11, emphasis added).

- **Increasingly joyful, not regretful:** "She shall rejoice in time to come [as she ages]" (Prov. 31:25). For believers, real joy comes only from knowing God is pleased with us because we have finished His will. As we age, we gradually reap either more joy or more regret: regret, if we consistently fail God's will; rejoicing, if we consistently fulfill it. Because this virtuous wife realized she had fully done God's will as a believer, wife, and mother, she ran the bell lap of her life-race with a reinvigorating and increasingly joyful sense of accomplishment, not with painful pangs of regret.

- **A rare find:** "Who can find a virtuous woman [wife]?" (v. 10). Fortune-tellers, lonely heart's clubs, Internet dating services, or eager Christian matchmakers cannot find a virtuous wife. But God can. He found Sarah for Abraham, Abigail for David, and Ruth for Boaz. His matchmaking is unmatched.

- **The most valuable jewel on earth!** "Her price is *far above rubies*" (v. 10, emphasis added). Among the Book of Proverb's repeated comparisons between spiritual and worldly valuables (Prov. 3:13–15), this statement looms large. It declares that a virtuous wife is "far" more valuable than "rubies"—precious earthly gemstones used in fine jewelry—and so hints that she is *the* most valuable jewel in the jewelry box of humanity.

> While the husband is the head of the family, the wife is far and away its most valuable member. Why? Because everything revolves around her, and rises or falls, succeeds or fails, with her virtue or lack thereof.

This proverbial virtuous wife is wisdom personified, or all the essential facets of godly wisdom manifested in a human being. While few wives master all these virtues, all Christian wives should strive to master as many as they can. Those who do so will be marked as foolish anachronisms, or people from a bygone era. A world full of coldhearted secular feminists and a church full of religious but worldly-minded Christians will laugh to scorn the humble Christian wife who sees her primary life work as being a loving companion and vital compliment to her husband and the guiding light of her children. But she'll weather the storm. Why? Because a virtuous wife has one additional feature not mentioned above: she's willing to be different—Amish, if you please—if that is necessary to please God.

Such a "wonder woman" is not only a personal and spiritual blessing to her man but also a very practical help to him in this very practical world. Her inspired partnership makes his life more comfortable, enjoyable, and fruitful in labor and ministry—and her life too as she receives God's fullest blessing for gladly fulfilling His will for her life.

Wisdom

When God joins a godly woman to a man, she brings her wisdom with her. Thereafter her intelligence and good judgment are new and useful resources for her husband. If he is wise, he will recognize this and draw upon this new thought-resource freely as needed. Though already wise, David was a wiser man after he united with Abigail.

First Samuel 25 states that Abigail was "a woman of good understanding" (v. 3) and showcases her exceptional wisdom and insight in the story it tells. Demonstrating acumen, Abigail quickly assessed the terrible danger Nabal's rudeness brought upon her household (vv. 17–18). Showing organizational skills, she planned and prepared a large shipment of food for David's men (v. 18). Wisely, she decided to seek mercy rather than defend Nabal's indefensibly insensitive actions: "Abigail...fell before David on her face, and bowed to the ground" (v. 23). Sacrificially, she offered her own life, should David require it, as a substitute for the innocents in her household: "Upon me, my lord, upon me let this iniquity be" (v. 24). Discreetly, she did not tell Nabal about David's great anger, her life-saving plan, or their rendezvous, until the time was right: "But she told not her husband, Nabal...she told him nothing, less or more, until the morning light" (vv. 19, 36). Thoughtfully, she exhorted David not to avenge himself upon Nabal, detailing the adverse consequences such action would bring upon him: "That this shall be no grief unto thee, nor offense of heart" (v. 31). Spiritually minded, she suggested that he let God fight for him, and, in faith, she assured him that God would do just that: "The souls of thine enemies, them shall he sling out, as out of the middle of a sling" (v. 29). Honestly, and opportunely, she asked David to "remember" her after God dealt with Nabal (v. 31). David immediately recognized Abigail's extraordinary wisdom and understanding, as well as God's hand upon her life and in her meeting with him: "Blessed be the LORD God of Israel, who sent thee this day to meet me" (v. 32).

When only days later she entered David's home, her wisdom came with her, a fresh and deep well of knowledge for Judah's king-in-training to draw from. And that wasn't all. She also brought meekness. Humble and thankful, Abigail came not to command but to cooperate with her new husband, not to compete against but to complement his other wives and servants: "She...bowed herself on her face to the earth, and said...let thine handmaid be a servant to wash the feet of the servants of my lord" (v. 41). A beautiful, wise, and humble lover, Abigail was more than a good wife. She was a great wife, a grand wife—the best.

Gifts

A spiritual wife brings God-given gifts, both natural and spiritual, to her husband and marriage.

Naturally, her domestic talents, as fully described earlier in this chapter, greatly bless a man. Most men (including this writer) aren't gifted cooks, homemakers, shoppers, decorators, seamstresses, or launderers. Truly, he is favored by God who has a lovely wife to lovingly care for his house, plate, wardrobe, and, yes, his socks. (And cursed be the thickheaded dummy that leaves them laying around the house!) But that's not all.

Godly wives also come bearing spiritual gifts. Besides an abundance of natural wisdom, Abigail possessed a divine gift of prophecy, as did Miriam, Hannah, Huldah, Anna, and Phillip's daughters. With penetrating prophetic insight, Abigail beheld David, who at the time looked like he would never rule anything more noble than a Judean cave, and proclaimed him the next king of Israel, even foretelling that God would raise a long line of kings from his posterity: "The LORD will certainly make my lord *a sure house* [royal dynasty]...When the LORD shall have...appointed thee *ruler over Israel*" (1 Sam. 25:28, 30, emphasis added). From this example, we may infer that her Spirit-given ability to tell forth God's will and foretell future events proved a timely blessing to David in many of his later crises.

Other benefits

There are at least four more benefits of a good wife.

Companionship and *consortium* are very human, earthy marital benefits, desired by even some of the most deeply spiritual men. Moses apparently married a second wife (probably after Zipporah's death), an "Ethiopian woman" (Num. 12:1, KJV), apparently for human companionship. And after Sarah's death, Abraham married an obviously younger woman, Keturah, by whom he fathered six sons (Gen. 25:1–4).

Human support is yet another meaningful blessing. When a man is besieged by adversities—challenged in his work or ministry, maligned by adversaries, misjudged by friends, resisted by his children, tried in health, and so forth—it's very comforting and reassuring to come home to a loving, loyal wife. Whatever the prevailing instability, she's there, like a rock, always by him and for him and for no other.

And godly wives occasionally increase their husband's estate with valuable monetary or material *assets*. When Caleb's daughter, Achsah, married the first of Israel's judges, Othniel, her dowry included a choice tract of well-watered land (Judg. 1:12–15).

Now a few words about bad wives. In this fallen world, there are not only Abigails, Ruths, and Esthers, but also Michals, Jezebels, and Athaliahs. Generally, a foolish wife's ways and influence are precisely the opposite of those of a good wife.

For instance, rather than bringing joy, a bad wife fills her spouse's heart with grief. Instead of helping, she hinders, competing with her husband instead of completing him, denouncing him instead of delighting in him. Driven by selfishness, she regularly counsels folly, not wisdom, and argues for her self-will, not God's will. Rarely do her suggestions come from above. Carnally minded, she despises, ignores, and wastes her God-given gifts. Instead of prudently increasing her and her husband's wealth, she senselessly depletes it. Rather than buying appropriate necessities as needed, she misspends her financial resources on unnecessary purchases and worthless pursuits. Instead of bringing her husband warm companionship and pleasure, she troubles him with constant and inescapable contention, frustration, and discouragement: "The contentions of a wife are a continual dropping" (Prov. 19:13). Rather than graciously submit and cooperate with her husband's leadership, she domineers either by relentless open challenges or subtle, sometimes sexually based, manipulations. Instead of respecting, she reproaches him—to children, friends, neighbors, and anyone else who will listen. Thus she brings him dishonor, not honor. Such a wife systematically destroys her own man, marriage, family unit, and children: "Every wise woman buildeth her house, but *the fool-ish [wife] plucketh it down with her hands*" (Prov. 14:1, emphasis added). And ultimately she destroys herself!

For these reasons, O unmarried man, don't rush to the altar: "Seek not a wife [hastily or without confirmed prayerful guidance from God]" (1 Cor. 7:27). Consider these truths now, while you're still single. Though a good marriage is better than the single life, a bad marriage is definitely worse—"It is better to dwell in a cor-ner of the housetop [alone!], than with a brawling woman in a wide house" (Prov. 21:9)—and may prove disastrous. So approach marriage with a spiritual, not a carnal mind; let your spiritual, not sexual, urges drive you. Walk closely with God and ask Him to lead you to a virtuous woman. Then believe, wait, and watch for His leading: "And…before he had finished speaking…behold, Rebekah came out…And he said…I being in the way, the LORD led me…" (Gen. 24:15, 27). And no matter how hard loneliness presses in, never settle for anything less than a wife "from the LORD" (Prov. 18:22). Why?

Because ultimately the happiness of your marriage depends upon only one question: "Lord, is this marriage *Your* plan for me?"

Chapter Twenty-three

PEOPLE, PLANS, AND PROVIDENCE

*A*h, the optimistic visions of youth! How strongly within our hearts beat a thousand wannabes in the bright, cloudless morning of young adulthood. Yet few of us end up at life's end as we foresaw ourselves at its beginning. Thus the hopeful plans of this world's children often fail to materialize.

The same phenomenon is often seen in the lives of Christians. After Christ enters our hearts and the Spirit fills and thrills our whole being, whatever our age, we sense again the surging of irrepressible hope for the future—our new future in God. Then curiosity begins working. What will we do in, with, and for the One who has saved us? That is the pressing question for which we have no immediate definitive answer. So we observe other Christians and reflect and think and dream. Then we make our plans: We'll do this for His kingdom, or that for the saints, or something else for His glory! Excited, we begin working and praying and waiting and watching. Yet, strangely, as time passes, we notice that God is withholding His blessing. Why is our hope deferred? One of two things is occurring.

First, the vision or calling we are pursuing is truly God's

initiative and plan, but He is testing our faith, patience, and loyalty, and preparing us as His servants by letting us pass through a season of the "death"—strange contradictory defeat and fruitlessness—of the promise, vision, or calling. (See John 12:24.) If we will just remain faithful and believing, and patiently and persistently pray, in God's time God's vision will speak and not lie: "For the vision is yet for an appointed time, but at the end it shall speak, and not lie" (Hab. 2:3). And our end will be exactly as God enabled us to foresee it in the beginning. Until then, however, God wants us to learn to walk very closely and humbly with Him and trust Him to fulfill the vision in His time and way. Or, to put it in Bible language, "The just shall live by his faith" (v. 4).

The second possibility is that our plan, however good and well intended, is not God's plan. The Book of Proverbs wisely notes:

> There are many devices in a man's heart; nevertheless, the counsel of the LORD, that shall stand.
>
> —PROVERBS 19:21

Paraphrased, this proverb states:

> A man has many plans [dreams, hopes, desires, initiatives] of his own, but God's plan for his life is the one that will ultimately "stand"—permanently planted, prolific, and prosperous.

Other excellent translations help us get a better grip on the inner meaning of this verse. *The Amplified Bible* states, "Many plans are in a man's mind, but it is the Lord's purpose for him that will stand." *The Living Bible* reads, "Man proposes, but God disposes," that is, decides, arranges, places in order. Moffatt's *A New Translation of the Bible* says, "Man thinks out many a plan, but 'tis the Eternal's purpose that prevails." So we see that if our plan isn't God's, He must have another life-course for us, one that He will bless and that will bless others and us. Ponder these convincing biblical and historical illustrations of how people and their plans are often overruled by Providence.

PEOPLE, PLANS, AND PROVIDENCE

The Old Testament begins to tell us this story. Young Moses surely thought he was destined for Egypt's throne, but God's unseen guidance led him to become a mighty prophet and dynamic spiritual leader. Joseph seemed content to feed his father's flocks, yet God's plan, revealed in repeated dreams, was that he feed his family, Egypt, and all nations during a terrible worldwide famine. Saul, son of Kish, assumed his life's work would be breeding donkeys, yet God's ordination was that he become Israel's first king. David probably expected to make a career of shepherding, psalmody, or military command, yet God willed that he too rule as king of the chosen nation. Ahimaaz, conversely, was sure he would make a fine royal messenger, but Joab, David, and God thought just the opposite...and eventually asked him to step aside. Even after his ordination Amos thought of himself as a mere fruit-picker, yet God's eyes and heart foresaw, called, gifted, and memorialized him as a prophet. Elisha was apparently content to be a farmer, but when the nation's mightiest prophet, Elijah, cast his mantle upon him, Elisha recognized heaven had other plans. Ruth accepted the life and place of a poor, unmarried, female laborer, but God's idea was for her to be a wife of wealth and mother of honor. In all these lives, God's will was at some point recognized, accepted, and fully done.

The New Testament continues the testimony of the Old. If asked, both Peter and John would have declared their vocation as simply "fishermen," yet Providence, through the unexpected invitation of an upstart Nazarene prophet, led them suddenly and unmistakably into the fledgling Christian ministry. Matthew probably thought he would retire a publican, but divine guidance led him from the accountant's office to another marked

"Apostle." Young Saul of Tarsus surely saw himself as a career Pharisee expounding the Law, the Prophets, and the Writings exclusively to Jews for the rest of his life, but on the Damascus Road the command from above was that he bear Jesus' gospel before kings, Jews, and primarily Gentiles! And so it was.

Post-Acts church history adds many chapters to the story. Martin Luther's father just knew his son was born to be a lawyer. After this hope fizzled, Luther became convinced that the monastery would be his permanent home and monkery his lasting ministry. But God's plan all along was quite different—that Luther become a revelatory scholar, a knowledgeable teacher, a powerful writer, a controversial reformer, a devoted husband, and a father of five! Freshly graduated from Oxford and ordained an Anglican priest, John Wesley thought his remaining duties would be those of a typical minister, but the counsel of the Lord was that he be an itinerate preacher, an anointed revivalist, a prolific writer, and an exceptionally gifted church builder. D. L. Moody seemed destined to sell shoes the rest of his days—until Providence interrupted his plans and set him on course to become a powerful and prolific evangelist. Oswald Chambers saw his destiny as bringing a Christian influence to the world of art...until God audibly called him to His service and began reshaping him as a profound Christian thinker, unorthodox minister, and extraordinary Bible teacher. His wife, Biddy, as a young woman had mastered shorthand (275 words per minute!) in hopes of becoming secretary to the prime minister of England. But God's idea was for her to be Chamber's loving help-meet, raise a daughter, take verbatim notes of all her husband's lectures, and, *after* his unexpected home call at age forty-three, edit and produce *My Utmost for His Highest* and some fifty others of Chamber's books—"a worldwide library from nothing but shorthand notes and a typewriter." And His will, not hers, was done.

America's national history adds a few more illustrations. George Washington was quite content as a "country gentleman" farmer, but God's plan was to uproot him from his peaceful Virginia estate and use him as an able wartime military leader and a wise and humble head of state in times of transition and peace. Abraham Lincoln had no higher ambition than to be a successful merchant, lawyer, and legislator, but higher wisdom chose to use his calm demeanor, passion for social justice, will for national unity, faith in God, and memorable rhetorical skills to lead a fledgling republic through its fieriest trial to date. And so he was used.

For an appendage to this story, just look around you. Ask your father, mother, uncle, aunt, or neighbor to describe their career path or life story. In most cases, theirs was not a simple, straight road to vocational or professional bliss or personal fulfillment. Or ask your pastor, teacher, missionary, or bishop to tell you about their pathway to the ministry. They will probably tell you their first choice and their present calling were *not* the same. And let me add my testimony to theirs.

Personally, my hopes were to excel in music...until the Lord unexpectedly disrupted my plans and began slowly but surely preparing me to become something I had never before considered: a writer and Bible teacher. As those described above, I too eventually discovered that when my plans fell by the wayside, His plans "stood"—permanently planted, prolific, and prosperous. They're still standing as I write. And by grace, so am I. How about you, my brother or sister?

Have your personal career or life plans collapsed beyond the possibility of repair? And after much prayer and waiting on God, has the Spirit confirmed that your plans were not His? If so, then take heart, be still, and listen.

Jesus is calling to you across the stormy seas of your disrupted life-plans: "Be of good cheer. It is I; be not afraid" (Mark 6:50). Yes, that's right, it's Jesus, not mere human forces, that are guiding you! Whatever human malice, manipulation, or madness is present, behind it *He* is controlling your circumstances, causing "all things" to "work together" for *His* good plan for your life (Rom. 8:28). (See also Genesis 50:20.) And if He is uprooting your plans, it is only to establish His. He has brought you to this end to give you a new beginning. He has blocked your path only to change your direction. And that direction can only lead to something better. God's plans aren't just good, they're the best, always. So don't look down in hopeless dejection. Look up and behold your way of escape, your "ram caught in a thicket by his horns" (Gen. 22:13), the new, joyful God-thing that awaits you. Trust in the Lord with all your heart and lean not to your own understanding. With the above examples in mind, completely abandon yourself to God's loving wisdom and all-powerful control.

By faith, let your plans go, and go with Providence—God and His predestined, perfect, and unfailing plan for your life and work. If you do so, you will find that "the counsel of the Lord, that shall stand" (Prov. 19:21). And you will stand with it, firmly planted. And your works will stand, blessing others. Then they will stand, doing God's will. And their works will help God's kingdom stand, forever. And you will rejoice!

And one day you will realize that God is making you a leader.

Chapter Twenty-four

TWO KEYS TO GOOD LEADERSHIP

*G*od seeks to accomplish a deep and abiding work in those He prepares to be leaders, whether their leadership is in the home, church, community, or nation. Why?

He does so to ensure that their leadership will bless, not curse, those they lead; that they will lead others in right, not wrong, paths. Also, He wants their benevolent leadership to last a long time, maximizing both their joy as leaders and the blessings of those they lead. Furthermore, He wants to receive honor for giving His people wise and caring leaders and to rejoice in their enduring godly prosperity. A monarch, monarch's son, and monarch's father, King Solomon was well qualified to discourse on matters of leadership.

Among the many proverbs he spoke and expounded, one specifically highlights two great keys of good leadership, mercy and truth:

> Mercy and truth preserve the king, and his throne is upheld by mercy.
>
> —PROVERBS 20:28

Paraphrased, this pearl of wisdom states:

> Merciful kindness and truthfulness [honesty and faithfulness] preserve the king [from harm], and by showing mercy he [maintains and] secures his moral authority, governing effectiveness, and full term of office.

Expounding this further, we may conclude that if a ruler consistently treats his (or her) people with kindness and honesty, demonstrating real respect for them and humble self-esteem, God will protect him. And by dealing kindly with his people, the ruler will command their respect and loyalty, thus securing his influence and position and protracting his and his people's joint prosperity.

Such behavior from an authority presupposes certain things. It assumes that he (or she) has real love, genuine humility, and a shepherd's heart—a mind-set that seeks and serves the welfare of his people first, before his own desires. Jesus encapsulated this philosophy of the ideal leader in His memorable sayings: "The Son of man came not to be ministered unto, but to minister, and to give" (Matt. 20:28); and, "The good shepherd giveth his life for the sheep" (John 10:11). The apostle Paul's heart was also gripped with this passion when he wrote, "I will very gladly spend and be spent for you; though the more abundantly I love you, the less I be loved" (2 Cor. 12:15). It was this selfless shepherd's love that frequently moved him to put himself in harm's way rather than fail to carry out his divinely ordained ministry to the churches.

Paul's ministerial trainee, Timothy, was also driven by the love of God. Of him Paul wrote, "I have no [other] man likeminded, who will naturally care for your state" (Phil 2:20). For most of his reign Solomon had this divine love, for during the Queen of Sheba's renowned state visit to Solomon's kingdom she observed, "Happy are thy men, happy are these thy servants...Blessed be the LORD thy God, who delighted in thee, to set thee on the throne of Israel. *Because the LORD loved*

Israel . . . therefore made he thee king, to execute justice and righteousness" (1 Kings 10:8–9, emphasis added). But we must also consider the opposite side of this shining pearl of wisdom.

It is equally true that callousness and falsehood put a king at risk, undermine his authority, and, if continued, bring both his reign and nation to ruin. Jewish history demonstrates that leaders who through hardheartedness and pride ignore their people's pressing needs and lie to them always lose their authority, eventually if not immediately. Strangely, Solomon himself also exemplified this implied darker side of our text. In his later years, Solomon turned to idolatry and, having broken fellowship with God, began to oppress the very people he had so greatly blessed. Thus the once-righteous leader became a ruinous misleader, promoting the falsehood of idolatry instead of the truth of God. After his death, his people protested to his son King Rehoboam, "Thy father [callously] made our yoke [tax burden] grievous" (1 Kings 12:4). Lacking in both mercy and wisdom, Rehoboam wasted no time in following his father's footsteps in folly. When the people asked him for a lighter tax burden, he arrogantly dismissed them with cruel words that swiftly boomeranged, bringing home a cruel and humanly unforeseeable surprise: ten of Israel's twelve tribes immediately defected, leaving Rehoboam with only two of the tribes his fathers had ruled. So his once-glorious throne ingloriously collapsed.

The dismal failures of the elderly Solomon and his youthful son Rehoboam were each threefold losses. First, the people lost benevolent, truth-loving leadership, as their kings' love and honesty turned to selfishness and hypocrisy. Second, two redeemed kings once beloved of God (especially Solomon; see 1 Kings 3:10) lost their moral authority and hence their ability to influence their people for God. And third, God lost the joy He otherwise would have had over His people's continuing godly unity, peace, prosperity, and joy and the glory He would have received had His two kings finished their courses of leadership in mercy and truth. So not only the blessings of kings and generations but also the blessing of God—His personal joy—fell by the wayside of history, another grand opportunity lost.

If we aspire to use and not waste our opportunities to serve God's people and bless and honor Him, we must fully understand and frequently practice mercy and truthfulness.

Mercy is kindness above and beyond what is fair. Showing mercy means doing something you don't have to do by normal standards of behavior. You make an exception, give something extra, waive your rights, or forbear, letting patience have her perfect work. Unloving leaders are always unworthy leaders and poor shepherds. To lead sheep, we must love sheep. The day we stop loving them, we begin misleading them, regardless of our previous anointing and fruitfulness. (See Proverbs 28:16; Ecclesiastes 10:16–17.) We stop focusing on ministering and look only to be ministered to. Pride rises and humility declines. Compassion wanes and callousness grows. And soon, just as this proverb warns, we've lost our "throne"—that is, the moral authority necessary to lead—or we've lost our office itself. Admittedly, most sheep aren't rocket scientists, but they know when their shepherd cares—and when he doesn't: "The hireling…careth not for the sheep" (John 10:13).

Like mercy, truth is required if we aspire to be good shepherds. We must face and speak the truth about everything: ourselves, family members, friends, the church, our nation, doctrines, fads, deceptions, genuine works of God, and so forth. We must also constantly seek and study eternal truth—God's Word—and then persistently obey it and share it with those we lead. We must never allow hypocrisy in ourselves or our associates, and we must always honor honesty, humility, and faithfulness. We must furthermore be thoroughly true, or faithful. If we make vows, we must keep them. If we accept responsibilities, we must discharge them. If we start tasks in God's will, we must finish them with God's help. If we sin, fail, or err in judgment, we must confess it immediately to God and to all people who are involved. And, finally, we must uphold the truth.

That is, we must courageously stand by true, not false witnesses. And we must insist that the high and authoritative standards of God's Word—"his righteousness" (Matt. 6:33)—be honored and obeyed in our personal "kingdom," or *sphere of personal influence*, making exceptions for none due to fear or favoritism. Such conduct keeps us living and leading in the truth: walking in the light, leading others into the light, and serving them in the light of God's favor. It also keeps us on our "throne," that is, securely in the position of authority, and the moral authority of that position, in which God has providentially placed us.

Now, Mr. "king," or Miss or Mrs. "queen," that is, *one in a position of authority or influence*, let me ask you a question. Whatever your title or position of authority—father, husband, mother, bishop, superintendent, pastor, teacher, mentor, elder, mayor, governor, congressman, judge, president—and whatever your "kingdom," *do you want to retain the authority God has given you and continue being a blessing to people?* Then heed, hallow, and hold fast Proverbs 20:28. That is, be kind, considerate, honest, and faithful in dealing with your subordinates, whether pastors, congregants, wives, children, students, constituents, litigants, or citizens. Never ignore their suffering. Never lie to them. Never be unfaithful to them. Never treat them unfairly. And if you should fail them, say so. Such living under God's authority puts you in God's authority. (See Matthew 8:9.) Then, like Christ's and the prophets' words, your sayings will be "with power," or spiritually explosive, deeply impacting, and permanent in influence.

In that day, God will personally cause your subordinates to respond to His authority vested in you—the supreme, irresistible power of love and truth: "Thy people shall be willing in the day of thy power" (Ps. 110:3). They will heed and hold your teaching. They will walk and minister in your ways in Christ. They will rejoice with you in victory, stand by you in adversity, and defend you before your accusers: "They shall speak with the enemies in the gate" (Ps. 127:5). In short, because you have first loved them, they will love you. And if at times they resist the truth you present, or the position or course you have taken in God's will (just as you and I have sometimes done to our leaders in the past), they will eventually recognize the correctness of your position and yield to the powerful, persistent persuasiveness of truth mercifully presented. And that's not all.

The King of kings Himself will pronounce a heavenly benediction upon you, His developing co-regent, the wise words He inspired Solomon's counselors to speak to Rehoboam:

> If thou wilt be a servant unto [the welfare of] this people this day, and wilt serve them [their needs], and answer them, and speak good [kind] words to them, then they will be thy servants [responsive to your godly authority] forever.
>
> —1 KINGS 12:7

Meanwhile, if you find you need some motivation, remember what happened to King Rehoboam when he *rejected* the foregoing heavenly counsel! A little holy fear never hurt, and always helps, any of us!

Specifically, it helps us bridle our tongues.

Chapter Twenty-five

WATCH YOUR WORDS!

*T*he Bible in general and the Book of Proverbs in particular have much to say about human speech. A vitally important issue, our talk can help or haunt us, bless or break others, and honor or dishonor God. Hence, God's Spirit aspires to teach us to speak rightly.

Specifically, His goal is to "bridle" our tongue, or *bring our words under His control.* If we will let Him, He will guide us ever so sensitively in what, when, how, and to whom we speak. In the Book of James, which unofficially is the proverbs of the New Testament, James teaches that a bridled tongue is a hallmark of a mature Christian: "If any man offend not in word, the same is a perfect [spiritually mature] man" (James 3:2). He also says a consistently unbridled, or uncontrolled, tongue is evidence of either self-deception or outright hypocrisy: "If any man among you seem to be religious, and bridleth not his tongue, but deceiveth his own heart, this man's religion is vain" (James 1:26). So he concludes we should listen carefully, think patiently, and then speak calmly: "Wherefore...let every man be swift to hear, slow to speak" (v. 19). Nothing new, James' findings simply restate the substance of many similar Old Testament declarations.

Among its numerous memorable sayings touching on our speech, the Book of Proverbs notes:

> Whoso keepeth his mouth and his tongue, keepeth his soul from troubles.
>
> —PROVERBS 21:23

Paraphrased, this pearly insight says:

> Whoever watches [guards, attends to] what he puts in his mouth [harmful or excessive food, drink, drugs, smoke] and what he says [ever speaking discreetly] will spare his soul from [needless and excessive] troubles [of mind, body, and life].

The word *keepeth*, used twice in this verse, is taken from the Hebrew word *shamar*, which means literally "to hedge about," and by extension, "to guard, protect, attend to, or watch."

We usually "hedge about," or watch and guard, things that we consider vital. Our mouths are certainly vital. With them we eat and drink and breathe—and live. But if on a regular basis we eat unhealthy foods, overeat, drink too much alcoholic beverages, take illegal drugs, exceed our prescription of legal drugs, smoke or chew tobacco, inhale bad air, or breathe toxic fumes, our troubles will increase and our health and happiness decrease. Why? Because we didn't guard our mouths.

We also *shamar* anything we consider very valuable or dangerous. For instance, heads of state, gold reserves, jewel or art collections, these precious things are closely guarded round the clock. Very destructive things, too, such as, radioactive materials, secret weapons, and nuclear missiles, are incessantly surveilled. Again, bringing this lesson home, the tongue—or our faculty of speech—is both valuable *and* volatile. Arguably our most precious assets, our tongues enable us to praise and worship God, share the gospel, profess our faith, confess our sins, communicate our thoughts and feelings, fellowship with friends, instruct, buy, sell, and work. Yet our words are also our greatest liability.

Hence this proverb points out the fact that, while some of our problems and trials arise because of our faith in or loyalty to God, others, perhaps many, arise because of loose speech—mocking, complaining, inconsiderate, arrogant, angry, condemning, revengeful, slanderous, flirtatious, or fearful talk. If we eliminate these problematic words, we eliminate the problems they create, which are unnecessary, unmeritorious, and reproachful in nature. That is, such problems don't have to occur, and God does not want them to occur. They do not win us any rewards and may cause us to lose some. And they bring shame, not honor, to the One whose great name and honor is at stake in our lives. Plainly, it is not God's will that we become snared in these verbal pitfalls. And we won't, if we *shamar* our tongues. How do we do that?

First, we should stay very close to Jesus. To try to conquer the troubles of our tongues without leaning on the Savior of our speech is to find frustration, not fulfillment, and vexation, not victory. Why? Because the full mastery of speech is humanly impossible: "The tongue can no [mere] man tame [bring under control]; it is an unruly evil, full of deadly poison" (James 3:8). Only *Christ in us* can fully master it. It is therefore a task we must take on with, not without Him. With Him, we can do "all things through Christ, who strengtheneth [us] [gives us of His own personal ability to overcome]" (Phil. 4:13). Without Him, well, to put it in His own words, "Without me ye can do nothing" (John 15:5).

Second, we should keep a close watch on our thoughts and emotions. Whatever they are, the thoughts and feelings that consistently occupy our hearts will eventually come right out of our mouths, ready or not. With unerring eternal wisdom, the Great Psychologist decreed, "Those things which proceed out of the mouth come forth from the heart" (Matt. 15:18). So to guard our mouth well we must diligently guard our "heart," or inward thinking and feeling: "Keep your heart with all diligence, for out of it spring the issues of life" (Prov. 4:23, NKJV)

Third, we must develop spiritual discretion. From the worldly standpoint, to speak discreetly is to be careful, not careless, about what one says. Spiritual discretion adds one more element to this worldly discipline, namely, letting the *Holy Spirit* rule our words, determining the substance, spirit, and timing of what we say. If we humbly yield to His subtle but distinct voice, He will gradually teach us to speak in a manner always pleasing to God. Eventually, we will consistently speak the truth in love, not in anger; correct with hope, not condemnation; warn with the fear of God, not threats. Note how the Paraclete instructs us.

If we will listen, He will teach us when to speak. Have we learned that there are moments when people are "ripe" for the right words, primed and ready to hear what we've been praying and waiting to say? "Sirs, what must I do to be saved?" (Acts 16:30). At such times, previously rejected words are presently received. Why? Because the words were different? No, because the time was different—and right. It was God's time: "To every thing there is a season, and a time to every purpose under the heaven…*a time to speak*" (Eccles. 3:1, 7, emphasis added). He will also show us how much to speak. Sometimes people have heard enough before we feel we have said enough. At such moments, the Spirit will check us, and, if we're wise, we'll stop speaking—in mid-sentence, if necessary. He will furthermore show us when we should say nothing at all, when it is time to keep our blessed mouths blessedly shut! "[There is] *a time to keep silence*" (Eccles. 3:7, emphasis added). In such moments, by saying nothing we accomplish something: we prepare the way for the Holy Spirit to open future "doors of utterance" by which our listeners will be helped, by us or by others, and God pleased.

However finely tuned our spiritual discretion, there will still be times when even our most gracious words will spark grievous troubles. But such tribulations, unlike those described in our text, are necessary, meritorious, and glorifying to God. That is, they are a part of God's plan for our life and necessary for our spiritual growth and maturation. They are also worthy of merit or reward in God's sight, and if we endure them in faith and patience, we will win divine approval for broader service, larger blessings, and promotions. And they bring honor to the Lord's name and deeply please Him if we "stand fast," loyal, loving, and laboring, in such fiery trials.

Take the incident recorded in Daniel 3 for an example. When commanded to worship Nebuchadnezzar's golden idol, Shadrach, Meshach, and Abednego uttered these incendiary yet inspired words:

> O Nebuchadnezzar, we are not careful [anxious] to answer thee in this matter. If it be so, our God, whom we serve, is able to deliver us from the burning fiery furnace, and he will deliver us out of thine hand, O king. But if not, be it known unto thee, O king, that *we will not serve thy gods, nor worship the golden image which thou hast set up [under any conditions]*.
> —DANIEL 3:16–18, EMPHASIS ADDED

Though personally placed in their mouths by the Spirit of the Immortal One Himself, their heavenly words brought them immediate, immense, and intensely hellish trouble. Their woes arose, therefore, not because of a stupid failure of discretion but because of a wise triumph of faith in and loyalty to God. They were not alone in their mastery of the art of bold speaking.

When the prophet Micaiah relayed his heavenly vision and message to Israel's King Ahab, he was promptly slapped (or punched!) by one of his hostile ministerial peers, the false prophet Zedekiah, and then mockingly sent off to prison by the most powerful—and deluded—man in the nation, King Ahab! When the Jewish leaders commanded the apostles to stop speaking and teaching in Jesus' name, the apostles "ceased not to teach and preach Jesus Christ" (Acts 5:42). In short order their holy words brought upon them horrific persecution, as Stephen was killed and many other Christians were either killed (2,000 according to *Foxe's Book of Martyrs*) or driven out of Jerusalem into neighboring provinces. (See Acts 6:9; 8:1–3.) When pressed to deny or disclose His deity, Jesus boldly declared He was indeed God's Son. Then the Jewish religious leaders promptly denounced Him as a demon-possessed Samaritan and began passionately plotting his death. (See John 8:48.) When the Holy Roman Emperor Charles V ordered Martin Luther to recant his radical but biblical teachings at the Diet of Worms, Luther refused, standing by his problematic words. For this stand, the pope excommunicated and denounced him as a "wild boar in the vineyard of the Lord," and Luther was thereafter hunted for execution and forced for a time to live in hiding.

In each of these examples, great professions of faith and truth, spoken graciously, opportunely, and with inspiration, caused great problems. No matter when, where, how, or to whom they said it, all these suffered for *what* they said, for speaking undiluted truth rightly divided to people who had come to hate the truth: "Take, my brethren, the prophets who have spoken in the name of the Lord, for an example of suffering affliction, and of patience" (James 5:10). This chapter reproves, not such heavenly inspirations, but human indiscretions.

So watch your words, my friend! With the Holy Spirit's help, hedge about and rule over your tongue. Stay very close to the Savior of your speech. Quickly expel the inward drivers of wrong speech: wrong thoughts, attitudes, and emotions. And let the Holy Spirit guide you whenever you speak. Then three great rewards will be yours.

First, Jesus will be pleased with you and will in some way commend you: "A man shall be commended according to his wisdom" (Prov. 12:8). Second, He will reward you, "Well done, thou good and faithful servant…I will make thee ruler over many things" (Matt. 25:21). And third, your words will no longer cause you needless, excessive troubles: "Whoso keepeth…his tongue, keepeth his soul from troubles." And that will make you one very happy Christian!

What a timely tonic! You'll need to be very happy to deal graciously with those who make indolence a way of life.

Chapter Twenty-six

THE SLOTH ETHIC

*E*veryone has a god, even if it's self. Everyone has a master, even if it's sin. And everyone has a belief, even if it's unbelief.

Similarly, everyone has an ethic, or rule or code of conduct by which he lives or works in the various fields of life. We readily accept that industrious people are driven by their "work ethic," but we may not realize that lazy people also have a clearly identifiable psychological driver. It is the "sloth ethic."

There are no less than eighteen references to laziness, described either as "slothfulness" or the ways of the "slothful" or "sluggard," in the Book of Proverbs. Along with its inspired commentaries on such ruinous vices as immorality, ignorance, indiscretion, alcoholism, pride, envy, lying, and vengeance, Proverbs cites indolence as one of the primary ways of folly and identifier of fools. One of its more interesting observations states:

> The desire of the slothful killeth him; for his hands refuse to labor. He coveteth greedily all the day long, but the righteous giveth and spareth not.
>
> —PROVERBS 21:25–26

211

Paraphrased, these precious pearls of knowledge teach:

> A lazy man's heart desires will eventually kill him, because [craving ease and comfort excessively] he surely will not work [and hence has little, and withholds due payments and needed donations]. But he will surely want [everything he sees, hears, and thinks of] all day long, while [by contrast] a man whose soul and living are right before God [works steadily all day long, and] gives [generously] and does not withhold [due payments and needed gifts].

Contrasted in these pithy sayings are the opposite lifestyles of indolence and diligence and the differing desires that drive them.

Examined first are the hearts of these two types of persons. The "desire" (lit. *longing*) of the slothful refers to the dominant desires residing in his heart—not his blood-pumping muscle, but his spiritual core, the nucleus of his personality, the center of his being and true source of his behavior. Jesus taught that whatever we are, say, or do is a direct result of whatever rests in our hearts: "Those things which proceed out of the mouth come forth from the heart" (Matt. 15:18). So our dominant desires determine who we are and drive everything we do. The heart desires of these two types of people, the lazy and the diligent, are key—and utterly different. One has the desires of a saint; the other of a slob. Let's consider other truths implied or stated in our text.

Implicitly, these proverbs reveal that laziness is sin, or rebellion against God's revealed will that sane, able-bodied people should work. Every human conscience innately records that the Creator made us to be about our business. We are here not just to live but also to labor, not just to enjoy pleasures but also to engage in productivity. Scripture corroborates this inborn revelation of conscience in both the Old and New Testaments. The psalmist wrote, "The sun riseth... [and] man goeth forth unto his work and to his labor until the evening" (Ps. 104:22–23). And the apostle Paul commanded Christians to be "not slothful in business; [but] fervent in spirit; serving the Lord" (Rom. 12:11). Indeed, the entire Word of God criticizes laziness and commends labor.

Jesus, who was God's self-revelation to mankind, revealed God as a working God and Himself as the laboring Son of His laboring Father: "My Father worketh hitherto, and I work" (John 5:17). As a boy, Jesus helped his supposed father, Joseph, in his carpenter's shop. As a young man, and after Joseph's death, Jesus continued Joseph's woodworking business in Nazareth. At age thirty, Jesus laid aside His manual labor to take up His ministerial labor and spend the rest of his days on earth busily engaged in teaching, preaching, and healing the sick and afflicted: "From that time Jesus began to preach, and...went about all Galilee, teaching in their synagogues, and preaching the gospel of the kingdom, and healing all manner of sickness and all manner of disease among the people" (Matt. 4:17, 23). His own words reveal that His personal satisfaction was inextricably linked to His labors: "*My food [soul satisfaction] is* to do the will of him that sent me, and *to finish his work*" (John 4:34, emphasis added). He also said that God has given Christians, His redeemed adopted children, specific works to fulfill in life: "For the Son of man is like a man taking a far journey, who left his house, and *gave...to every man his work*" (Mark 13:34, emphasis added). If God's Word reveals that He is a worker, His Son is a worker, and He has given us works to do, our refusal to work is rebellion against God's revealed will. Hence, laziness is sin.

THE COMPANION SINS OF SLOTHFULNESS

Our text from Proverbs 21:25–26 also reveals six companion sins, or sins that always accompany a slothful heart.

1. Most obviously, lazy people simply and stubbornly reject work: "...his hands *refuse* to labor" (emphasis added). This refers not to inability but unwillingness to perform any labor, either for pay or to maintain one's

possessions in good repair. (See Proverbs 24:30–34.) Why? Slothful ones crave ease and comfort, and they sleep excessively. They are irresponsible, refusing to carry their own weight financially. And they are selfish, completely unconcerned with helping truly needy people. (We must not confuse these obstinate unemployables with those who are innocently unemployed due to war, a poor economy, physical sickness, mental or emotional illness, injury, youth, or agedness.)

2. Wherever there is laziness there is covetousness: "...he *coveteth* greedily" (emphasis added). Despite their aversion for honest wage earning, slothful people are avidly hungry for money and the material things it buys. Besides being the root of all kinds of evil, excessive craving for money is a violation of the tenth commandment, "Thou shalt not covet...anything" (Exod. 20:17).

3. Wherever slothfulness is, idleness is also. Note the sluggard covets greedily "all the day long." This implies he regularly wastes his workdays. When he should be industrious, he's inactive; when he should be doing, he's dreaming; when he should be focused, he's faraway somewhere lost in the idle thoughts of his indolent heart. Idleness is always the flip side of the coin of irresponsibility. If we don't use our work time rightly, we misuse it.

4. Lazy people invariably become financially delinquent. Note the contrast in our text. The righteous man "spareth not," that is, he does *not* withhold payments that are due. By contrast, we may infer that the slothful person does withhold paying his bills. This makes sense. If he refuses to work, he lacks an income. He then lacks financial resources, so he doesn't pay his bills and excuses his negligence, saying, "Sorry, I don't have the money."

5. Lazy people withhold tithes and offerings from God's house. By refusing to earn an income, they deny their hardworking pastor and church the tithe of their income, not to mention the offerings they could otherwise give to God's work. In God's sight, their plight is not pitiful but pitiless. In fact, He goes so far as to call it a criminal act, specifically robbery! "Will a man *rob* God? Yet ye have *robbed* me...in [withholding your] tithes and offerings" (Mal. 3:8, emphasis added).

6. Slothful ones don't give to the poor when God gives them opportunities to do so. Why? To give they must have, and to have they must work—and they've ruled out the work option! So they can't give to the needy.

Besides these undesirable manifestations, our text also discloses the surprising lethality of laziness: "The desire of the slothful *killeth him*" (Prov. 21:25, emphasis added); or "the sluggard's craving *will be the death of him*" (NIV, emphasis added). Most of us would readily agree that laziness causes trouble, but *death?* That seems a bit strong. Will laziness really kill us? Immediately, no; eventually, yes. Why? Because turning off the highway of labor puts us on the road to ruination: "There is a way that seemeth right unto a man, but the end thereof are the ways of death" (Prov. 16:25). For instance, laziness leads to unemployment, which leads in turn to financial indebtedness, desperation, and despair; and that may result in foolish or criminal behavior, excessive danger, and premature death or suicide. Want confirmation? Read your newspaper.

How many obituaries would have been deferred ten, twenty, thirty, or forty years, if only the subjects had chosen diligence over slothfulness at an early age? Steady work would have kept them from the idleness that spawned their depressing descent into destruction. Review their biographical sketches backwards,

215

from finish to start, and see what you find at the beginning of their death trek. How many get-rich-quick schemers have lived get-ruined-quick lives? How many who would not patiently work for a decent living turned instead to fraud, embezzlement, theft, robbery, or drug trafficking, and ended up with lengthy prison sentences? How many have been driven to kill to obtain unjust wealth—and have ultimately killed themselves by causing their own capital punishments? What drives otherwise normal people to such abnormal extremes and sensible souls to such senseless behavior? Greed? Yes. Poor choices? Yes. Bad friends? Surely. Poor parenting? Probably. But unquestionably, one key factor is the sloth ethic: they just won't work! Let's examine this in greater detail.

The lazy person is infected with a twisted view of himself, others, and the historic pattern of life in this world. He (or she) never accepts the most basic and timeless truth of adult society: we must work to live. Arrogantly, he feels he can circumvent this common way, that he can have wealth without work, gain without pain, even luxury without labor. Ignorantly, he ignores the examples of what laziness has done to people all around him. Pitying himself, he feels that because he, his family, nation, or race has experienced injustices in life, real or imagined, someone else—parents, relatives, the wealthy, the government, anyone, everyone!—owes him a living. Envying others, he boils with angry discontentment at others having and enjoying the things he wants but will not earn. Also dubbed the "welfare mentality," this toxic mixture of arrogance, ignorance, self-pity, and envy consumes his healthy desire to work, earn, and provide. (This is not intended to condemn those who, as stated previously, for legitimate reasons need temporary government assistance to help them through extraordinary adversities, but to expose those who seek to make a career of it.) So his hands refuse to work. So he wants. So he doesn't pay his bills. So he doesn't give to God or share with men. And so he is a fool, or one who consistently chooses to believe lies instead of truths and so deceives himself. But he doesn't fool God or the wise.

"But the righteous giveth and spareth not," our text adds, contrasting the philosophy and lifestyle of the wise. Observant, the wise notice the ways of hard workers all around them. Humble, they accept that they too must work to live. Responsible, they diligently pay their bills and tithes. Generous, they give offerings. Thankful, they refuse to pity themselves, choosing to count their blessings rather than mourn their disadvantages. Honest, they acknowledge that no ones owes them anything. Believing the gospel, they realize they owe *God* everything—their spirit, body, and labor! So they work, demonstrating John Wesley's doctrine, "Earn all you can; save all you can; give all you can." And daily their good works shine in this dark and confused world.

Despite these luminous examples of healthy industry, the sloth ethic remains very real, very deadly, and very universal. So never again think lightly of laziness. Never tolerate it in yourself or indulge it in others. Don't lust to expose others' indolence, but ever leap to expel it from yourself. Lovingly exhort friends, family, and fellow Christians if they begin succumbing to sloth: "Exhort one another daily...lest any of you be hardened through the deceitfulness of sin" (Heb. 3:13). Who knows? Yours may be the antibiotic words that, when injected into their minds, save them from the lethal disease of laziness. (See James 5:19–20.) Intercede for those who buy into the lie of laziness, that God will goad them to diligence. And remember, our working heavenly Father has left us here on earth not just to believe in Him but also to walk and work with Him.

The Father finished His work of creation and rested on the seventh day. Jesus finished His work and rests now at the Father's right hand. Let's finish our work and enter into the rest of the righteous.

Let's work at knowing God ever more deeply. Let's work at pursuing our calling and finishing it. Let's work at studying the Bible to show ourselves approved unto God. Let's work at intercession until our prayers change individuals, families, cities, and nations. Let's work at worship until God's presence powerfully inhabits our praises. Let's work at demonstrating Jesus—His mercy, truth, holiness, justice, and wisdom—to a world that doesn't know Him and will never know Him this side of Armageddon unless it sees Him walking and working in the earth *in us.*

And as we adopt this, God's work ethic, let's remember that the Son of God is working with us: "And they went forth...*the Lord working with them*" (Mark 16:20, emphasis added). With His constant help, and by His amazing grace, we will one day finish our greatest work: glorifying Him! And in that day we will say with Him:

> Father...*I have glorified thee* on the earth; *I have finished the work* which thou gavest me to do.
> —JOHN 17:1, 4, EMPHASIS ADDED

If we persistently practice it, God's work ethic will prepare us for the greatest event of our times—the appearing of Jesus Christ!

Chapter Twenty-seven

PREACHING AND PRACTICING PRUDENT PREPARATION

*S*ome well-meaning Christians mistake caution for fear of evil. But proper caution is evidence of wisdom, not fear. Fear is unbelief, or lack of trust in God, and is never wise. Do we understand the difference between prudent preparation, which is foreseeing and faithful, and fearful forethought, which is foreseeing and faithless?

Jesus clearly condemned the latter. He lived by a one-day-at-a-time philosophy based on the comprehensive care and ability of His heavenly Father to meet all His earthly needs. And in His loving lectures, He advised us to do the same. "Take therefore no [anxious] thought for the morrow" (Matt. 6:34, KJV) was His watchword to all His followers, yesterday, today, and forever! Resounding this theme, the apostle Paul's sweeping injunction to the church is, "Be anxious for nothing," followed by his recommendation that we follow the wiser way of trusting in God, "but in everything, by prayer and supplication with thanksgiving, let your requests be made known unto God" (Phil. 4:6). Together these sacred sayings teach us we should deal with today's problems today, trusting God to guide and help us through believing

219

prayer, but we should never worry or fret ourselves because of what we imagine will be tomorrow's problems. Jesus concluded, "Be, therefore, not anxious about tomorrow; for tomorrow will be anxious for the things of itself" (Matt. 6:34). But does this command to not *worry* today about tomorrow mean we are not at all to *think or work* today to prepare for tomorrow?

No. Solomon, the wisest man who ever lived, makes it clear that God wants us to be prudent, or *careful, cautious, and exercising good judgment in preparing for foreseeable future occurrences.* In the Book of Proverbs Solomon preached prudent preparation, writing:

> A prudent man foreseeth the evil, and hideth himself; but the simple pass on, and are punished.
> —PROVERBS 22:3

Paraphrased, this pearl of truth tells us:

> A person who is prudent [reasonably and wisely foreseeing] recognizes approaching troubles and prepares for them [trusting God to then help and bless his efforts] and so hides [covers, protects] himself [from needless harm, loss, or failure]; but someone who is simple [careless, thoughtless, or naïve] walks straight into trouble unprepared, and suffers for it.

This truism, which is repeated verbatim in Proverbs 27:12 for emphasis, illustrates a key point of both worldly and biblical wisdom. Everywhere in life and in Scripture prudent preparation is commended and unwise unpreparedness condemned.

If you have any sense at all, you prepare yourself, your family, and your property when a powerful tornado or hurricane bears down on your community. If a nation has any prudence in these perilous times, it is busy making its passengers, ports, and borders as secure as possible against terrorists. When a long-quiet volcano begins rumbling and spewing steam and ash daily, wise nearby residents evacuate. When winter comes to the upper elevations of the North American Rocky Mountains or the European Alps, observant mountaineers and tourists begin preparing and watching for blizzards, drifts, and avalanches. When a nation's economy plunges into a deep recession without any signs of quick recovery, sensible individuals and corporate leaders do not take on large new amounts of unnecessary debt. When a wise nation sees another nation's military forces poised to attack its border, it readies its military forces and initiates a preemptive strike. When a besieged and dismantled combatant nation realizes its military defeat is impending and unavoidable, if it is foreseeing, it sues for peace rather than blindly fighting on to utter annihilation. When a young wife becomes pregnant, she and her husband are wise to immediately begin planning, buying, and preparing for their upcoming venture into parenthood. When we are elderly, it's prudent to clear our debts and make arrangements for our passing, so that our families will not be excessively burdened by our departure. But not all people are foreseeing and proactive. As stated in our text, the "simple" prefer to ignore indicators of imminent change, especially when they announce that "evil," or trouble, is on the way.

"A prudent man foreseeth the *evil*..." (emphasis added). The Hebrew word here translated "evil" means literally something *bad*, naturally or morally. It connotes anything unpleasant, adverse, unjust, troublesome, dangerous, or trying. Many Christians get very uncomfortable, even agitated, when told they must face adverse things, imagining that if they ignore them they will evade them. But God's Word takes quite the opposite approach. From cover to cover, the Bible is filled with warnings, not denials, of approaching adversity. It teaches preparation and faith, not as conflicting but as complementary practices. In Scripture, it's not preparation *or* trust, but preparation *and* trust. Always, the infallible word of faith urges us to make wise and full preparations now for all our approaching battles, natural or spiritual: "The horse is prepared for the day of battle" (Prov. 21:31). Yet with equal emphasis it urges us to remember, and fully trust, that, even with our best preparations in place, God alone determines if our efforts succeed or fail: "But safety [victory, deliverance, rescue] is from the LORD [alone]" (v. 31).

One of the Bible's most princely characters, Joseph, was hailed by men and honored by God, not for denying Pharaoh's dark dream and its ominous prediction of an approaching seven-year famine, but for helping the Egyptians, the Israelites, and really, the whole world, prudently prepare for it: "Now therefore let Pharaoh seek out a man discreet and wise, and...let Pharaoh do this...gather all the food of those good years that come, and lay up grain...and that food shall be for storage in the land against the seven years of famine" (Gen. 41:33–36). Moreover, God's prime spokesperson, Jesus, openly promised Christians that evil would come our way.

In John's Gospel, Jesus pledged, "In the world *ye shall have tribulation*" (John 16:33, emphasis added). In Mark's, He promised that we would be widely detested for professing Him: "*Ye shall be hated of all men* for my name's sake" (Mark 13:13, emphasis added). In Luke's, He warned we would be ostracized for our commitment to Him: "Blessed are ye, when men shall...*separate you from their company*" (Luke 6:22, emphasis added). In the same verse, He also warned that we would be bitterly criticized: "Blessed are ye, when men shall...*reproach you*" (emphasis added). And He foretold that we would at some point suffer betrayal, or surprising bitter attacks from formerly close friends: "*Ye shall be betrayed* both by parents, and brethren, and kinsfolk, and friends" (Luke 21:16, emphasis added). He further prophesied that, due to our loyalty to His Word and calling, some of our families would be split right down the middle: "Suppose ye that I am come to give peace on earth? I tell you, Nay; but rather division; for from *henceforth there shall be five in one house, divided*; three against two, and two against three" (Luke 12:51–52, emphasis added). He compared these and other exceptionally strong trials of faith to spiritual hurricanes, forecasting that we would at times be psychologically and emotionally pounded by the brutal pressures—"winds, rains, and floods"— of adversity. (See Matthew 7:24–27; Luke 6:47–48.) Through the pen of James, the risen Christ told us to rejoice, not reel, repent, and reverse our courses, when we meet these and other "various trials" (James 1:2–4). Through Peter, He forewarned us that our faith must be "tried with fire" because of its immense and eternal value (1 Pet. 1:6–7), and that we should "think it not strange" when we meet "fiery trial[s]" (1 Pet. 4:12). That's a lot of "evil," and straight from the mouth of our Savior. But it's not all.

The great Prophet also forewarned us of a coming time of unprecedented trouble, the Tribulation period: "For then shall be great tribulation, such as was not since the beginning of the world to this time, no, nor ever shall be" (Matt. 24:21, emphasis added). To avoid this final time of testing, we must overcome our present Christian tests and so qualify to be taken in the rapture of the church, which will in one event remove the Holy Spirit, translate Jesus' Bride to heaven, terminate the Church Age, and initiate the seven-year Tribulation. (See Revelation 3:10.) In His parable of the Ten Virgins in Matthew 25:1–13, Jesus taught that, at the rapture, He will appear to take spiritually prepared disciples ("wise" virgins) to the marriage supper of the Lamb, but unprepared ("foolish") Christians will be left behind. Why will they be left? Because they are, as our proverbial text describes, "simple"—careless, thoughtless, and naïve. They foresee the evil time clearly enough in Bible prophecy, but they don't seriously prepare themselves to be "hidden" from it. So they will "pass on" and be "punished" by being subjected to a period of peril God never intended Christians to experience: "For God hath not appointed us to wrath but to obtain salvation by our Lord Jesus Christ" (1 Thess. 5:9). That's too bad for them.

But what about us? Are we wise or foolish virgins? Are we prudently preparing for or unwisely ignoring the various evils the Word foresees in these end times? Our answer will determine whether we are hidden from or exposed to needless future loss and whether we will help cause others to be prepared or unprepared. It will also determine if we have, at the very least, the wisdom of a squirrel.

As I write, autumn is visiting my dear North Carolina. The air is getting cooler and the leaves are turning beautiful colors. It's obvious that winter is not far away. Just this week I noticed that the squirrels are very proactive regarding the approaching "evil," or season of potentially lethal cold. They're scurrying about, stuffing their cheeks with prime food—fat acorns from the bountiful crop that's fallen from my red oak trees. Driven by instinctive sensible caution and far-seeing wisdom, they're hiding acorns everywhere: under leaves, in piles of pine needles, in holes, and in the mud, stick, and leaf "condominiums" they've constructed on the upper branches of my trees. Why all the activity? Because squirrels aren't simpletons. They're prudently preparing for the evil day. The good Lord must shake His head at this anomaly: redeemed man, made in God's very image at the top of His order of created beings, often doesn't prepare for approaching seasons of adversity; little squirrels, who are well down the line in creature sophistication, do. May God help us manifest the wisdom of a squirrel.

That is, may He stir us to be equally proactive, so we may escape our evil day—the Tribulation—when Jesus appears: "Watch ye, therefore, and pray always, that ye may be counted worthy to escape all these things that shall come to pass, and to stand before the Son of man" (Luke 21:36). And just how may we do this? We prudently prepare ourselves by abiding closely to the Lord. We abide closely by praying and feeding on His Word daily; accepting and overcoming our present trying circumstances; yielding to the Holy Spirit's correction; building our knowledge of and faith in God's Word through study; learning to handle difficulties by prayer, not mere reason; loving our neighbors as ourselves; speaking the truth in love; faithfully fulfilling our current God-given duties and ministries; and, when Jesus requires us to do so, keeping "the word of my patience," or patiently enduring very lengthy difficulties until the Lord releases us from them. Then we won't worry about tomorrow, because we'll know we're preparing for it—and that our "safety," or deliverance, will come from the Lord.

To his eternal credit, Solomon preached prudent preparation to God's people. Let's go one step further. Let's preach and practice it, today, tomorrow, and forever.

But we won't, we can't, do this if there is vengeance in our hearts.

Chapter Twenty-eight

THE SPIRIT OF REVENGE

swald Chambers, an expert in biblical studies, human understanding, and spiritual living, concluded, "Vengeance is the most deeply rooted passion in the human soul." The spirit of revenge is a bitter determination to redress a wrong, loss, or defeat. In making us "a vessel unto honor, sanctified, and fit for the master's use" (2 Tim. 2:21), the Holy Spirit seeks to purge us of this satanically stubborn root sin. Hence He inspired Solomon to address it in the Book of Proverbs.

There David's sagacious son ordered us not to plan or execute any acts of retaliation: "Say not, I will do so to him as he hath done to me; I will render to the man according to his work" (Prov. 24:29). The New Testament continues Solomon's line of thought. Jesus explicitly commanded non-retaliation, "But I say unto you that ye *resist not evil*" (Matt. 5:39, emphasis added; see vv. 38–48). And the apostle Paul repeated the substance of Christ's doctrine by writing, "Recompense to no man evil for evil" (Rom. 12:17; see. vv. 17–21). But overt acts of full-blown retaliation are not the only ways the spirit of revenge manifests. It also betrays its presence by subtle acts of spite, apparently accidental but actually deliberate hurtful comments, costly oversights, and other "mistakes." One of its most common yet least

226

detected manifestations occurs when it prompts us to celebrate openly or to be glad secretly when our enemies fall into trouble, harm, dishonor, or defeat. Solomon also describes this:

> Rejoice not when thine enemy falleth, and let not thine heart be glad when he stumbleth, lest the LORD see it, and it displease him, and he turn away his wrath from him.
> —PROVERBS 24:17–18

Paraphrased, this priceless proverb says:

> When your adversary stumbles or falls [into trouble, loss, dishonor, or defeat], don't celebrate or even subtly be glad; if you do, God will see you [or your spirit of revenge], and, displeased with you, stop [defending you by] punishing your enemy.

In this iridescent pearl of wisdom, we can see a virtual rainbow of colorful spiritual truths: warnings, commands, questions, assurances, and hints. Let's describe them.

Two warnings are readily seen, as God here alerts us to the immediate adverse consequences of holding or displaying vengefulness. First, the spirit of revenge displeases Him: "Lest the Lord see it, and it *displease* him [lit. be evil in his eyes]" (emphasis added). This causes us to lose God's full approval for fellowship and service—which spoils our intimate communion with Him, reduces our effectiveness in prayer, blunts our ability to hear His voice, blocks our insight into His Word, and hinders our usefulness in His service. Second, vengefulness causes God to stop defending us: "…and he [God] turn away his wrath from him [your enemy]." When people are obsessed with defaming, discouraging, and defeating us, we need God on our side *actively* confusing, thwarting, and limiting them and dividing their alliances, so we can continue moving forward in His will. As long as we continue pleasing Him, He continues helping us by resisting our adversaries. Sometimes this brings them to contrition and repentance, as we discussed more thoroughly in an earlier chapter: "When a man's ways please the LORD, he maketh even his enemies be at peace with him" (Prov. 16:7). But if we harbor vindictiveness, He stops defending us with His full powers. That will result in one of two undesirables: our deliverance is delayed or it is canceled, unless and until we repent.

Besides these sober warnings, this passage in Proverbs 24:17–18 contains five precise commands. The first two are explicitly stated, while the other three are clearly implied. They are:

1. *Do not celebrate* your enemy's adversity: "Rejoice not…"

2. *Do not be glad* when your enemy is sad: "…and let not thine heart be glad."

3. *Do not harbor* a spirit of revenge, for to think sin is sin.

4. *Cultivate* goodwill, or a desire for repentance and reconciliation, which is like God, who desires for all men to come to repentance. (See 2 Peter 3:9.)

5. *Receive* the fullness of the Holy Spirit—and *obey* Him, who alone is the source of the overcoming love of God.

In the first two commands God orders us not to party, grin, or gloat when evil befalls our bitterest enemy. Note He speaks not only to the outward display of revenge but also to its inner presence known only to us and the Holy Spirit.

The only way to avoid delighting in the demise of our detractors is to not allow the cause of such reactions—the spirit of revenge—to rest in our hearts. If you want to terminate a tree's bad fruit, pluck up its roots. But removal is not the full solution.

We must also refill our hearts with something of God, namely, goodwill. When the apostle John hastily requested that heavenly fire be called down on the Samaritans, the Jews' longstanding religious enemies, Jesus reminded the embryonic apostle of love that the purpose of His mission was blessed reconciliation, not bitter revenge: "Ye know not what manner of spirit ye are of; for the Son of man is not come to destroy men's lives, but to save them" (Luke 9:55–56). We too must remember this and pray regularly for our enemies to repent: "Pray for them who despitefully use you, and persecute you" (Matt. 5:44).

To live in this conciliatory spirit, or the love of God, in this bitter, revengeful world, we need to be filled with a new spirit—the Holy Spirit. Why? Because only He imparts and helps us cultivate God's own love, which enables us to permanently conquer the spirit of revenge: "The love of God is shed abroad in our hearts by the Holy Spirit who is given unto us" (Rom. 5:5). And merely receiving the Spirit of love is not enough. We must consistently *yield* to Him if we want His love to be manifested in us on a regular basis. Hence the five commands listed above.

WHY GOD COMMANDS US TO ABANDON THE SPIRIT OF REVENGE

When God commands, men question: "But why, God? Why should I neither celebrate nor be glad when my enemies fall?" Here are three good reasons.

1. To conform us to Jesus' image

Though at times He was very bold and blunt-spoken, Jesus was never vindictive. To the contrary, He wept streams of tears for His enemies when He pondered the awful judgment awaiting them (Luke 19:41–44) and prayed, even while dying, that God would forgive their sins against Him. He was the express image of His compassionate Father, who said, "Have I any pleasure at all that the wicked should die?" (Ezek. 18:23). And conforming us to His character image is *the* primary goal of the Holy Spirit in all His work in and for us: "For whom he did foreknow, he also

229

did predestinate to be *conformed to the image of his Son*" (Rom. 8:29, emphasis added).

2. To release God to fully defend us

As stated above, when we're harassed and persecuted by adamant adversaries, we need help very badly! And God wants very much to provide that help whenever and wherever it is necessary. He freely offers His services as our all-powerful Defender and the just Arbitrator of all our disputes: "I will contend with him that contendeth with thee" (Isa. 49:25). But to receive His defense, we must forfeit our self-defense and the spirit of revenge. Then He will step in and do for us what we cannot do for ourselves, making a way out for us through a deep, wide Red Sea of slander, persecution, injustice, illegality, and oppression.

His promises make it abundantly clear that He is both willing and waiting to intervene, provided we do not disqualify ourselves as stated above: "And I will…curse him that curseth thee" (Gen. 12:3); and again, "I will be an enemy unto thine enemies…mine angel shall go before thee…and I will cut them off" (Exod. 23:22–23). (See also Luke 1:74–75.)

3. So we won't be like our enemies

We must understand that this divine ban on the spirit of revenge is not binding on our enemies. Presently free to be as wicked as they will, they will sing, dance, and party freely when we are persecuted and beam with joy when we are crestfallen. David knew all about this. He apparently received reports that King Saul's loyalists were delighting in his purported demise: "But in mine adversity they rejoiced, and gathered themselves together…with hypocritical mockers in feasts" (Ps. 35:15–16). The Philistines freely made sport of Samson after his defeat. They made a grotesque trophy of King Saul's severed head after his death on Mount Gilboa. And the Edomites freely rejoiced when Judah fell to the Babylonians. But one day God freely judged both of these nations for their unchecked vengefulness against His children.

Do we want to be like them? Or, to bring us up to date, do we want to be like the rabid Palestinians who sang and danced in the streets when the World Trade Center towers were destroyed? If not, we should *thank God,* not complain, that He has commanded us to abandon the spirit of revenge.

There is also a powerful assurance hidden in this proverb. It is this: one day God will reckon with our vengeful enemies. Note Solomon's inspired use of the word "when" instead of "if": "Rejoice not *when* thine enemy falleth...*when* he stumbleth" (Prov. 24:17, emphasis added). It is a strong, sustaining comfort to know that, if our offenders remain bent on viciously harming us and those we love, God has promised to eventually right every wrong done against us: "Vengeance is mine; I will repay, saith the Lord" (Rom. 12:19). Jesus personally assured us that our heavenly Father would ultimately give us perfect justice: "And shall not God avenge his own elect, who cry unto him day and night, though he bear long with them?...I tell you that he will avenge them speedily [suddenly]" (Luke 18:7–8). Confidence in God's unchanging, unfailing righteous judgment releases us to fully and deeply rest in the day of our sufferings. It gives us a peaceful sense of psychological closure the moment we believe, long before closure comes in our actual circumstances. As a result, we don't have to think a thought, speak a word, or lift a finger in retaliation. (And as time passes and God's love grows in us, we have less desire for God's judgment and more for our adversaries' repentance, as Romans 9:1–3 illustrates.) Our Father will take care of that for us in His own time and way. We are free to leave our enemies in His hands and focus all our attention on knowing God more intimately and pursuing His will for our lives. Hence, unshackled by vindictiveness, we vigorously press toward the mark set before us.

And finally, this proverb is pregnant with a big hint. Because God's commands are His enablings, every one of us can and should confidently confess, "Because God can do this in me, I can do this in God!" That is, by the power of His Spirit God can enable me to live absolutely free of the spirit of revenge and full of the spirit of reconciliation—not in the hereafter but now in this time. He did this in David, who progressed from haltingly cutting off a piece of King Saul's robe to publicly renouncing his right to take revenge on the "Lord's anointed." (See 1 Samuel 24–26.) When Saul finally died, David wept, not with feigned mourning but with real poignant grief over what Saul could have been had he not turned from God. God did the same work of grace in Stephen, who prayed for his raving murderers, "Lord, lay not this sin to their charge" (Acts 7:60), and centuries later, in William Tyndale, who, with his dying words, prayed for the very monarch who had long and strongly opposed him, and, it is believed, had instigated his execution, "Lord, open the King of England's eyes." If God's grace was sufficient for them, it will be sufficient for us, too.

But we need to understand something. The amazing grace of David and Stephen and William Tyndale manifests not instantly, but gradually as day by day we repeatedly reject the spirit of revenge and choose the spirit of mercy. So if we're wise, we'll begin our transformation process now. Why not practice this proverb today? And again tomorrow? And the next day, and the next...until God perfects His grace in you?

Then He will send you to teach others what He has taught you.

Chapter Twenty-nine

TO BE A TEACHER

*T*eaching is undoubtedly one of the most honorable professions. To have the joyous privilege of sowing into other lives the information, skills, methods, values, beliefs, insights, and wisdom one has discovered and proven is indeed a noble and fulfilling station in life.

To be called to the Christian teaching ministry (Eph. 4:11) is an even greater honor, because it is a heavenly summons to practice, and in a sense continue, the very primary lifework of Jesus of Nazareth. Jesus spent much of His daily ministry teaching—by the seashore, on mountainsides, and in boats; by fields, roads, and wells; and in houses, synagogues, and the temple courts. Look over these illuminating sample texts:

> And Jesus went about all Galilee, *teaching*…
> —MATTHEW 4:23, EMPHASIS ADDED

> And he opened his mouth, and *taught* them, saying…
> —MATTHEW 5:2, EMPHASIS ADDED

> And he began to *teach* them many things.
> —MARK 6:34, EMPHASIS ADDED

He *taught* in their synagogues…and *taught* them on the Sabbath days.
—LUKE 4:15, 31, EMPHASIS ADDED

He sat down, and *taught* the people out of the boat.
—LUKE 5:3, EMPHASIS ADDED

Nicodemus…said unto him, Rabbi, we know that thou art a *teacher* come from God…
—JOHN 3:1–2, EMPHASIS ADDED

Early in the morning he came again into the temple, and all the people came…and he sat down, and *taught* them.
—JOHN 8:2, EMPHASIS ADDED

Jesus answered…I ever *taught* in the synagogue, and in the temple…
—JOHN 18:20, EMPHASIS ADDED

Jesus' innate teaching Genius and Successor, the Holy Spirit, is presently the chief Dispenser of divine wisdom and Interpreter of the divine Word. Of His basic work in this age Jesus said, "He shall teach you all things" (John 14:26).

By the mystical work of the Spirit, many masterful Christian professors have been trained, not physically but spiritually, "at the feet of Jesus." Among these lofty lecturers on divine things, who to a man were not merely taught of men but *taught of God,* were the original apostles, including Paul; the church fathers, including Augustine; key reformers, such as Martin Luther; gifted scholars, such as Matthew Henry; empowered revivalists, such as John Wesley; princely pulpiteers, such as Charles H. Spurgeon; masterful writers, such as F. B. Meyer and A. B. Simpson; extraordinarily insightful Bible expositors, such as Oswald Chambers; and many other less famous but equally gifted instructors of the Christian way. The Lord's current corps of teachers—including those through whom He has often enlightened and edified us—follows in the wake of these specially inspired and inspiring instructors.

While every Christian is not called by the Spirit to the five-fold ministry of "teachers" (Eph. 4:11), every Christian is called by the Scripture to minister through teaching; that is, to become "apt to teach." Paul informed Timothy, "The servant of the Lord must...be...*apt to teach*" (2 Tim. 2:24, emphasis added); "ready and able to teach" (PHILLIPS); or "skilled in teaching" (MLB); or "gentle, patient teachers" (TLB). This includes foremost pastors, because teaching is the most central pastoral duty: "A bishop [minister] then must be...apt to teach" (1 Tim. 3:2). It also includes a whole host of lay-teachers, such as, elders, counselors, mentors, Sunday school teachers, and parents.

It further extends to cover *any Christian who shares with another any truth God's Spirit has shared with him (or her)*. Jesus alluded to this aspect of the believer's service in His "teacher's commission" recorded by Matthew:

> Go ye, therefore, and *teach* all nations...*teaching* them to observe all things whatsoever I have commanded you.
> —MATTHEW 28:19–20, EMPHASIS ADDED

This ability to invest in others what the Spirit has invested in us was on Paul's mind when he instructed Timothy to train lay-teachers: "And the things that thou hast heard from me...the same commit thou to *faithful men, who shall be able to teach others also*" (2 Tim. 2:2, emphasis added). By inspiration the writer to the Hebrews disclosed that this ability and privilege to share spiritual truth should be the normal experience of every mature believer in due season: "By this time you ought to be teaching others" (Heb. 5:12, AMP). *Should be*, that is, if he or she complies with God's essential and nonnegotiable requirements for teaching. What are they?

The Spirit of God moved King Solomon long ago to inscribe a pair of proverbs that point out these divine requirements for becoming "apt to teach." And the teacher of Israel wrote:

> Bow down thine ear, and hear the words of the wise, and apply thine heart unto my knowledge. For it is a pleasant thing if thou keep them within thee; they shall be fitted in thy lips.
>
> —PROVERBS 22:17–18

Paraphrased, this priceless pearl of truth states:

> Humble yourself [by assuming your teachers know more than you] and [deeply, respectfully, and attentively] listen to their wise words, and apply your whole mind and will to [study and obey] them. If you continue doing this, it will be very pleasant [deeply satisfying to you and pleasing to God]; and you will become qualified and able to teach the same truths [to other humble disciples].

These two verses reveal four required steps by which humble learners may become holy teachers.

BIBLICAL STEPS TO BECOMING "APT TO TEACH"

The steps by which we ascend to the teacher's chair are attitude, attention, application, and adherence—and they all lead to approbation. Let's examine them in greater detail.

Attitude

Wisdom's first command is, *"Bow down thine ear"* (v. 17, emphasis added), or "consent and submit" (AMP). "Bow down" is God's call to intellectual submission and personal humility, both of which are required if we are to be teachable—an essential for any successful student. Why is teachability so important? Because we must be good students before we can be good teachers.

Good students of Jesus Christ freely submit to two recognized authorities, God's Word and God's teachers; they have total trust for the one and sincere respect for the other.

The "words of the wise" refers primarily to God's Word, the Bible, which the wise are ever interpreting and applying to their students. The Scriptures are given by the infinitely higher wisdom of the Creator, who said, "My thoughts are not your thoughts...for as the heavens are higher than the earth, so are...my thoughts [higher] than your thoughts" (Isa. 55:8–9). Therefore, the Scriptures are to be trusted absolutely, with child-like simplicity, not vetted with academic skepticism: "Except ye be converted, and become as [simple and trusting as] little children, ye shall not enter into the kingdom of heaven" (Matt. 18:3). If we doubt the integrity of God's Word, we forfeit the right to explore and grasp its literal and figurative meanings and expound them to others.

As to the human teachers of God's Word we listen to or read, we must respect them: "Know them who labor among you, and...esteem them very highly in love for their work's sake" (1 Thess. 5:12–13). Universally, good students assume that their teachers know more than they do about the subject at hand, and Christian students should do the same. We must guard against mental insubordination, the subtle uprising of petty judgmentalism, personal contempt, or intellectual envy. We may be very successful or knowledgeable in other, perhaps many, fields of human knowledge or endeavor, but we should always consider our teachers in Christ to be ahead of us in understanding the Words, ways, and Spirit of God. If they aren't, we should prayerfully seek other instructors who are. Always, we should expect our teachers to either inform us of things we have never known or give us fresh insights and new perspectives on familiar truths and doctrines.

If we ever stop "consenting and submitting"—agreeing with and receiving the truths presented rather than doubting and rejecting them and disrespecting the presenters—we cease being hungry children of God searching for truth and become arrogant critics searching for faults. And we fail as students of God and potential teachers of His people. Why? Because to God a humble attitude is more important than a high aptitude.

What is your attitude to the Word and workmen of God?

Is it teachable or terrible? Humble or haughty? Bowed down or stiff-necked?

Attention

"And *hear* the words of the wise" (Prov. 22:17, emphasis added). "Hear" is God's call to become a good listener. To a person, good students are good listeners. Listening has become a rare skill, probably because it demands patience and sustained focused attention—a considerable mental effort many of us are simply unwilling to expend. Our "sound-bite" generation is fast becoming infamous for its juvenilely short attention span. If a book, article, speech, documentary, or commercial advertisement is lengthy, you can safely predict it will be ignored by the childishly unfocused majority. Why? Because we are frenetically impatient and simply refuse to wait for anything we deem too slow or lengthy—moneymaking, sex, scandal, and sports excepted, for which things we have an inexhaustible appetite and endless energy. But God is looking for Christians of a different mold.

The Berean Christians fit God's preferred pattern perfectly. When the apostle Paul spoke (and his heavenly homilies were *not* brief!), they listened "with all readiness of mind" (Acts 17:11). That is, their attention was alert, focused, and sustained. When they tired, they didn't turn off; they took breaks for refreshment, to be sure, but afterwards they returned, refocused, and kept listening. Thus, in the fullest sense, they "heard" the words of the wise—deeply, respectfully, and attentively. Consequently, nothing Paul said went over their heads. Everything went straight into their hearts, took root, grew, and produced lush fruit of the Spirit.

Are you a Berean Christian, my friend? That is, do you listen well and listen long as they did? Remember, you'll reap the attention you sow. If you want others to listen to you attentively, listen to your teachers attentively. Never tune them out if they talk longer than you anticipated. Remember, you're listening to eternal truth and "all the things thou canst desire are not to be compared" to it. (Or, if that motivation fails, pretend you're at a sporting event that goes into overtime or you're listening to a protracted segment of fascinating breaking news. Whatever it takes, don't stop listening!) And keep listening well, and learning deeply, and becoming a more focused listener.

Application

"And *apply thine heart* unto my knowledge" (Prov. 22:17, emphasis added). "Apply thine heart" is God's call to respond correctly and fully to the teaching we have received, to apply our entire minds and wills to studying and obeying it. To humbly receive teaching is one thing; to diligently respond to it is another. Jesus taught this at the close of the Sermon on the Mount.

There, after He had finished giving us many mighty truths with which to build our lives, including a string of milky white proverbial pearls known as the Beatitudes (Matt. 5:3–10), He challenged us to immediately start building our houses of personal character. To hear His Words was not enough, He assured us. We must also do them: "Whosoever heareth these sayings of mine, *and doeth them*, I will liken him unto a wise man, who built his house upon a rock" (Matt. 7:24, emphasis added). Hence, He requires that we convert our theological knowledge into practical obedience in the tests the Spirit of God arranges for us daily. This is the only way we can build our houses of personal character—and of future ministry.

There are therefore two parts to the divine construction plan: personal study and personal obedience. Again, the Bereans show us the way. After Paul taught them, they followed up their public instructional meetings with private study sessions: "They…searched the scriptures daily, whether those things [which Paul taught] were so [or biblically accurate]" (Acts 17:11). In this way they confirmed that Paul's teachings were indeed scriptural, and they made them their own by patient, prayerful research, reflection, and probably also recording (writing). Paul ordered all

Christians to follow this example: "Study [research, review, record] to show thyself approved unto God" (2 Tim. 2:15). To humbly receive teaching is to receive the building materials for our houses of character. To then obey those truths as we have opportunity is to use them to actually construct personal character. Hence James charged us: "Be ye doers of the word, not hearers only" (James 1:22). This gives us something a mere academic student of Scripture will never have: an experiential knowledge of God.

This aspect of ministerial preparation is often overlooked in this day when academic qualifications are in such high demand in the house of God. But God never overlooks it. He chose the Levites to teach Israel solely because they obeyed His Word at a great cost: "*They have observed thy word*, and kept thy covenant. *They shall teach Jacob* thine ordinances, and Israel thy law" (Deut. 33:9–10, emphasis added; see vv. 8–11). And the New Testament reveals that He hasn't changed His mind. Though the apostle Paul had studied at the feet of Gamaliel, the most renowned rabbi of his day, God did not release him to teach until he had for years proven himself a "doer of the Word" in Tarsus. Even Jesus was not exempted from this requirement to apply the Word in his daily living, but was held back eighteen long years in Nazareth until He had fully proven not his heavenly knowledge, but His earthly obedience.

Why does God insist that teachers of His Word be doers of His Word? Because many Christians will study God's Word, but few will surrender to it. Many will talk it, but few will walk it. Many declare their respect for it, but few demonstrate it. Are you correctly and fully responding to the truths you have received, applying your whole will and mind to not only studying but also obeying them? Or have you neglected applying the powerful Word to your personal world?

Adherence

"If thou *keep them* within thee" (Prov. 22:18, emphasis added). "Keep them" is God's call to retain what we have received by *continuing* to respond to it correctly and fully. It's one thing to receive knowledge and another to retain it. And it's one thing to study and obey God's truth and another to *continue* studying and obeying it—through tests, tribulation, and time.

Jesus emphasized this imperative of spiritual adherence: "If ye *continue* in my word, then are ye my disciples indeed" (John 8:31, emphasis added). Many begin but few persevere in private study and personal obedience. We may stop at any time, if we wish, but if we do, we'll forfeit our right to be an effective teacher. In all fields of knowledge the best teachers are continuous learners. Their passionate pursuit of knowledge inspires an insatiable passion for more knowledge in their students. Everything and everyone will at times try to hinder us from *going on* in knowledge and obedience. Caustic critics and envious enemies will arise to withstand us. The worst enemies—impatience, doubt, pride, rebellion, judgmentalism, anger, vengeance, laziness, and sheer weariness—will arise from within to hinder us. Deceivers will persistently try to turn us from our devotion and duties with an alluring array of good but not best interests and activities. And God will allow baffling disappointments and defeats—the triumphing of deceivers and prosperity of the wicked—and not explain His actions for years. (See John 11:1–46.)

In that hour will we choose to take or forsake offense at Christ? Reaffirm or question His integrity? Abandon or adhere to His way? Fall away fast or "hold that fast which thou hast, that no man take thy crown" (Rev. 3:11)? It's up to us to graciously press through this opposition and continue becoming "disciples indeed." Those who persistently adhere will find theirs is a most rewarding quest. Two rewards come immediately to mind.

First of all, it is pleasant: "For it is a pleasant thing" (Prov. 22:18). By "pleasant," we mean deeply satisfying to our souls and pleasing to God. God is satisfied with us when we continue in His Word, just as He was when Jesus, after He already possessed great knowledge of Scripture, continued in His hidden, humble obedience for eighteen long years in Nazareth: "In thee I am well pleased" (Luke 3:22). And knowing that our heavenly Father is pleased with us gives us the greatest possible human satisfaction.

Second, perseverance in obedience gives us moral authority. Just as knowledge gives intellectual authority, obedience gives moral authority, and that alone causes our instruction to leave a lasting impression on souls. It was not Christ's divinity but His moral authority that made His teachings powerfully impact his hearers' hearts—"The people were astonished at his doctrine [teaching]; for he taught them as one having authority..." (Matt. 7:28–29)—and permanently alter their lives. Such authority can't be replicated in those who have only studied the lives and teachings of the great masters of Christianity or those who have had a close walk with God themselves in the past but have since turned back to mere religion: "...and not as the scribes [who had religious but not moral authority]" (v. 29).

This spiritual adherence leads us in God's time to divine approbation. God, having approved us for His service, releases us to begin releasing truth to His people. For Jesus, this period began when He left Nazareth to teach in Capernaum and the surrounding cities of Galilee: "And he taught in their synagogues" (Luke 4:15). For Saul of Tarsus, it began when Barnabas called him to come to Antioch, where "for a whole year they assembled themselves with the church, and taught many people" (Acts 11:26).

Approbation

"They shall be *fitted in thy lips*" (Prov. 22:18, emphasis added); "ready on your lips" (NAS); or "prepared in you for your lips to teach" (paraphrased). "They shall be fitted in thy lips" is God's promise to one day permit us to teach others the very truths—prepared first in our hearing, then in our living, and now in our teaching—we have persistently studied and lived in. This is divine approbation, or God's approval, to teach. While God's salvation is given freely by His grace, His approval for service is reserved for those who subsequently qualify for it.

The Bible constantly challenges us to seek God's full approval for service: "Study to show thyself *approved unto God*, [as] a workman that needeth not to be ashamed" (2 Tim. 2:15, emphasis added); and again, "Wherefore, we labor that...we may be *accepted [approved] of him*" (2 Cor. 5:9, emphasis added). Though he had long been approved for service, the apostle Paul wisely retained a healthy, holy dread lest he ever turn aside and lose, not his salvation, but his approval for divine service: "But I keep under my body, and bring it unto subjection, lest...I myself should be a *castaway* [lit. *disapproved*]" (1 Cor. 9:27, emphasis added). That is exactly what Jesus alluded to in symbolic language in John's Gospel: "If a man abide not in me, he is *cast forth* as a [disapproved, severed, fruitless] branch, and is withered" (John 15:6, emphasis added).

Approval for service seems to come in two stages:

1. God's approval (divine ordination)
2. Man's official recognition of God's preexisting approval (human ordination)

While Jesus was diligently applying and adhering to the Word in Nazareth, His heavenly Father was gradually approving Him (as a man) for divine service. Luke puts it, "And Jesus increased in wisdom [through prayerful study] and stature [physically, by growth; spiritually, by humble obedience], and *in favor with God...*" (Luke 2:52, emphasis added). Then, when the Father released Him to teach His word, others saw and approved of the Father's preexisting approval: "...and [in favor with] man." The Book of Proverbs promises a similar path to all who seek and retain God's wisdom: "So shalt thou find favor and good understanding in the sight of *God [first] and man [second]*" (Prov. 3:4). In His case, Jesus' divine approval was further confirmed by the marvelous and compassionate miracles God granted through His ministry: "Jesus of Nazareth, a man *approved of God* among you by miracles and wonders and signs, which God did by him" (Acts 2:22, emphasis added). In Paul's case, when after years of powerful and fruitful ministry he reported to the ecclesiastical authorities what God had done through him among the Gentiles, they unanimously and heartily confirmed the divine approval that for years had rested upon him: "When James, Cephas, and John, who seemed to be pillars, perceived the grace that was given unto me, they gave to me and Barnabas the right hands of fellowship" (Gal. 2:9). This act was more than an act of fellowship. It was tantamount to their official ecclesiastical endorsement, or ordination, of his apostolic ministry.

Human appointment to ministry must not be confused with divine approbation. Without God's approval—which always develops as declared in our proverbial text and generally as expounded in this chapter—man's ordination is, frankly, meaningless. Mere religious officials, with varying degrees of academic distinction, religious training, and cultural polish, are produced. But with it, we are fit to serve in whatever duties the Spirit deems appropriate and His anointing and gifts enable us to discharge. I would be remiss if I failed to note that God has shown an undeniable tendency to anoint and send qualified teachers who, for whatever reasons, have been raised up by Him without official ecclesiastical overseership.

When God needed a prophet to replace Elijah, He chose Elisha, a simple but highly devout farmer and non-cleric who surely had practiced the right attitude, attention, and application of God's Word. Elisha was a much less likely candidate than the least of the sons of the prophets who lived and studied at the prestigious ministerial schools of his day located in Jericho, Bethel, and Gilgal. John the Baptist, Jesus, and the apostles did not enjoy the approbation of the religious authorities of their day. To the contrary, they suffered the caustic condemnation of the ruling but apostate scribes and chief priests, whose official evaluation of

Jesus read as follows: "He hath Beelzebub [an epithet for Satan], and by the prince of the demons casteth he out demons" (Mark 3:22). Many of the church's greatest reformers and revivalists, such as Martin Luther, George Whitefield, and John Wesley, suffered the same rigorous rejection from religious authorities at the very time God was most evidently approving and powerfully using them. We get into trouble if as denominational leaders, ordaining boards, and ministerial overseers, we declare that God *can't* use someone unless *we*, or another ecclesiastical body, have ordained them. Clearly, there are times when He prefers someone from the ecclesiastical desert. And what God has cleansed, we must not call common; unless, of course, we wish to foolishly forbid those who "followeth not with us" (Luke 9:49–50). Why does God do this? I'm not sure. Perhaps at times He has no other choice. Or perhaps He wishes the mighty established religious apparatus to taste and remember this rather large piece of humble pie—to know that, while it cannot function without Him, He can function without it if He has to.

Do we believe God's promise, that He will make His truth "ready on our lips"? Are we seeking to be "approved of God" as set forth in this chapter? Why not?

So the Book of Proverbs has set before us the way to become "apt to teach." It is up to us now to grasp it.

So let us heed God's calls to the right attitude, the right attention, the right application, and the right adherence. And let us earnestly believe His promise, that He will cause His Word to be "fitted in our lips." Then, in God's time and way, whether as clerics or laypersons, we will find the Holy Spirit prompting us to share with other hungry, humble disciples the truths He has shared with us. And they will be blessed. And we will be blessed. And God will be blessed, and say of us, "My son, my daughter, in whom I am well pleased." It's time to pray:

Lord, may Your Spirit work in us mightily until we are "faithful men [and women], who shall be able to teach others also." Amen, Lord, so be it.

Part of your training for service will involve learning the delicate task of correcting God's people with grace.

Chapter Thirty

THE MINISTRY OF
COURAGEOUS HONESTY

*W*hen we see family, friends, or fellow Christians turn aside from righteousness, how should we respond? And, God forbid, if we ourselves should turn to sin, stubbornness, bad advice, evil influence, or selfish folly, what do we need most in that perilous hour?

Foreseeing these two questions by the Spirit, King Solomon gave an answer that is direct and unequivocal: in the first case we need to render, and in the second receive, the ministry of courageous honesty. The insightful son of David put it this way:

> Open rebuke is better than secret love. Faithful are the wounds of a friend, but the kisses of an enemy are deceitful.
> —PROVERBS 27:5–6

Paraphrased, this pearl of wisdom reveals:

> It is better to politely but bluntly rebuke someone [with the truth] than to hide [hold back, repress] such correction in the name of love. Such verbal "wounds" from a true friend are faithful [restorative, edifying, healthful], while

247

the "kisses" [audible or silent agreement] of enemies are unfaithful—false, misleading, and harmful.

To help us better understand this paraphrase, let's define some of the key words and phrases of this text as it appears in the King James Version of the Bible.

The "love" spoken of is *loving correction*, or, in the language of Scripture, "the love of the truth" (2 Thess. 2:10). This is the kindness of accurate, corrective (or constructive) criticism, spoken to one who is straying from God, His righteousness, guidance, or call, and intended to keep or release him from the bondage and destruction of sin. The Bible here brings out something we almost completely overlook in the psychologically soft Western world today; namely, *it is always an inherently loving act to speak the truth.* This is so whether the truth is spoken politely or impolitely; whether our sin or error is pointed out with carefully worded euphemisms or in the form of a tough, blunt rebuke, or "dressing down." However it is delivered, we are always better off for having heard the truth—the way things really are. Why? Because Jesus taught that only "the truth [God's Word or the realities of life, once accepted,] shall make you free" (John 8:32). Without truth, we abide in deception and spiritual bonds.

"Secret" means literally *hidden* or *concealed* and is so rendered in numerous translations (for example, NIV, NAS, AMP). "Secret love" is, therefore, loving correction that is undisclosed, held back, or suppressed. Just as it is a token of developing spiritual maturity to "[speak] the truth in love" (Eph. 4:15), it is an equally sure indicator of inadequate love to repress the truth, which, if released, would deliver those who are lying to themselves, to others, and to God. Another translation of Proverbs 27:5 reads:

Better a frank word of reproof than the love that will not speak.

—MOFFATT

The "love that will not speak" is clearly not God's kind of love, because it is selfish, not sacrificial, in nature. It is more interested in saving itself from potential rejection than in saving its loved ones—straying friends, family, and fellow believers—from ruin.

Conversely, God's love is passionately, not passively, corrective. The Book of Proverbs makes this unmistakably clear. Not content to silently observe people walking down the road to folly, sin, and destruction, the Spirit of wisdom, represented as a godly, wise, and vigilant woman, cries out to everyone who avoids or forsakes God and His wisdom, "How long, ye simple ones, will ye love simplicity and...hate [the] knowledge [of God]? *Turn you at my reproof*" (Prov. 1:22–23, emphasis added). As an incentive, God offers all who turn to Him an immediate refilling of His Spirit and a rich, new understanding of His Word: "Behold, I will pour out my spirit unto you, I will make known my words unto you" (v. 23). To further motivate the straying reader to begin fearing the Lord and loving His correction, the Spirit of wisdom warns that all who reject correction will come to ruin—"Because I have called, and ye refused...but ye have set at nought all my counsel, and would have none of my reproof... [therefore] your destruction cometh as a whirlwind" (vv. 24–25, 27; see v. 30)—while all who receive correction will live in peaceful, confident security: "But whoso hearkeneth unto me shall dwell safely, and shall be quiet from fear of evil" (v. 33). As the main point in this lecture, God emphatically declares that His corrections and rebukes prove that He loves, not loathes, us; that He delights in, not despises, us; that He considers us worthy children, not worthless castaways: "Whom the LORD *loveth* he correcteth, even as a father the *son* in whom he *delighteth*" (Prov. 3:12, emphasis added). And He urges us to neither be offended nor exhausted by His continuous corrections: "My son, despise not the chastening of the LORD, neither be weary of his correction" (v. 11).

This truth is so important to God that He ordained its

restatement in Hebrews 12, the prime New Testament passage revealing His plan to purify Christians through constant corrective criticisms, and, if necessary, rebukes and punishments (Heb. 12:5–17). It was this divine love that filled and motivated the prophets to correct patiently and plead passionately with the Jewish people. It also moved Jesus to repeatedly correct His apostles (Luke 9:46–56), and, later, the churches of Asia (Rev. 2–3). And it stirred the apostle Paul to persistently correct the errors, faults, and abuses in the churches he oversaw: "O foolish Galatians, who hath bewitched you, that ye should not obey the truth?" (Gal. 3:1).

Divine love, therefore, is selflessly committed to others' highest good and willing to risk rejection in order to speak the truth that frees the soul. So motivated, the prophets, Jesus, and Paul spoke correction, suffered rejection—and kept on speaking. (See James 5:10.)

The "wounds" referred to in our text are injuries to our pride caused by open rebuke. While all wounds are painful, some are ruinous and others restorative. If you are shot at close range with a large-caliber gun and one of your vital organs is pierced, you will likely die, but if a surgeon cuts you with his scalpel to remove a malignancy, his incision is likely to prevent death and restore health. I never thought of a surgeon's incision as a "wound" until my daughter Sarah needed surgery when she was only three days old. In his detailed pre-op presentation of the risks and rewards of the proposed procedure, Dr. Charles Turner of the Brenner Children's Hospital in Winston-Salem, North Carolina, described the incision he planned to make in Sarah's tiny abdomen as "the wound." I realized then that a surgeon's love wounds his patients in order to heal them. And God, the heavenly Surgeon, sometimes finds it necessary to do the same if we turn from Him to sin, folly, bad advice, or error and don't quickly correct ourselves. At such times, He sends our friends to minister faithful verbal "wounds" that ultimately heal our sin-sick, self-deceived souls.

In our text, the word *faithful* is taken from a Hebrew word (*aman*) meaning, "to build up or support." Hence, it speaks of that which is edifying (building up) or helpful (supportive), or, in keeping with the medical analogy we are using, that which restores full health. Wounds from godly rebukes may hurt, but if received, they will faithfully restore our spiritual health. Thus, we should see open rebukes as positive, not negative, forces; as building us up rather than tearing us down. Or, as our text denotes, we should consider them "better" than secret love.

Why are open rebukes "better" than secret love? Because the former leads to life and the latter to death. The Book of Proverbs declares, "Reproofs of instruction are the way of [and to, more] life" (Prov. 6:23). Heavenly correction through human correctors, if received, keeps us on the straight and narrow way to more life-joy, more insight into God's Word, more unshakable confidence in Him, more of His presence and peace, and more usefulness to Him. Rejecting "the love of the truth" strengthens deception and invites delusion and judgment. (See 2 Thessalonians 2:10–12.) Hence, the ministry of courageously honest correction is always better than the miserableness of cowardly silent love. This issue of frank vs. false kindness is one that defines wise and foolish Christians.

Wise, humble, God-fearing believers soon learn that God's love is passionately corrective. Hence, they choose to love correction and both give and receive it freely as needed. David wrote, "Let the righteous smite me [with corrective criticism or open rebuke]; it shall be a kindness. And let him reprove me; it shall be an excellent oil, which shall not break [harm] my head [mind, soul]" (Ps. 141:5). Note these excellent renderings of this verse:

> Let the righteous man smite and correct me—it is a kindness. Oil so choice let not my head refuse or discourage...
>
> —AMP

Let the godly smite me! It will be a kindness! If they reprove
me, it is medicine! Don't let me refuse it…

—TLB

When good men wound us and reprove us, 'tis a kindness;
I would pray ever to have their goodwill.

—MOFFATT

Though observant, the true sons of correction aren't judgmental. They have no desire whatsoever to find fault in matters
not clearly defined as sin in the Bible. Lovers of liberty, they've
learned to leave the debatable issues to God. Whatever is acceptable to Him is acceptable to them. (See Acts 10:15.) Reproving
others is the last, not the first, thing they prefer. Nor are they
fanatical. They don't pretend to enjoy being criticized or rebuked
by others. But, wisely, they realize two key facts: (1) God has
ordained correction when necessary; and, (2) it always helps
them. For these reasons their appreciation of open rebuke out-
weighs their aversion to it. Hence, rather than reject those who
love them enough to offer corrective criticism, they respect
them—if not immediately, then eventually, after their "wounds"
heal: "He that rebuketh a [wise] man *afterwards* shall find more
favor than he that flattereth with the tongue" (Prov. 28:23, emphasis added). Sometime after the apostle Paul publicly rebuked his
ministerial peer, Peter, over a vital sin-issue that was adversely
affecting not only Peter but also the church (Gal. 2:14), Peter
described Paul with glowing admiration as a "beloved brother," a
recipient and writer of divine "wisdom," and one whose epistles
were to be considered as inspired as "the other scriptures" (2 Pet.
3:15–16). Why? Because Peter was no fool. He respected those
who practiced courageous honesty and humbly received their
ministry when needed.

But fools see this issue quite differently. Gripped and ruled
by personal pride, they despise any form of correction: "Correction is grievous unto him that forsaketh the way" (Prov. 15:10).

Hence they reject all corrective counsel and those who offer it. A prime fool, King Ahab had this to say about Micaiah, the man God regularly sent to correct him: "I hate him; for he never prophesied good unto me, but always evil" (2 Chron. 18:7). To Ahab, and all the arrogant fools he typifies, a "good" word is any message that is complimentary or pleasant whether true or not, and an "evil" word is any message that is unflattering whether true or not. Also, as our text illuminates, fools refuse to give correction to those needing it. Theirs is "the love that will not speak," a miserably lame, deaf, and dumb companionship. Though they could release words of exhortation that would turn erring souls back to life, and even consider doing so, they prefer to repress their righteous rebukes. This brings us to the heart of this chapter and to our initial two questions.

First, our text teaches us how to react when our friends, family, or fellow Christians turn from faith in and obedience to God. If their actions merely do not suit our religious scruples, personal ideas, or preferred methods of operating, we should check our judgmentalism and tend our business. But if they break clearly established, biblically stated standards of conduct or abandon their vows, covenants, or ministries, *we must not be silent* and conceal loving correction. No, that is the time to remember the surgeon's love and politely but bluntly "wound" our spiritually sick friends with the truth, knowing that their wound will heal, their walk with God will recover, and, ultimately, they will respect us for our courageous honesty, regardless of their immediate reaction.

Make no mistake, this will demand courage—the willingness to face duties recognized as difficult, painful, or risky rather than flee from them—for more often than not we will meet adverse reactions. They range from denial, "No, you're wrong; I haven't thought, said, or done that"—to deflection, "I couldn't help it, it's his fault; he forced me to make this decision"—to denunciation, "How dare you! Who are you to correct me?"—to derision, "Oh, so you're perfect, are you?"—to defamation, "Did you hear what he (or she) said to me?" Are we prepared to quietly accept reactions like this and trust the power of the spoken truth to break the rockiest rebellion and burn away the chaff of carnality? "Is not my word like a fire: saith the LORD; and like a hammer that breaketh the rock in pieces?" (Jer. 23:29). Do we love Jesus and the fellow Christian we have corrected more than we love being loved? Paul did: "Though the more abundantly I love you, the less I be loved" (2 Cor. 12:15). There are other options, of course.

We can always just "kiss" our erring friends with religiously correct soft words: "Oh, I guess it doesn't really matter, sister; the Lord will love you whatever you do. He just wants you to be happy." Or we can simply say nothing—the lukewarm Christian's option of choice. But if we give such audible or silent approval of their sinful behavior, or worse, defend or assist them in their folly, we become their enemy, not their friend; a false, not a faithful, brother or sister in Christ. Why? Because we're encouraging them to continue their journey to the land of no return.

Second, our text teaches us what we need most if we should turn away from the Lord: the ministry of courageous honesty! When we are on the receiving end of the "wounding," *we must never reject the unvarnished truth about ourselves*, however distressing to our pride, but rather learn to receive our "wounds" as tokens of God's passionately corrective love and our friends' genuine concern. And in that perilous hour, should our long-standing adversaries "kiss" us with friendly approval of our choices, we must beware, not be fooled, knowing they don't have our best interests at heart. We can trust a friend's criticisms, but never an enemy's favor. And any Christian who refuses to tell me the truth is my enemy.

Summing up, this lustrous proverbial pearl shines with the knowledge that *the truth is the best "love" we can render or receive.* However they package it, in smooth euphemisms or stingingly direct words, the people who courageously tell us the unpleasant truth when we're pleasantly ignoring it are our most faithful friends. Where do we stand in regard to the ministry of courageous honesty? Are we giving and receiving "open rebuke" as needed? Or are we silent when others need it and sullen when we receive it? It's time we fully embrace godly correction. Why?

Because we need it to withstand the hostility of the spirit of envy.

Chapter Thirty-one

CAN YOU STAND BEFORE ENVY?

*A*n astute and inspired observer of the human experience, King Solomon spoke often about the most universally problematic and pernicious human attitudes and emotions. While he dissertated often against common vices such as covetousness, vanity, lust, and anger, he seemed to put one attitude, envy, in an entirely different category. His language reveals that he considered envy—angry discontentment at others' possession of things we desire ourselves but which rightfully belong to them—to be one of the most troublesome satanic catalysts, that when it influences people to persecute us, we experience adversity on an entirely new and often shocking plain.

Let the exceptionally insightful son of David speak for himself:

> Wrath is cruel, and anger is outrageous, but who is able to stand before envy?
>
> —PROVERBS 27:4

Paraphrased, this pearl of truth tells us:

> It is hard to stand against merciless wrath [vengefulness] in an opponent, and standing against a [furiously] angry

256

adversary is outrageously difficult [lit. a "flood; overwhelming"; or like facing a huge tsunami], but it is even harder to stand [unmoved, undiscouraged, and spiritually undefeated] before someone who bitterly envies you. Who can do this?

Consider just how radical a comparison Solomon uses here. After naming two seemingly impossible situations, handling attacks by vengeful opponents and raging enemies, he names a third that he considers to be even *harder*. Harder? Yes, he is focused upon something he considers more demanding than facing either cruelty or rage. What is this monstrous force? It is envy! Envy is unreasonable, groundless anger at those who have the things we want. Those desirables may be material, such as money, possessions, property, clothes, and physical beauty. Or they may be immaterial, such as success, love, friendship, favor, honor, and natural abilities. They are not only worldly but spiritual objects also, such as spiritual gifts, wisdom, peace with God, spiritual maturity, and biblical insight. The original language helps us understand Solomon's conception of envy even more perfectly.

The word *envy*, as used in this text, is translated from the Hebrew word *ginah*, which means "jealousy or envy; also zeal." This word is derived from another Hebrew word, *gana*, which means, "to be zealous" (in a bad sense), or obsessed. This definition is very accurate to life. Those who give way to envy zealously wage spiritual war against the very people they envy. With impish persistence (and in some cases demonic possession; see James 3:14–15), they obsessively and compulsively compete, criticize, argue, accuse, attack, defame, challenge, or rebel against them. They are committed, consumed really, with a totally unreasonable and groundless, yet very real, hatred. In the same way that deeply committed, spiritually minded disciples of Christ are zealous to fully know Him and fully do His will, so these are incessantly preoccupied with desires, plans, and attempts to trouble or ruin the people they envy. So Solomon puts at the top of his list of the difficulties we face in this world the tribulation and persecution that is driven by zealously, or obsessively, envious enemies.

The other sixty-five books of the Bible consistently corroborate this profound observation. Arguably the worst persecutions recorded in Holy Scripture were caused by envy.

THE PEERLESS PERSECUTIONS PROVOKED BY ENVY

Consider the experiences of these who stood before the relentless and at times overwhelming onslaughts of envious adversaries.

Abel

The first righteous procreated man, Abel, was overwhelmed by envy. Genesis 4 tells how the first family and first siblings became divided when Adam's first son, Cain, envied his younger brother Abel's right standing with God. This led to the first instance of divine correction, as God tried to counsel Cain into conviction and repentance (vv. 6–7). When Cain rejected God's correction, the first persecution and first murder soon ripped apart the first family, resulting in the first death, Abel's.

In His Book of Beginnings, God is speaking to us about the seriousness of envy. Are we listening?

Joseph

In a sadly enlarged reenactment of the Cain-Abel incident, Joseph's ten brothers envied his favor with his earthly father and his heavenly Father and the choice gifts they each bestowed upon him, a long-sleeved tunic and dreams of exceptional favor. (See Genesis 37:1–11.) When his brothers chose, as Cain had centuries earlier, not to repent, envy "moved" (Acts 7:9) them to sell their younger brother into slavery and, as far as they hoped, oblivion. *Good riddance!* they surely thought, as they justified their unjustifiable sin and increased their self-deception. "The dreamer" had gotten what he deserved!

Moses

Both Miriam and Aaron's surprising criticism of Moses (Num. 12) and Korah's deadly rebellion (Num. 16) were prompted by envy. In the first case, Moses' exceptional prophecies were the arousing object, and in the other, his and Aaron's divinely ordained positions of leadership: "They *envied* Moses also in the camp, and Aaron..." (Ps. 106:16, emphasis added).

David

King Saul envied his young son-in-law David because of the many ways in which he was evidently superior to the king. David was courageous and Saul cowardly. David behaved wisely and Saul foolishly. The Lord's Spirit rested upon David while demons harried Saul. David was a gifted musician and natural leader of men, and Saul was neither. Saul's son Jonathan and his daughter Michal respected Saul, yet they both openly loved David. And the list goes on. But when the women publicly praised David's exploits in battle more highly than Saul's, that was it. Something snapped in the carnally minded monarch, and for the next ten years he was zealously driven to kill David: "And Saul watched enviously David, from that day and onward... and Saul became David's enemy continually" (1 Sam. 18:9, 29).

Meshach, Shadrach, and Abednego

The three Hebrew boys' famous visit to the infernal interior of King Nebuchadnezzar's crematorium resulted from allegations made by the "Chaldeans" (Dan. 3:8), who surely envied the three youths for the superior wisdom that had won them greater favor, fame, and position than that which Babylon's renowned sages had long enjoyed (Dan. 1:20).

Daniel

Daniel's excellent attitude and faultless employment record consumed his occupational rivals with envy so much that they dedicated themselves to the task of eliminating him—so they could be elevated in his place. (See Daniel 6:1–15.)

Paul

The disbelieving Jews of Antioch in Pisidia were "filled with envy" (Acts 13:45) when they saw "almost the whole city" flocking to hear Paul preach the gospel they had already heard and rejected. They became so obsessed with stopping the apostle that they pursued him to other cities and finally caused his stoning in Lystra (Acts 14:19).

Jesus

Burning with envy at Jesus' blossoming public popularity, supernatural powers, heavenly messages, beautiful compassion, and gracious nonresistance toward them, the Jewish scribes and Pharisees hatched a plot to eliminate Him and retake the religious honors they felt were rightfully theirs. Pilate discerned the true motive behind their trumped-up charge that Jesus was an insurrectionist worthy of death: "For he knew that for *envy* they had delivered him" (Matt. 27:18, emphasis added).

Now you should be able to understand Solomon's radical language and his rhetorical question, "Who is able to stand before envy?"

Primarily, for Christians in these last days, this query asks, "Who can 'stand,' spiritually victorious, close to Jesus, unmoved from faith, undiscouraged by contradictions, unhindered in labor, and strong in the Holy Spirit, when the spirit of envy arises *against* them with the full brunt of its demonic fury?" The answer is this: We can, in Jesus! How can we be sure of this?

Because the inerrant Word declares, "I can do all things through Christ, who strengtheneth me" (Phil. 4:13), and "all things" includes standing against envy. It also teaches, "Greater is he that is in you, than he that is in the world [working in and through our envious adversaries]" (1 John 4:4). Who is "he" that is in us? The very Son of God is in us—and all His irresistible power and limitless grace. The Logos also reveals, "He giveth more grace [to overcome the opposition caused by human envy]" (James 4:6).

To fully access this overcoming grace, we must receive the fullness of the Holy Spirit and carefully, humbly, and persistently obey the instructions of God's Word regarding how we are to react to injustice and trouble for Christ's sake.

This involves seeing all our circumstances spiritually, or being "spiritually minded" (Rom. 8:6). We must understand, and remember often, that "we wrestle not against [mere] flesh and blood, but against...spiritual wickedness" (Eph. 6:12). And we'll need to forgive...a lot. Dropping anger toward our impenitent enemies is not our option; it is our obligation. (See Mark 11:25–26.) We must learn to act on our will, not on feelings only, to choose to give God sacrifices of thanksgiving in unpleasant situations daily: "In everything give thanks; for this is the will of God in Christ Jesus concerning you" (1 Thess. 5:18). (See also Hebrews 13:15.) Time and again we will have to exhort ourselves to wait patiently for God's help: "Let patience have her perfect work" (James 1:4). And to wait perfectly, we will have to endure, quietly and diligently pursuing our God-given duties while the persecutions of envy continue. We must learn to live by prayer, to discover that we prevail not by contentious conversations but by persistent supplications in the Spirit: "Praying always with all prayer and supplication in the Spirit...with all perseverance" (Eph. 6:18). And there's more.

We will also need to live by faith, that is, to trust God to control what we cannot control, to believe He will faithfully make a "way to escape" (1 Cor. 10:13) from every test, and that in the meantime He is working "all things," even those that seem accidental, hindering, and spiteful, for our ultimate good (Rom. 8:28). We'll need to "in all thy ways [circumstances] acknowledge him [God's presence, control, and will]" (Prov. 3:6), or discover that everything God sends our way, including suffering for Jesus' sake, is a very positive part of our overall Christian development. Paul lists "long-suffering," the ability to endure unjust opposition and difficult people for long periods without succumbing to offense at God or bitterness at people, as the fourth "fruit of the

Spirit" (Gal. 5:22–23). This valuable evidence of Christ within us is required for translation. (See Revelation 3:10.) As we thus "stand," letting patience have her perfect work, the Spirit of God is putting the finishing touches on our developing Christian character. And eventually we will emerge, "perfect and entire, lacking nothing" (James 1:4) and thoroughly "sanctified, and fit for the master's use" (2 Tim. 2:21). In the end we will see, just as Joseph did, that God has sovereignly used the author and agents of envy to do His own good will. They meant to destroy us, but God meant to develop us—and He did! That's how to "stand" when envy arises against us.

We must also know how to "stand" when the spirit of envy arises *within* us. Ever sufficient for every human need and problem, the Bible shows us God's way to deal with our own carnal, or old, nature, which is strongly inclined to envy others. Note these five scriptural instructions.

First, we must fully accept the fact of envy. That is, we must understand that envy is an integral part of the sin nature and hence of the prevailing behavioral patterns of the world, the carnal church, and each one of us, until we learn to walk consistently in spiritual mindedness. By constantly warning us, His children, not to envy, God and His Word assume the preexistence of envy in everyone, saved and unsaved. (See Psalms 37:1; 73:1–28; Proverbs 23:17–18; 24:1.) Facing this truth is the first step to freedom (John 8:32). We can't be liberated from a sin if we deny its existence. To heal a disease, we must first face it, then treat it.

Second, every new revelation of sin is yet another call to vigilance. Once informed of a transgression, we must thereafter watch for it, and diligently! Hence Solomon commands, "Keep thy heart with all diligence; for out of it are the [sin] issues of life" (Prov. 4:23). Are we examining our hearts for envious reactions when others are promoted, prospered, or preferred? We should. In *He Shall Glorify Me,* Oswald Chambers said:

Envy…may remain entirely latent until competition is launched on a certain plane and I recognize someone else's superiority; there is no getting away from it, I recognize that in the particular quality on which I prided myself, the other person is superbly my superior. How do I know when I am envious…of someone being what I am not? When I am secretly rather glad, though my lips say the opposite, when that one stumbles.[1]

Third, whenever we become aware that envy is stirring, however subtly, within us, we must quickly and firmly reject it. "Envy will *not* rest in me! I *refuse* envy!" must be our immediate and adamant internal reaction. Experience has taught me that when envy is first aroused, it is extremely subtle, almost subconscious, and only the Spirit of God will detect it. Then it is up to us to frankly face it and firmly dispatch it.

Fourth, if instead of doing this we allow envy to remain in our hearts, we must confess this to God as "sin" (1 John 1:9) in order to be cleansed and fully reunited with Him. And if envy has "moved" us to speak or act wrongly toward someone we envy, we must also ask their forgiveness and be reconciled (Matt. 5:22–24). Failure to do either of these things prolongs our separation from God, gives Satan a spiritual "place" (foothold, advantage) in our souls, and makes us exceptionally vulnerable to his subtle tricks and strong attacks. (See Romans 6:16; Ephesians 4:26–27.)

Fifth, we must remember again just who is in us: "Greater is he that is in you." The very Son of God is in us, and all His amazing love. And "[God's] love envieth not" (1 Cor. 13:4). His overcoming grace is also in us. Note how James connects our human propensity to envy others with God's provision of divine grace (impartation of His ability) that enables us to reject and overcome our envy: "Do you think Scripture says without reason that the spirit he caused to live in us envies intensely? But he gives us more grace" (James 4:5–6, NIV). Hence we always have an alternative when envy arises within us. We can choose to walk in God's grace rather than our carnality, and in the humility of love rather than the pride of envy. It is this meek Christlike disposition that enables us to see God's hand in the blessings, advantages, and superiority of others and fully accept it. John the Baptist took this humble line of thought when the Jews tried to stir envy in his heart in order to create hostility and division between him and Jesus. When told of Jesus' rising ministry, John calmly acknowledged that it was God's will, "A man can receive nothing, except it be given him from heaven" (John 3:27), and then went one step further in the humility of Jesus by choosing to be glad about it: "The friend of the bridegroom... rejoiceth greatly... this my joy, therefore, is fulfilled" (v. 29, emphasis added). If we follow John's example, we will become and remain free from the tyranny of envy and continue walking closely with the God of love and grace. That's how to "stand" when envy rises within us.

So we return again to Solomon's probing question, "Who can stand before envy?" Well, now we know not only the answer to His query—that we can—but also the "how to." If envy arises against us, by God's grace we can understand and endure it and develop our Christian character by being persistently spiritually minded. If envy arises within us, by God's love and grace we can discern and dispatch it and walk on with God. But will we? Will we "stand," perfectly unmoved by envy's workings while God perfects His workings in us? That remains to be proven. So, let's first say to God, and then prove to Him, that we will!

Conquering envy will help us teach our children about, and free them from, "sibling rivalry." And that will make us good parents.

Chapter Thirty-two

ON GOOD AND POOR PARENTING

*G*odly parenting is a recurring theme in the Book of Proverbs. Why? Because parenting, whether good or poor, is the single most important human factor in our natural character development.

Character training is a kind of psychological procreation. In physical procreation, we reproduce our own kind physically, replicating our physical features in our children. In character training, we reproduce ourselves psychologically, replicating our life values and habits in our children's thoughts and ways of living. While there are exceptions, the general rule is that wise parents produce wise children and foolish parents mold foolish ones. Why is this? Largely because wise parents believe in and practice godly discipline and foolish ones don't.

Speaking to this very issue, King Solomon wrote:

> The rod and reproof give wisdom, but a child left to himself bringeth his mother to shame.
>
> —PROVERBS 29:15

Paraphrased, this pearl states:

> Steady discipline by the "rod" [of firm authority and consistent appropriate punishments] and by godly corrections and rebukes teach a child how to live wisely [responsibly, obedient to all authority, and in awe of God] but a child left without such discipline and training will [live foolishly—irresponsibly, irreverently, and perhaps illegally—and so] bring shame to his mother [whose primary maternal responsibilities are not only to bear but also to train her children].

This proverb uses key biblical symbols for godly parental discipline and foretells their effect.

The "rod" speaks of *firm parental authority*. Just as Jesus, as the King of kings, will rule all nations in the thousand-year Day of the Lord with His "rod of iron," or inflexible authority, so the Christian parent must exert, not shirk, his or her authority in the home. The "rod" also speaks of the *predictable appropriate punishments* that are given to the children for deliberately breaking known household rules. In the Christian home, all the functions of orderly government—law making, law enforcement, and judicial judgments and punishments—are replicated in miniature in the parents, who set the rules, enforce them, judge the "cases" presented them in their home, and execute the "sentences" of their decisions. If they are consistent, their children will learn how to live under authority and law in the home first, and, once grown, they will easily and subconsciously transfer their acquired attitude of respect for authority to the societal, occupational, and ecclesiastical authorities that oversee them for the rest of their adult lives.

"Reproof" speaks of *calm, compassionate, verbal correction*; that is, constructive criticism, or the corrective truth, spoken in love. When children have done something the wrong way, parents must take the time to tell them the right way...again... and again...and again. This demands vast amounts of love and patience, the two golden requisites of good parenting. Matthew Henry wrote insightfully of the correlation between the use of a parent's rod and his reproof:

> If a reproof will serve without the rod, it is well, but the rod must never be used without a rational and grave reproof;...then it will give wisdom.[1]

Henry suggests that we begin disciplining our children with verbal corrections, but if this is ineffective, we should then apply appropriate, carefully measured punishments, such as calm, controlled, and discreetly limited spanking (corporal punishments). Or if we prefer, we should administer other punishments, such as loss of privileges, loss of allowance, "time out" alone in a chair, and so forth. Whatever punishments we choose, with them we should also explain straightforwardly to our children precisely why they are being punished, point out to them again the benefits of obedience, and encourage them to seek them. And this must be done with both a loving heart and tone. If practiced steadily, this firm but loving discipline will produce a very valuable human product: a wise child. Thus our text concludes, "The rod and reproof give *wisdom*" (emphasis added).

Conversely, withholding such discipline from our children, or abandoning it after a season because of its inherent difficulty, invariably leads us and our offspring to two very unpleasant destinations: their foolishness and our shame. Again, our text sums this up, "A child left to himself bringeth his mother to *shame*" (emphasis added). Parents, wake up and take note! There is no uncertainty here. Solomon's word is inspired: "All scripture is given by inspiration of God, and is profitable" (2 Tim. 3:16). We're presenting sure theology here, not unsure theories.

CAUSES OF PARENTAL NEGLECT

With the sure consequences of both good and poor parenting before us, let's consider some common causes of parental neglect.

Apathy

Reasonable indifference is the spirit of this modern age. We're calm, cool "centrists" these days, not too strongly for or against anything, but comfortably—and too often callously—in the middle of everything. So many parents take the attitude that parenting isn't really a vital issue. Life and death don't really hang in the balance. Why become a parental alarmist or "extremist"? If we just feed, clothe, house, transport, and educate our children until they reach adulthood, they'll make it. Somehow. Sometime. Some way. Thus states the prevailing lukewarm parental philosophy.

But here's some breaking news! The Bible says they *won't* make it unless we become passionate about good parenting. Are we passionate or passionless about our children? Their temporal lives? Their eternal destinies?

Selfish ambition

Parents consumed with occupational, professional, or ministerial ambitions are rarely good character trainers. Why? Their minds, affections, and time are wholly sacrificed to the demands of the great god Self-Interest. From within, this modern slave-master drives them daily to seek personal achievements, accolades, advancements, and assets, all to satisfy their insatiable appetite for the fleeting and futile "pride of life" (1 John 2:16).

Sorry, kids, Mom and Dad don't have time for you today, or tomorrow, or ever! They're glassy-eyed with career-worship. You'll just have to wait "until…" But sadly, tragically, in most cases "until" never comes this side of the grave.

Impatience

Successful parenting demands not only passion but also patience and perseverance. It takes many long years of commitment, not days, weeks, or months. Therefore, we must patiently persist at child care. It is a very long labor of love, and few of us practice the love that labors long. Typically, farmers exercise "long patience" to harvest the "precious fruit of the earth" (James 5:7). But tragically, many Christians grow impatient with parenting and give up long before they receive the *most* precious and rewarding fruit of the earth: godly character in their children. Godly parenting will force us to go beyond our current limits of patience and kindness again and again.

Are we ready to run with patience the parental race set before us? Will we steadily cultivate our family "field" until one day we reap our, and God's, precious "fruit"?

Laziness

Good parenting demands maximum physical exertion. It is very draining to constantly listen to, teach, and correct children morning, noon, and night. Sharing activities with them—athletic events, concerts, educational exhibitions, travels, recreational activities, sports, walking, and so forth—requires us to be more active ourselves. Unless we are athletically or recreationally inclined, this disturbs our preexisting adult comfort level and forces us to become much more mobile than we were "B.C." (before children). Now, reasonable rest periods for weary parents are fully in order, but lazy parents repeatedly and unashamedly indulge themselves at the expense of their kids' healthful development. While they luxuriate, their little ones stagnate.

Are we loving or lazy parents, active or inactive, sharing or shunning meaningful parent-child activities? May God stir us to get out and do things with our kids now, before the advent of retirement, rheumatism, and rigor mortis!

Unbelief

Many neglect parenting because they simply don't believe the Book of Proverb's numerous plainly stated commands, principles, and prophecies concerning parenting. For instance, they're not at all sure that good parenting:

- **Gives parents rest and delight:** "Correct thy son, and he shall give thee *rest*; yea, he shall give *delight* unto thy soul" (Prov. 29:17, emphasis added).

- **Imparts wisdom to children:** "The rod and reproof give *wisdom*" (Prov. 29:15, emphasis added).

- **Delivers children from the folly of stubbornness and rebellion:** "*Foolishness* [rebellion] is bound in the heart of a child, but the rod of correction shall *drive it far from him*" (Prov. 22:15, emphasis added).

- **Saves children from early death and eventual damnation:** "Do not withhold discipline from a child; if you punish him with the rod, he will *not die*. Punish him with the rod and *save his soul from death*" (Prov. 23:13–14, NIV, emphasis added).

Nor are they convinced that negligent parents will reap the following:

- **Sorrow:** "He that begetteth a fool doeth it to his *sorrow*; and the father of a fool hath no joy" (Prov. 17:21, emphasis added).

- **Grief:** "A foolish son is a *grief* to his father" (Prov. 17:25, emphasis added).

- **Bitterness:** "A foolish son is . . . *bitterness* to her that bore him" (Prov. 17:25, emphasis added).

- **Shame:** "A child left to himself bringeth his mother to *shame*" (Prov. 29:15, emphasis added).

- **And, in some cases, calamitous tragedy:** "A foolish son is the *calamity* of his father" (Prov. 19:13, emphasis added).

Every day these same parents fully believe the findings of scientific and even nonscientific studies and promptly change their beliefs and behavior accordingly. But they forget that God has done His own wide, scholarly, and credible study on parenting. Consequently they fail or refuse to believe His superbly accurate "report." "Who hath believed our report?" (Isa. 53:1). What about us?

Do we believe God's report on parenting? Or do we, as so many of our peers, consider His views antiquated and His methods questionable?

Rejection

In these last days, many parents lack natural affection: "In the last days...men shall be...without natural affection" (2 Tim. 3:1–3). Some actually despise their own children—upon whom they should dote! Hardhearted parents cruelly reject children for a variety of unreasonable reasons, such as:

- Their *physical appearance* (too fat, skinny, short, tall, or homely)

- Their *behavior* (habitual, or sometimes occasional, misbehavior)

- Their *failures* (in academics, athletics, hobbies, etc.)

- Their *social life* (inability to get along with other kids, parents, or teachers)

No matter how different, difficult, or dysfunctional our children, rejecting them is always profoundly wrong—and ruinous to their self-image, natural development, and eventual conversion to our Christian faith. To a person, parents who reject their children suffer amnesia: they forget the imperfections and rejections they struggled with as children!

Are we rejecting and dejecting our young ones, or receiving and developing them?

Sinful addictions

When parental addictions persist, parental attention desists. Parents who give themselves to sinful pastimes can't simultaneously give themselves to their little ones. As long as they hold their bad habits, they can't help their children form good habits. Uncured alcoholism, unchecked drug addiction, and unforsaken adulterous affairs have robbed many children of their greatest earthly need: a sober, sane, responsible parent, disentangled from his or her own evil distractions and focused on their children's welfare.

Are we a distracted or devoted parent? Are we addicted to our sins or attentive to our children's needs?

Ignorance of God

Some Christians neglect parenting because they never realize that their heavenly "Father" is not only their creator but also their *parent*. And they've never considered just how passionately, patiently, and persistently He parents them every day: "As a father pitieth his children, so the LORD..." (Ps. 103:13). Having given us life, our Father is unwaveringly committed to the task of training us to walk in that life and building our characters to be like His own, so we can walk and work with Him forever. The Book of Proverbs states, and the Book of Hebrews confirms, that God is constantly training us with his "rod and reproof." "My son, despise not the chastening [rod] of the LORD, neither be weary of his correction [reproof]; for whom the LORD loveth he correcteth, even as a father the son in whom he delighteth" (Prov. 3:11–12). (See also Hebrews 12:5–6.)

If God is passionate about parenting, shouldn't we be also?

Stress

When parents are stressed out, children are left out—in the cold of neglect, where they are exposed to bad influences, wasted time, psychological and physical dangers, and dangerous people, such as child predators. At best, family life in this twenty-first century is super-stressful. If we fail to learn how to walk closely with God and cast all our burdens on Him, we will eventually be overwhelmed with stress and become *unable* to give the attention, energy, counsel, time, and intercession to our children that they need. When we break down, our parental influence breaks down with us. And our children, God bless them, will suffer the consequences of our parental impotence. This is happening with disturbing frequency in our generation, largely due to unnecessary divorces.

Single parenting, especially when raising two or more children, is excessively stressful and even in the best scenarios significantly reduces the amount and quality of our parental training. Maybe this is why from the beginning God's idea was for two, not one, to raise children! Mounting parental failures are teaching us daily that, while a devoted single parent can get by with help from friends, family, and church, a stable, two-parent home is necessary for Christian parenting to truly thrive. This is why separation or divorce should never be pursued hastily or without clearly irremediable biblical cause. It is also why God recommends Spirit-led remarriage for young widows with children: "I will, therefore, that the younger women [widows] marry [remarry], bear children, rule the house..." (1 Tim. 5:14). It furthermore provides Christians considering marriage or remarriage food for thought: Is that man or woman you love and who loves you willing also to love your children? Is he or she the kind of believer and personality that will passionately, patiently, and persistently parent them? Or does he or she clearly manifest one or more of the causes of parental neglect mentioned above? Think about it now, before you commit to a marriage covenant. *Never marry someone with glaring faults, expecting them to change after you marry them!* In most cases, they stay the same.

So pray long and well about any proposed marriage. Someone's counting on you to make the right decision.

Tonight, go into your children's bedrooms and slowly gaze at their faces as they sleep. There they are, created in God's image and procreated in yours. They're innocent, dependent, vulnerable, and completely at your mercy. Their future in this life, and to some degree the next, is largely in your hands and prayers.

So don't be idle and leave them to themselves. Love them now, while they're with you. Don't procrastinate; proactively seek their highest good. And don't leave them undisciplined; prayerfully, patiently, and purposefully use your "rod and reproof" as needed, expecting God to bless your obedience and watching for Him to give your children wisdom—and you joy!

> I have no greater joy than to hear that my children walk in truth.
>
> —3 JOHN 4

And one day you'll eat the fruit of, and be honored for, your labors.

Chapter Thirty-three

ATTEND TO YOUR MASTER— AND FIG TREE!

*H*imself a man of faith and duty, King Solomon believed firmly that if God's servants faithfully attended to and served God, God would give them sure rewards. So firm was Solomon's conviction that he made it the subject of one of his timeless maxims of wisdom:

> Whoso keepeth the fig tree shall eat the fruit thereof; so he that waiteth on his master shall be honored.
> —PROVERBS 27:18

We may paraphrase this as follows:

> Whoever [faithfully and diligently] tends to a fig tree [or orchard] shall [as his reward] eat the fruit of it; in exactly the same manner, the believer who [faithfully and diligently] attends to [the will of Jesus] his master [and to the work He assigns him] shall [as his reward] be honored.

Let's examine this rather large and valuable proverbial pearl in more detail.

The first half of this saying describes the natural rewards of natural labors. Those who maintain fig trees have the right to eat their fruit, or receive income from its sale. Paul asserted, "The hardworking farmer should be the first to receive a share of the crops" (2 Tim. 2:6, NIV). But there is also a figurative application. Our text implies that caring for the fig tree is the duty of the keeper assigned to it, either due to his ownership of the fig tree or his relationship to or employment by its owner. Spiritually speaking, then, the "fig tree" (or orchard) represents *our divinely appointed responsibilities,* whatever work the Lord of the harvest assigns us in the present season of our lives, whether secular or religious in nature.

These responsibilities include all kinds of family, occupational, church, and ministerial duties. As believers in secular employments, our "fig trees" are the daily jobs we hold. Scripture enjoins us, "Whatever ye do, do it heartily, as to the Lord, and not unto men...for ye serve the Lord Christ" (Col. 3:23–24). Wherever God puts us, on a farm or in a factory, on the road or in an office, there we are serving the Lord by what we do and how we do it. If we are parents, our children are "fig trees." As stated in the previous chapter, our children's very lives, especially in their early years, depend completely on how well we care for them. If we hold a job, office, or ministry in our church, that is our "fig tree," as is any ministry to the larger body of Christ to which we are called and in which we are actively engaged. As an anointed reformer and restorer of his people, Nehemiah's "fig tree" was, as he described it, his "great work" (Neh. 6:3) of rebuilding Jerusalem's walls and restoring obedience to God's law among the discouraged remnant of Jews in Israel's post-exile period. Just as an orchard has many trees, so we may have two or more "fig trees" committed to our care. Whatever our "fig trees," if we keep them well, in God's time and way we will receive a sure reward. Our text proverb promises we "shall eat the fruit thereof"; and Paul's epistle to the Colossians adds, "Knowing that of the Lord ye shall receive the reward of the inheritance" (Col. 3:24). Thus this maxim assures us that in some way God will cause our faithful, diligent labors to return to bless us. Though keeping fig trees sounds simple enough, it isn't as easy as we might think.

Indeed, the orchard keepers of ancient Israel worked hard to reap their fruit. Always they were busy either protecting or maintaining their trees.

To protect them, they had to construct walls and watchtowers around their orchards. These were built of either stones or mud bricks and required hours of backbreaking labor in the hot sun. And when these structures were damaged by animals, humans, or erosion, the orchard keepers had to repair them. Thus they protected every tree they planted.

Initial preparation and planting and seasonal maintenance also kept the orchard keepers in constant motion. The soil had to be prepared for planting by painstakingly removing roots, rocks, weeds, and bushes. Then the trees had to be planted, with proper spacing. If rainfall was sufficient, watering was not necessary. If it was insufficient, water had to be supplied by one of two labor-intensive processes: digging irrigation ditches and rerouting water courses or pumping water into them; or, if there were only a few trees, drawing and carrying clay pots or goatskin containers of water. Periodically the trees had to be fertilized, which involved working animal dung into the soil and mulching each tree with available ground covers. Pesky weeds, thorns, and thistle bushes had to be constantly identified and uprooted. Every day the keepers examined their trees, especially the leaves, for evidence of diseases, worms, or parasites; these enemies within the orchard were as dangerous as any without. When the fruit was ripe, the orchard keepers carefully harvested each tree's produce by hand and then prepared it for market by grading, sorting, and storing the figs in baskets. Afterward, they carefully pruned the limbs to induce new and stronger growth and more fruit the next season. And finally, ever zealous to obtain the most fruit possible from their orchards, they judged their trees, removing any that failed to produce and replacing them with new, healthy, fruitful trees. All this, and nothing less, was required to "keep" a fig tree or orchard properly. Are we working this diligently and thoroughly at keeping our "fig trees"? Thus says, and probes, the first half of this proverb.

The second half describes a servant waiting on his or her master: "…he that waiteth on his master." *Waiteth* is translated from the Hebrew word *shamar*, which, as stated previously, means "to hedge (about)." By extension, this means, "to guard, protect, or tend to." Why? Because we put hedges, walls or fences around things we wish to guard, protect, care for, or attend to; for instance, dwellings, children, fields, flocks, wells, or orchards. To "hedge about" our master, then, is to care for or attend to our master's needs; or *to attend to every aspect of our master's will.* Like the first half of this proverb, the second promises a sure reward, namely, honor: "He that waiteth on his master shall be *honored*" (emphasis added). Literally, this applies to every diligent, faithful servant or employee. Such subordinates will surely receive recognition, favors, and advancement from their gratified superiors. But the most important application is figurative. Believers who constantly tend to their relationship to and service for their Master, Jesus, will be honored by Him in this life and the next. Matthew Henry wrote, "God is a Master who has engaged to put an honor on those who serve him faithfully."[1]

To receive such honor from Jesus, we must "wait on our master." Do we fully understand what this involves?

ATTENDING TO OUR MASTER'S WILL

To wait on Jesus, our Master, requires steady attention to every aspect of His will. This requires us to attend to His presence, His Word, His voice, His call, His interests, and His challenges. Let's consider these key responsibilities more closely.

Attending to His presence

Insightfully, the Book of Psalms speaks of "the secret place of the Most High" (Ps. 91:1). Invitingly, it reveals that "in thy presence is fullness of joy" (Ps. 16:11). Insistently, it challenges us to "seek the LORD, and his strength; seek his face evermore" (Ps. 105:4); or "seek and require His face and His presence [continually]" (AMP). Clearly, through His Word our Master is calling us to come and wait—spend a large quantity of quality time—in His presence: "Come unto me..." (Matt. 11:28).

From Mount Sinai He called Moses to draw near, and he responded. From a Galilean mountain He called his first disciples to "be with him" (Mark 3:14), and they responded. And from the highest mount, heavenly Zion, He's calling us today to "seek and require...His presence continually." Are we responding? Are we forming the habit of entering into our private chambers, shutting our doors, and spending time in intimate fellowship with our Master? Every time we experience that still, quiet, mystical communion, our spirits and His are fused, and we emerge more like Him. There we learn to open our hearts to Him in frank, childlike prayer, listen for the response of His still, small voice, and persistently intercede in the Spirit for everyone He brings around us. And there the Holy Spirit, the great Teacher, inspires and instructs us to worship our heavenly Father in the way He desires, "in spirit and in truth" (John 4:24). Oh, how blessed they are who respond to the Master's call by attending to His presence daily: "Blessed is the man whom thou choosest, and causest to approach unto thee, that he may dwell in thy courts [or presence]" (Ps. 65:4). Are we so "blessed"?

Are we responding to or running from Jesus' invitation to intimacy? Are we experiencing full joy in His presence or full frustration in other good but unedifying interests and pastimes? Have we made His presence the "one thing" we cannot live without daily? "*One thing* have I desired of the LORD, that will I seek after: that I may dwell in the house [presence] of the LORD all the days of my life, to behold the beauty of the LORD, and to inquire in his temple [presence]" (Ps. 27:4, emphasis added).

Attending to His Word

"In the beginning was the [living] Word," declared the apostle John (John 1:1). Thus the living Word of God—Jesus, the perfect expression of the divine thought and being—not only predated but also produced every good thing that followed in earth and Eden: "All things were made by him; and without him was not anything made that was made" (v. 3). So before there was light, life, order, and progress in the pre-Fall world, there was the mighty, creative living Word. The same is true with us and God's written Word. If we are to have light, life, order, and godly success in our lives, we must begin with the written Word of God. Are we learning to attend to God's written Word, which is the literary expression of the living Word?

As discussed in a previous chapter, are we prayerfully, patiently, and persistently studying the Bible so that we might understand, practice, and teach it with God's full approval? "Study to show thyself approved unto God, a workman that needeth not to be ashamed, rightly dividing the word of truth" (2 Tim. 2:15). Are we reading the Word devotionally, for personal edification and communion with and communication from its Author? "Seek ye out of the book of the LORD, and read" (Isa. 34:16). Are we meditating on the Word as we walk, travel, or pass the free moments of the day? "In his law doth he mediate day and night" (Ps. 1:2). Are we speaking God's Word to ourselves to release its full power in our souls and circumstances? "With the mouth he confesses, resulting in salvation" (Rom. 10:10, NAS). And, as expounded earlier in this book, are we freely sharing the light of our Master's Words with others of like faith and commitment? "They that feared the LORD spoke often one to another" (Mal. 3:16). If so, we have a reward coming.

If we attend to God's personal Word, our creative Master will attend to our personal world in a distinctly new and more intimate way, filling it with His inextinguishable light, irrepressible life, flowing peace, productive order, and divine prosperity. The result will be nothing short of a wonderful new genesis or beginning! How can we be sure? We have His word for it: "Then [when steadily meditating in and obeying God's Word] thou shalt make thy way prosperous, and…have good success" (Josh. 1:8).

Here's food for thought. God's angels are His historians, the designated inscribers of eternal literature. Will the angels write of your life, "In the beginning [of his or her walk with God] was the Word," or, "In the beginning there was no Word"? Think about it.

Attending to His voice

To glorify God, we must do His will. To do His will, we must be led by Him. To be led by Him, we must attend to His voice—that is, recognize and respond to His guidance.

There is nothing more precious than being able to hear God's voice guiding us through the long, dark, dangerous, and deceptive valley of this world. Only by the quiet, inward prompting of our supernatural Helper, the Holy Spirit, can we detect that God is speaking to us and discern what He is saying. But once He prompts us—to be silent, speak, go forward, stop, reverse our steps, or wait for further instructions—the rest is entirely up to us. We are perfectly free to obey or disobey His guiding voice. Christians who disobey the Master's guidance dishonor and grieve Him and bring on themselves needless troubles. But those who obey His leading, especially when it crosses their will or contradicts their wisdom, highly honor and deeply please the Lord. And for that, He delights to honor them with stunning blessings and surprising fruitfulness.

When Jesus guided Peter to cast his nets again into Galilee's blue depths, despite the utter improbability of success, Peter obeyed. Immediately, he received an astonishing blessing, two boatloads of his heart's and business's desire—fish! (See Luke 5:1–11.) When the Holy Spirit distinctly called Philip to go into the desert, despite his current notable success in the city of Samaria, he obeyed with childlike, unquestioning faith.

Immediately, he received a surprise: more fruitfulness! Once in the desert, he met and ministered to a key man in God's plan, the Ethiopian eunuch, through whom God established the gospel and a fruitful church in a faraway land. Similarly startling blessings and remarkable fruitfulness await those who attend to the Master's voice of guidance. Why? Because He has promised, "Them who honor me I will honor" (1 Sam. 2:30).

Are we honoring or dishonoring God's guiding voice? Our response will determine whether we grieve or glorify Him, and whether at last we reap remarkable fruit or failure for God's kingdom.

Attending to His call

Jesus, our Master, calls each of His servants to specific duties or ministries in every season of our lives. Whether in the fivefold ministry or not, we are all equally called of God and given a gift from the Spirit, or talent or ability with which to serve God and bless His people: "He gives them to each one, just as he determines" (1 Cor. 12:11, NIV). We should ask Him, therefore, as Saul of Tarsus did, "Lord, what wilt thou have me to do?" (Acts 9:6). If we continue attending to His presence, Word, and voice, one day the Master's call will come: "Separate me Barnabas and Saul for the work unto which I have called them" (Acts 13:2). Then it's up to us to diligently attend to His call.

Whatever it is, His call is the primary "fig tree," or orchard, we must keep. As described earlier, that will require us to expend much steady, hard work—building, planting, cultivating, watering, guarding, examining, etc. Satan's objective is to distract or divert us from our calling, and he will use anything and everything—sin, disappointment, laziness, enemies, friends, spouses, children, pleasures, prosperity, even religious activity—to achieve his ends. His temptation of Christ was an attempt to divert Jesus from His Father's call to go to the cross. Are we turning from our Master's call, or are we tenacious, holding fast to the duty or ministry He put in our hands? Oswald Chambers wrote, "Paul had received a ministry from the Lord Jesus, and in comparison of accomplishing that, he held nothing else of any account."[2]

Are we equally committed to our Master's call? Are we persistently focused and working hard to attend to our "fig tree," whether we're prosperous or persecuted, famous or forgotten? Or, as time wears on, are we being worn down and diverted to other activities, however popular, honorable, or religious?

Attending to His interests

In a word, our Master's dominant interest in this world is not property or prosperity or politics but _people_. He died to save all kinds of human beings—smart, stupid, weak, strong, religious, irreligious, Jewish, Gentile, male, female, Caucasian, African, Indian, Asian, Middle Eastern—and transform them into His own wondrous character image. Oswald Chambers taught that we should always identify ourselves with God's interests in other people. Are we doing that?

Are we treating our Christian brothers and sisters gently and kindly because Jesus said: "A new commandment I give unto you, that ye love one another..." (John 13:34)? Are we loving them with the same patient, forbearing, forgiving love with which He has loved, and is still loving, us? "...as I have loved you" (v. 34). Are we helping the sin-wounded strangers He puts before us on our Jericho roads? Are we counseling those who ask us for advice and giving to those who ask us for provision because our Master said, "Give, and it shall be given unto you" (Luke 6:38)? Are we preparing ourselves to feed His sheep, because Jesus said, "Lovest thou me?...Feed my sheep" (John 21:16)? Are we ready to drop our chosen careers and comfortable settings in life, if necessary, to go into desert-like scenes of service because there are people there He is interested in saving, delivering, healing, counseling, or teaching through us? Or are other things more interesting to us than the Master's interests?

We better get interested in this subject quickly, because one day we'll give account of our lives to Jesus: "Every one of us shall give account of himself to God" (Rom. 14:12). In that day, He will honor those who faithfully attended to His interests in the people He brought to them. And there's more: He will also honor them in this day. The day we set aside our private interests to begin attending to His personal interests in others, He will begin attending to our private interests in a special way...and eventually give us our hearts' desires: "Delight thyself also in the LORD [and his interests], and he shall give thee the desires of thine heart" (Ps. 37:4). I find that very interesting.

Attending to His challenges

After saving us, our Master's burning perpetual passion is to transform us, His raw Christian converts, into seasoned spiritual overcomers. He emphasized this, His great goal, in His messages to the seven churches of Asia, in which He repeatedly challenged ordinary believers to become extraordinary overcomers. (See Revelation 2–3.) To this end He steadily tests us. Every trying circumstance He sends us is a silent challenge, which, if it could speak, would say, "Will *you* be one of My overcomers, proven, wise, and ready to rule with Me forever? Here, this difficulty in your marriage, family, church, job, or ministry, is your chance to become one." Thus through adversity He seeks to stimulate us to leave the valley of ordinary Christianity and climb the demanding and dangerous mountain of extraordinary Christianity. Because the Good Shepherd is leading, ours is a controlled, gradual ascent, so none of us need be discouraged or intimidated.

In the initial stages, He sends elementary trials, mild in difficulty and brief in duration: "Count it all joy when ye fall into various trials" (James 1:2). As we pass these, He sends intermediate level tests, which demand more of us and last longer: "Though now, for a season...ye are in heaviness through manifold trials" (1 Pet. 1:6). If we remain faithful, He sends advanced tests, intense, protracted trials of fiery opposition that expose our latent faults and sins, purify our thoughts and motives, prove our loyalty to the hilt, polish our patience to perfection, open our inner eyes to fully see God's will, and melt and mold us to forever establish us in the character image of the Son of God: "Beloved, think it not strange concerning the fiery trial which is to test you" (1 Pet. 4:12). The final stages of these master trials require us to "endure unto the end [of our tests]" (Matt. 24:13) and keep the "word of my patience" (Rev. 3:10). We learn then not only to wait *on* our Master in daily fellowship but also to wait *for* Him to come to our aid in distress. If we meet all these challenges, enduring until He terminates all our difficult and lengthy tests, the rare fruit of "long-suffering" (Gal. 5:22), a hallmark of the prophets, will be developed in us. But the looming question is, "Will we?" Will we endure to the end—or stop short?

At any point in this challenging testing process we may turn back. And many do just that: "From that time *many* of his disciples *went back*, and walked no more with him" (John 6:66, emphasis added). For every Ruth that remains loyal there's an Orpah that turns back (Ruth 1:15); for every Timothy that stands by Paul there's a Demas who forsakes him (2 Tim. 4:10). If we also go back, we limit God's work of grace in our souls and forfeit our right to rule and reign with Christ. That privilege is reserved for those who attend to all His challenges: "If we suffer, we shall also reign with him; if we deny him [to avoid suffering], he also will deny us [our right to reign with him]" (2 Tim. 2:12).

Are we attending to or abandoning our Master's challenges? Overcoming or succumbing to the difficulties He has designed and sent into our lives? Fulfilling or frustrating His passion to make us overcomers?

Today, just where you are, commit yourself anew to wait on your heavenly Master. Persistently attend to every aspect of His will—His presence, His Word, His voice, His call, His interests, and His challenges. And diligently keep the "fig tree(s)" He has committed to your care. When difficulties visit and linger, remember the deep, abiding consolation found in the core of this priceless proverbial pearl: *You will be rewarded, both now and later, for your faithfulness!* For the present time, your reward will be that you "eat" of your "fig tree"—that is, God will provide all your needs as you provide all its needs. And ultimately, because you honored Him by waiting on Him, your Master will honor you.

> If any man serve me, him will my Father honor.
> —JOHN 12:26

Notes

Chapter 3
Why Am I Doing This?

1. A. W. Tozer, *The Root of the Righteous* (Camp Hill, PA: Christian Publications, 1986).

Chapter 4
Attitudes, Attitudes, Attitudes...

1. A. W. Tozer, *The Best of A. W. Tozer* (Camp Hill, PA: Christian Publications, 1995).

Chapter 7
Understanding: A Wellspring of Life

1. *Webster's Unabridged Encyclopedic Dictionary of the English Language* (New York: Gramercy, 1996), s.v. "insight."
2. James Strong, *Strong's Exhaustive Concordance of the Bible* (Peabody, MA: Hendrickson Publishers, 1988), s.v. "*maqowr*."
3. A. W. Tozer, *Of God and Men* (Camp Hill, PA: Christian Publications, 1995).
4. Tozer, *The Best of A. W. Tozer*.

Chapter 10
The Ministry of Conscience

1. *Webster's Unabridged Encyclopedic Dictionary of the English Language*, s.v. "conscience."
2. Oswald Chambers, *Oswald Chambers: The Best From All His Books*, ed. Harry Verploegh (Nashville, TN: Thomas Nelson, 1987).
3. Ibid.

Chapter 14

PUT OFF THAT WEIGHT!

1. W. E. Vine, *Vine's Complete Expository Dictionary of Old and New Testament Words* (Nashville, TN: Thomas Nelson, 1992), s.v. "*ewil.*"

Chapter 22

GOOD WIFE, GOOD BLESSING

1. Matthew Henry, *Matthew Henry's Commentary on the Whole Bible* (N.p.: Hendrickson Publishers, 1991), s.v. "Proverbs 31:10."

Chapter 31

CAN YOU STAND BEFORE ENVY?

1. Oswald Chambers, *He Shall Glorify Me* (N.p.: Marshall Pickering, 1965).

Chapter 32

ON GOOD AND POOR PARENTING

1. Henry, *Matthew Henry's Commentary on the Whole Bible*, s.v. "Proverbs 29:15."

Chapter 33

ATTEND TO YOUR MASTER—AND FIG TREE!

1. Henry, *Matthew Henry's Commentary on the Whole Bible*, s.v. "Proverbs 27:18."
2. Chambers, *He Shall Glorify Me.*

OTHER BOOKS
BY GREG HINNANT

alking in His Ways (Creation House). This twenty-four chapter work sets forth the essential principles for true biblical discipleship, guiding the reader through the successive stages of spiritual development, from spiritual infancy to spiritual maturity. It is the textbook for Greg's course on Biblical Discipleship taught through Beacon Institute of Ministry. Every serious-minded believer is sure to find timely instruction or comforting confirmation in this book. (Trade paperback, 280 pages)

Walking on Water (Creation House). This twenty-chapter study on the Christian testing process identifies many tried and true biblical principles that enable us to walk on—rather than sink beneath—the turbulent waters of life. It offers aspiring overcomers tested truths for these trying times. (Trade paperback, 240 pages)

DanielNotes: An Inspirational Commentary on the Book of Daniel (Creation House). An exposition of the Book of Daniel unlike any other, this inspirational commentary will guide readers to the spiritual high ground upon which Daniel lived and labored. With numerous Bible references given to illustrate and corroborate most entries, this is an excellent resource for study and teaching. It is the textbook for Greg's course on The Book of Daniel taught through Beacon Institute of Ministry. (Trade paperback, 320 pages)

Spiritual Truths for Overcoming Adversity (Greg Hinnant

Ministries). This twenty-six chapter, plainly written book offers strong meat for strongly tried believers and ministers. Its numerous biblical principles help frustrated, overwhelmed Christians drop carnal attitudes and grasp new spiritual attitudes that will enable them to endure and grow in any adversity. (Trade paperback, 217 pages)

Key New Testament Passages on Divorce and Remarriage (TEC Publications). Petite but powerful, this small book is a colorful verse-by-verse exposition of the two most vital New Testament passages bearing on the timely subject of divorce and remarriage, Matthew 19:3–12 and 1 Corinthians 7:1–40. It will be enlightening and helpful to any believer, but especially to those being challenged in this area of life or ministry. (Trade paperback, 55 pages)

About This Ministry...

Mission Statement

GREG HINNANT MINISTRIES exists to train believers to walk in New Testament discipleship by teaching the timeless, priceless, and unfailing principles of the Word of God. By doing so we are contributing to the spiritual preparation of the body of Christ for the appearing of our Lord Jesus Christ. "Prepare ye the way of the Lord" (Isa. 40:3).

Ministries Available

We presently offer a *monthly Bible message* (hard copy or e-mail) to interested believers. Pastors and others in Christian ministry are particularly encouraged to take advantage of this mailing. Foreign readers are also served, preferably by e-mail.

We presently offer for sale six *books* and numerous *audio-cassette tapes* of Greg's messages. Current price lists are available upon request.

Or visit us at our Web site: www.greghinnantministries.org

To Contact This Ministry

Mail: Greg Hinnant Ministries
P. O. Box 788
High Point, NC 27261
Tel.:   (336) 882-1645
Fax: (336) 886-7227
E-mail: rghinnant@aol.com or rghministries@aol.com